UNDERSTANDING RELIGIOUS EXPERIENCE

In this book, Paul K. Moser offers a new approach to religious experience and the kind of evidence it provides. Here, he explains the nature of theistic and nontheistic experience in relation to the meaning of human life and its underlying evidence, with special attention given to the perspectives of Tolstoy, Buddha, Confucius, Krishna, Moses, the apostle Paul, and Muhammad. Among the many topics explored in this timely volume are religious experience characterized in a unifying conception, religious experience naturalized relative to science, religious experience psychologized in merely psychological phenomena, and religious experience cognized relative to potential defeaters from evil, divine hiddenness, and religious diversity. *Understanding Religious Experience* will benefit those interested in the nature of religion and can be used in relevant courses in religious studies, philosophy, theology, biblical studies, and the history of religion. The book will enable enquirers about religion to:

- understand the importance of religious experience;
- identify where key religious evidence can be found in religious lives;
- and understand how religious experience bears on the meaning of human life from a range of diverse and influential religious perspectives.

Paul K. Moser is Professor of Philosophy at Loyola University Chicago. He has published widely, most recently as author of *The God Relationship* (Cambridge University Press, 2018) and co-editor of *The Cambridge Companion to the Problem of Evil* (Cambridge University Press, 2017). He serves as editor of Cambridge Studies in Religion, Philosophy, and Society and Cambridge Elements in Religion and Monotheism.

Understanding Religious Experience

From Conviction to Life's Meaning

PAUL K. MOSER
Loyola University Chicago

CAMBRIDGE
UNIVERSITY PRESS

CAMBRIDGE
UNIVERSITY PRESS

University Printing House, Cambridge CB2 8BS, United Kingdom

One Liberty Plaza, 20th Floor, New York, NY 10006, USA

477 Williamstown Road, Port Melbourne, VIC 3207, Australia

314–321, 3rd Floor, Plot 3, Splendor Forum, Jasola District Centre,
New Delhi – 110025, India

79 Anson Road, #06–04/06, Singapore 079906

Cambridge University Press is part of the University of Cambridge.

It furthers the University's mission by disseminating knowledge in the pursuit of
education, learning, and research at the highest international levels of excellence.

www.cambridge.org
Information on this title: www.cambridge.org/9781108471428
DOI: 10.1017/9781108558785

First published 2020

Printed in the United Kingdom by TJ International Ltd. Padstow, Cornwall

A catalogue record for this publication is available from the British Library.

Library of Congress Cataloging-in-Publication Data
NAMES: Moser, Paul K., 1957– author.
TITLE: Understanding religious experience : from conviction to life's meaning /
Paul K. Moser, Loyola University Chicago.
DESCRIPTION: Cambridge, United Kingdom ; New York, NY, USA : Cambridge
University Press, 2020. | Includes bibliographical references and index.
IDENTIFIERS: LCCN 2019040711 (print) | LCCN 2019040712 (ebook) |
ISBN 9781108471428 (hardback) | ISBN 9781108457996 (paperback) |
ISBN 9781108558785 (epub)
SUBJECTS: LCSH: Experience (Religion)
CLASSIFICATION: LCC BL53 .M7125 2020 (print) | LCC BL53 (ebook) |
DDC 204/.2–dc23
LC record available at https://lccn.loc.gov/2019040711
LC ebook record available at https://lccn.loc.gov/2019040712

ISBN 978-1-108-47142-8 Hardback
ISBN 978-1-108-45799-6 Paperback

All religious expressions are an expression of a sense of meaning, and a penumbra of mystery surrounds every realm of meaning.

—Reinhold Niebuhr (1966)

Contents

Preface   *page* ix

1   Religious Experience Characterized   1

   1 The Maze of Human Life   1
   2 Core Religious Experience and Life's Meaning   7
   3 Concepts and Diversity   21
   4 Whither Religion?   24
   5 Why Be Religious?   33
   6 Two Extremes on Religious Experience   37

2   Religious Experience Interpreted   42

   1 Experience beyond Interpretation   42
   2 Interpretation and Sensemaking   49
   3 Nontheistic Religious Interpretation   52
   4 Theistic Religious Interpretation   67
   5 Prospects and Questions   96

3   Religious Experience Practiced   100

   1 Practice in Action   100
   2 Practicing Religion   104
   3 Peril in Religious Practice   128
   4 Lessons for Religious Practice   135

4   Religious Experience Naturalized   137

   1 A Natural World   137
   2 Agents in Nature and Religion   153
   3 The Bearing of Naturalism   177

5 Religious Experience Psychologized   180

    1 Freud's Psychological World   181
    2 Religion after Freud   199
    3 Religious Experience in Psychology   208

6 Religious Experience Moralized   209

    1 Religion Moralized Reductively   209
    2 Religion Moralized Nonreductively   221
    3 Moralizing without Replacement   238

7 Religious Experience Cognized: Foundations   239

    1 Cognized Religious Experience   240
    2 Interpersonal Inquiry   241
    3 Tested in *Agapē*   247
    4 Led by God   254
    5 Convicted in *Agapē*   258
    6 Discerning God   268
    7 Convictional Knowledge   272
    8 Gift for Imitation   277

8 Religious Experience Cognized: Defeaters   283

    1 Skepticism and Defeaters   284
    2 Explaining God and Evil   293
    3 Divine Hiddenness   313
    4 Religious Diversity   316
    5 God's Gambit in Redemptive Duress   320
    6 Normative Meaning in Religious Experience   327

References   335
Index   341

Preface

"Religious experience," as commonly understood, includes the bizarre and the banal, among other things. Many inquirers wonder if any religious experience is reliable, and many are altogether skeptical in this area. This book identifies a unique value in *some* religious experience, including as evidence for some people about the real world. So, it offers a positive approach to some religious experience on the basis of positive evidence. In doing so, it gives special attention to core religious experiences involving Tolstoy, Gautama, Confucius, Krishna, Moses, Paul, and Muhammad.

The book explains religious experience as one's experience of the sensed value underlying life's overarching meaning for one. It does so in connection with these topics: religious experience characterized in a unifying conception (Chapter 1); religious experience interpreted as theistic or nontheistic (Chapter 2); religious experience practiced with distinctive intentions (Chapter 3); religious experience naturalized relative to science (Chapter 4); religious experience psychologized in terms of merely psychological phenomena (Chapter 5); religious experience moralized reductively or nonreductively (Chapter 6); religious experience cognized, or made cognitively relevant, by its role in a person's foundational evidence (Chapter 7); and religious experience cognized relative to potential defeaters from evil, divine hiddenness, and religious diversity (Chapter 8).

The book explains how religious experience and commitment differ from scientific experience and belief. It identifies why they do not either reduce to or yield to evaluation as scientific phenomena, contrary to various critics of religion. A distinctive feature of religion consists in the role of *experienced religious meaning* as overarching existential meaning for a person's life. Such meaning is formative in a person's existence and identity, and thus it does not figure *just* in a general explanatory hypothesis, let alone a hypothesis just in terms of general laws. In the book's approach, religion should be *conservative* in conforming to supporting evidence from actual experience, but it also should be *progressive* in pursuing and considering new evidence from experience. In being guided by overall evidence, religion can avoid a charge of being dogmatic, authoritarian, or vulnerable to wishful thinking. It thus can save its experienced existential value and meaning from easy dismissal by critics. This benefit is needed and overdue for religion.

The book introduces a notion of *convictional knowledge* to clarify how religious experience can be cognitive, including well grounded in experiential evidence. Such knowledge goes beyond factual knowledge, in one's being convicted in moral conscience. A key issue is whether being thus convicted can supply evidence of a God worthy of worship. The book contends that it can, owing to a unique intentional component in the relevant evidence. It also contends that the familiar defeaters of evidence for God fail to undermine the intentional convictional evidence in some contexts. So, the book offers a distinctive approach to the evidential foundations of theistic religion. In doing so, it seeks an audience not just in scholars and teachers but also in college students and readers outside the university. The topic of religious experience has importance that merits a wide audience.

Chapters 7 and 8 rework some parts of my following essays: "Doxastic Foundations: Theism," in *Theism and Atheism*, ed. Joseph Koterski and Graham Oppy (New York:

Macmillan, 2019), pp. 103–118; "Divine Hiddenness, Agapē Conviction, and Spiritual Discernment," in *Sensing Things Divine*, ed. Paul Gavrilyuk and Frederick Aquino (Oxford: Oxford University Press, 2020); and "Theodicy, Christology, and Divine Hiding," in *The Expository Times* 129 (2018), 191–200.

I have benefited from questions, comments, and suggestions from many people, including Simon Babbs, Aaron Bartolome, David Bukenhofer, Tom Carson, Blake Dutton, Harry Gensler, Todd Long, Chad Meister, Linda Moser, Ben Nasmith, Clinton Neptune, and various anonymous referees. I thank them for their kind help. I also thank my students at Loyola University Chicago for being a helpful audience for presentation of some of the book's material. For excellent assistance at Cambridge University Press, I thank Beatrice Rehl, Publisher, and Katherine Tengco Barbaro, Senior Content Manager.

∾

Religious Experience Characterized

Religion chases, and sometimes catches, life's meaning in the hallways of human experience. What, however, empowers religion and keeps its quest alive, despite its notorious failures and crimes throughout history? The answer lies, at least partly, in religious *experience* of a distinctive *power* that supplies life's *meaning* in a morally relevant way. So, the answer is not in mere beliefs, creeds, theories, or rituals. Religion without experience is thin on motivating evidence, whereas experience without religion is short on life's meaning.

The meaning in question is not reducible to human desires, intentions, or pursuits. Instead, it represents "the meaning *of* human life," in a morally relevant sense. It thus goes beyond anyone's "meaning *in* life" that stems just from one's desires or intentions. Mere desires or intentions for something will not yield the kind of meaning suited to religion. They do not include the powerful *experience of life's overarching meaning* found in religion. We shall see whether this approach to religion and meaning is tenable, given our relevant evidence.

1 THE MAZE OF HUMAN LIFE

Religion, religious experience, and life's meaning do not arise in a vacuum. Instead, they emerge, if they emerge at all, in a context of action-options for humans, indeed in a seeming maze of such options. The maze experienced by humans presents ongoing options for decision-making: to act this way or that way, or (perhaps) not at all – where refraining from acting can be a matter of decision, too. The maze of options comes with one's dynamic, wavering experience of the world, in relation to how one is to respond to that experience. Either one can ignore an experience (say, a taste experience), or one can seek to prolong it, cooperatively. Taking a third option, one can seek an alternative to the experience, say, in another kind of experience. Such options continue for one experience after another, and a person often responds with subconscious decisions. So, one can be in a maze of decision-making without being aware that one is. Even so, a person's decisions are ongoing, prompted by the maze of options in experience. These decisions are not just about experience, given that one's life is not reducible to experience, but they often have a basis in experience.

We find ourselves in the maze, on reflection, although we did not choose to enter it. It comes to us uninvited, and it persists at least for a time, without our invitation. The maze seems, in addition, to be part of our lot as intentional agents, as no conscious intentional agent seems immune to it. In some people, it yields decision fatigue, a weariness about the parade of options for decision. The fatigue can overwhelm if one's decisions are felt to be dangerous or frustratingly uncertain. Such decisions can wear one down under stress, perhaps even to the point of decision paralysis. One then can form a habit of indecision as a protective measure, although this habit itself may be initiated by a decision. A question arises: Is there any way out of the stress of the maze, short of one's ceasing to be an agent at all? The answer will not come easy, if it comes at all. Even so, the question merits our attention, and it will get it in due course.

Many people in the maze will raise a natural question: What, if anything, is the purpose, point, or goal for us in the maze of action-options? In particular, is there such a singular thing as "the purpose" in the maze generally, perhaps emerging from the overall purpose *of*, or *for*, the maze? Some people hold that there are only various *purposes* inside the maze, stemming from individual human goals in it. There is, in that view, no overall purpose, point, or goal of the maze, regardless of what people intend to do in the maze. So, any talk of what the maze overall is intended to accomplish would be misplaced, if that view holds. I might intend to accomplish various things with my decisions in the maze (such as survival and the common good), but my intention would not generalize to the maze overall, or to everyone in it, as an overarching value or norm. I, among others, lack the needed authority or normative value for such a broad role.

People disagree over whether the maze of action-options has overall value, that is, comprehensive, overarching value for the maze as a whole. Such value would be desirable for many people, because it would underwrite overall meaning for the maze and thus for human life in the maze. In that case, the value would be *sensemaking,* or meaning-making, for the maze, by giving sense or meaning to it overall. The overall sense, meaning, or point of the maze then could be to realize, or to actualize, the overarching value of human life. (Even so, we sometimes use "the value of life" and "the meaning of life" interchangeably.) While acknowledging controversy over the existence of overarching value for human life, we shall explore whether a case can be made for it.

Overarching meaning for the maze and human life would be personal if grounded in the valuable intentions of a personal, intentional agent, such as a God who is personal. In that case, the overall *personal* meaning *of* the maze would depend on an intentional agent who can give such overall meaning or purpose. This agent, having a special role in giving meaning, thus could be sensemaking for the maze overall and for the human lives in it.

Individual humans fall short of that general role, because their intentions do not bear normatively, in their value, on the maze overall, or on everyone in it.

We may think of "the actual meaning of human life" (or of the maze) as identifying what actually makes it *worthwhile* overall, that is, *worth our living* overall, despite its pain, frustration, and evil. So, if nothing makes our living our lives worthwhile overall, or on balance, then there is no "actual meaning of human life." In that case, one still might talk of "the meaning of human life" or of "life's meaning" *for certain people* in a less objective sense, relative to their (perhaps subjective) experiences and commitments. Such talk, however, would have no requirement of a sensemaker that actually makes living human life worthwhile overall.

The kind of sensemaker in question goes beyond various values in human life to an overall value that is meaning-making for living human life overall. Such an overall value and the corresponding meaning of human life, at least under certain hospitable circumstances, would be available to be discovered and received by humans. It would not be fully or even largely created by them in the way a *merely* perceived meaning of life would be. Meaning for life, or life's meaning, *endorsed by a person* thus can rest on merely perceived value that is not actual. In that case, we have something other than the actual meaning of human life. Someone might propose the meaning of an individual human life without extending this to human life generally. Even so, we would need to identify the relevant sensemaker and explain its restriction to an individual life. It will not do to claim simply that the individual endorses a particular sensemaker, because a merely perceived sensemaker could be at work. In any case, our interest is now in the prospect for an overarching meaning for human life in general, and not just for an individual life.

A God who is personal (i.e., a personal agent) could supply an overall value for human life and sustain human lives via the value of God's perfect moral character. Indeed,

God could supply *lasting* value and meaning for human lives in a way that short-lived humans, with their temporary purposes, could not. In addition, God could issue commands on the basis of a perfect moral character, and thereby create or at least clarify and motivate morally grounded duties for humans (thereby avoiding the arbitrariness threatened by Plato's Euthyphro problem). God would not face a regress problem of further mazes, because God's perfect moral character would suitably ground divine decisions and commands. It would be premature, however, to assume that only a personal God could provide overall value for human lives. Other options await our consideration. It also would be premature to assume that the human maze exists in isolation from mazes of action-options facing other species. For all we know, mazes for responsible decision-makers extend beyond the human maze, but we cannot digress.

People inside the maze can experience value and meaning for their lives. They also can be convicted to give the value and meaning an overarching role in guiding their lives, covering all aspects of their lives. Perhaps, however, this would be just *self*-conviction, merely an individual's decision to value certain things for his or her life. Some interpreters, in contrast, will propose a role for values that does not depend on such a human decision but entails value *realism*: the view that the values are independent of human decisions and attitudes. Whichever position one favors, any overarching meaning of the maze, bearing on the maze overall, would not arise without *something* transcending the maze that gives it such meaning and is thus sensemaking for it. For instance, an intentional agent who "guides" the maze with an overarching purpose for it could give it overarching meaning. In the absence of such a purpose, the maze could have only internal meaning, courtesy of the agents inside. We shall ask whether religious experience bears on the issue of the breadth of such meaning. Our question will be whether such experience underwrites overarching meaning for human life beyond the purposes of individual humans.

A thought experiment can illuminate our perspective on the maze. Imagine a visitor who finds herself on planet Earth with no historical experience here. She does have, however, a typical level of human intelligence and a moral perspective acceptable to morally decent humans. What would our visitor think about the goodness and badness of the planet, and about its meaning and hope for the future? Suppose that, after due examination, she finds it to be a mixed bag regarding goodness and badness; it would be hard to fault her for that. Would she, however, find its future meaningful or hopeful for any kind of overall triumph of goodness over badness? Perhaps not, after due examination. Still, she would have other questions, similarly in need of careful examination. She would not assume, in any case, that human life has overall meaning only if it has an overall triumph of goodness over badness.

One pressing question would be: Is this planet subject to any overarching purpose, beyond that of its human citizens, individually or group-wise? Its citizens disagree on this matter, but our visitor still wants to know the fact of the matter. Where would she begin, after her consultation with the available citizens? Where, in particular, would she look for relevant evidence? Perhaps she would canvass a range of people about their various moral experiences, including her own. It is unclear, however, that she would agree with the following bold statement by H. H. Farmer: "Our minds are so made – and after all we must in the end accept our minds – that we cannot but believe that the Universe in which we find ourselves is somehow in its real nature a suitable stage for the fullest realisation of ourselves" (1929, p. 21). Perhaps our visitor would lack adequate evidence for such a striking claim, as, I suspect, many of us do. We seem not to be required to believe that our universe is a good stage for our "fullest realisation." Many people are crushed

by the evil of our universe in a way that blocks such realization for them, at least in their earthly lives.

Our thought experiment raises the question of how one
can discern, if one can, whether our planet is under an
overarching purpose, beyond the goals of its human citizens. Perhaps there is an overarching purpose, but we are
unable to discern it. This seems to be a live option, but it
also seems questionable. One might suppose that the source
of the relevant purpose would enable us to discern that
purpose, if only to contribute to its realization in human
lives. Even so, we should not reduce a question about an
overarching purpose for the planet to a question about such
a purpose for human life; the former would be broader than
the latter. (Chapters 7 and 8 return to the matter of discerning an overarching purpose for human life.) Our immediate
effort, however, will be to identify some approaches to
religious experience that may illuminate the topic of overarching meaning for human life.

2 CORE RELIGIOUS EXPERIENCE AND LIFE'S MEANING

We may think of a *core* religious experience as one *characteristic* of *religious* experiences. The latter experiences bear
on a person's perceptual or sensory awareness, including
experiential direct attention-attraction, in a way pertinent to
religious matters. They involve the presence of something
(understood broadly) to one's awareness, and thus cannot
be reduced to an inference or a judgment. The relevant
presence to awareness in direct attention-attraction is qualitative in experience in a way that mere inference or judgment is not. To the extent that we understand direct
attention-attraction in awareness, we understand the relevant kind of experience. So, it would be misguided to
suggest that a suitable notion of experience is not available
to us (contrary to Aubrey 1933 and Lash 1990).

Lev (Leo) Tolstoy has described his life-changing religious experience in a way that qualifies it as a core religious

experience. Tolstoy was not only a theist but also a Christian. Even so, his core religious experience is understandable without his commitment to Christianity or even to theism. It centers on *overarching meaning* for human life and includes an indispensable ethical component, without being reducible to that component or to a philosophy. It is a core religious experience, because some of its aspects are characteristic of religious experiences in general.

Tolstoy describes his transformative religious experience in abridged form:

All that was around me came to life and received a meaning.... And I was saved from suicide. When and how this transformation within me was accomplished, I could not say. Just as [earlier in my life] the life force within me was gradually and imperceptibly destroyed, and I encountered the impossibility of life, the halting of life, and the need to murder myself, so too did this life force return to me gradually and imperceptibly.... I returned to the conviction that the single most important purpose in my life was to be better, to live according to this. (1882, pp. 76–77; trans. first two sentences, Aylmer Maude, and remaining sentences, David Patterson)

Tolstoy had struggled with the option of suicide, but this struggle, like his Christian theism, is not crucial to his core religious experience. The core of his religious experience lies elsewhere.

Something *happened*, or *was presented*, to Tolstoy in his experience, including in his qualitative awareness; it attracted his attention directly, with qualitative content. So, it was not just a thought, a belief, or anything else simply intellectual. He directly *experienced* the emergence of *meaning*, and thus sensemaking, for his life. This meaning figured for him in all surrounding things as well as "within" him, particularly in the "transformation within" him. It thus was overarching meaning for his life. He reports: "All that was around me came to life and received a meaning." This was something Tolstoy directly experienced in a powerful way. The relevant meaning was person-engaging in a practical manner that included and even prompted Tolstoy's forming an intention to become conformed to it, that is, to become "better." It thus was valuable for his practical life; it was not merely speculative or abstract in the way many ethical and philosophical reflections are.

Whatever else the meaning in question includes, it is practical and *self-involving* for Tolstoy by its becoming action-guiding and life-guiding for him. It figured centrally in his primary intention and goal to become better. As Tolstoy explains, in response to experiencing meaning for his life: "I returned to the conviction that the single most important purpose in my life was to be better, to live according to this." So, his core religious experience of meaning gave him the conviction that the primary purpose of his life is to become *better*. This purpose is, in his conviction, *morally* relevant, bearing on how he ought to be and to live. It concerns his life overall, and not just some part of it. In addition, the conviction went beyond reflection to Tolstoy's intention to direct his life in a particular way. We sometimes use "religious experience" when no experience of overarching meaning is indicated, but that falls short of a *core* religious experience in the sense proposed. I aim to separate peripheral matters from the core, in order to illuminate what motivates some prominent religious figures and their religions.

The role of *conviction* is important in a religious experience of meaning for a human life. It distinguishes an experience from a mere belief, creed, theory, or ritual. A religious experience of meaning for life includes one's being convicted by the experienced meaning for one's life: in particular, one's being convicted by its primary *value* for one's life, and one's being convicted to intend to form one's life in a corresponding way. Being thus convicted differs from a simple "conviction" (as a mere belief) *that* something is true. It includes one's experience of the value, or at least the sensed value, of the overall meaning of one's life. Tolstoy's direct experience of the value of becoming better serves as a good example. Such an experience can motivate and guide one in forming beliefs and plans about one's life. When one forms an intention to conform to the value, the experience also can prompt actions in one's life, particularly actions suited to the overall meaning of one's life.

One's experience of overall meaning for life can mislead regarding what is the *actual* meaning of human life overall. This can result from an experience that misleads one regarding the actual value of human life overall and relates one at best to *merely sensed* value. For instance, I might sense that the acquiring of personal power is the value and meaning of human life overall. The relevant notion of "sensed" does not rely on a familiar notion of "sensory"; it is more akin to a notion of "sensing a duty" or "sensing a need." A *merely* sensed value of human life overall (as we shall use the language) includes one's sensing *something* that fails to be the actual overarching value of human life. Even if it is not that actual value, one can sense it to be such and thereby take it to be such, fallibly and thus perhaps erroneously.

Interpretation of *something experienced* figures in one's sensing something to be life's value and meaning. So, we will distinguish between religious experiences that mislead regarding reality, such as the reality of life's value, and those that do not. The same distinction applies to the corresponding sensed values and meanings bearing on human life. A *veridical* core religious experience would include an experience of the actual overarching meaning of life, but a nonveridical religious experience would not. The means for distinguishing the two in an actual case is a separate, epistemological matter (to which Chapters 7 and 8 return).

Being convicted by life's meaning has the following variations: (a) being convicted of *the primary value* underlying life's meaning, (b) being convicted of *falling short* of life's meaning, and (c) being convicted *toward conforming* to life's meaning. Being convicted of the primary value underlying life's meaning, such as the value of becoming better, can be an opening to either or both of the other two variations. Having been convicted of the primary value underlying life's meaning, one then could be open either to being convicted of falling short of life's meaning or to being convicted toward conforming to life's meaning. In that case, one also could be open to being convicted of both options, and one could proceed accordingly in one's practical life.

One would conform in a practical and responsible way to life's meaning by making decisions and forming intentions to actualize in one's life the values that set life's meaning for one, such as the value of becoming morally better. (Chapter 3 will clarify the difference between decisions and intentional states, while allowing that people sometimes use "decision" and "intention" interchangeably.) These decisions and intentions would be at the discretion, or the will, of a person, if they are responsible, and thus they would not be set coercively by nature or anything else that overrides a human will. A person therefore could decide to reject being convicted in a practical way (a) of the primary value underlying life's meaning, (b) of falling short of life's meaning, or (c) toward conforming to life's meaning. So, being convicted in a practical and responsible way would not be a mechanical process. It would require human cooperation via exercise of a human will. The conviction in question, then, bears on intentional agents who are responsibly self-directed in their responses. (Chapters 7 and 8 return to the role of conviction in religious experience.)

We have suggested that a core religious experience relates one directly to life's meaning and *perhaps* even to actual value for one that are overarching, primary in value, and self-engaging in a transformative, existential manner for one. Here is a summary characterization of what we shall call "religious life's meaning," or "life's meaning," for short:

Life's meaning for a person: Something meaningful for a person is life's meaning for that person when it is:

(a) *life-directed* for that person in that it is (based on the person's intentions) action- and goal-directed for that person's life (and death); in this respect, it is *practical* and *life-guiding* for that person's life (for instance, toward becoming better, in Tolstoy's perspective)

(b) *overarching*, or *life-encompassing*, and thus life-integrating for that person in that it bears on all of that person's life, leaving out nothing of that life, thereby bringing a kind of unity to that life

(c) *of primary value* for that person in that its experienced value for that person would not be overridden now by any other value for that person

(d) *self-engaging* for that person in that it challenges the person to be transformed, as a person, toward the realization or the goal of the meaning in question (for instance, to become better, in Tolstoy's perspective).

In this regard, religious life's meaning for a person is inherently life-directed and thus intentional and practical for that person. So, it is not just a subject of reflection or contemplation for that person. We can recommend this approach for its illuminating a key feature of religious commitment.

What one person experiences and takes to be life's meaning need not be life's meaning for another person, given variation in experiences and intentions among people. Even so, there can be, at least in principle, such a singular thing as "the meaning of life" for all humans, and people can share religious experiences and corresponding religious meaning for their lives. As a result, religious experiences and meaning can be socially important. They also can bear

on a person without that person's categorizing or classify-
ing them for what they actually are. We thus can distinguish one's experience of *something meaningful* for one and
one's experience of *something as meaningful* for one. The
former allows for one's not categorizing the thing experienced *as meaningful* at all; the latter does not allow for this,
as it requires such categorizing. This distinction bears on
how intellectual, in terms of categorizing, a person's religious experience is. We shall identify variation among the
religious experiences of people in this regard.

We now can see how religious experience and its corresponding life's meaning differ from what ordinarily tran-
spires in ethical theory and philosophy. For instance,
Tolstoy's core *religious* experience of conviction by life's
meaning does not reduce to a feature of either ethical theory
or philosophy. Instead, it is a direct experience of a sensed
value accompanied by an interpreted practical meaning and
a corresponding intention for his life (in short, to become
better). So, the relevant religious experience of conviction is
not *just* an ethical or philosophical insight or judgment.
Tolstoy's religious experience bears on his life in a manner
guided by an interpreted overarching meaning that is intentional, and thus practical, for his life. This kind of all-
encompassing intentional phenomenon is absent from a
mere ethical or philosophical insight or judgment. Neither
ethical theory nor philosophy, as typically understood,
offers a sensed value that bears in a practical manner on
all of life's meaning for one. (Chapter 3 returns to the topic
of how practical factors relate to religious experience and
life's meaning.)

In the tradition of Plato and Aristotle, ethical theory and
philosophy do not depend on a sensed value that underwrites life's overarching meaning in the practical way suggested by Tolstoy. They do depend, according to Plato and
Aristotle, on *intellectual* insight toward Forms or Essences of
reality, but such insight is more narrowly intellectual than
the religious experience identified by Tolstoy as grounding

overarching practical meaning for life. So, something more than ethical theory or philosophy occupies Tolstoy's transformative experience of conviction: namely, distinctively *religious* experience and its bearing on life's overall practical meaning.

Tolstoy acknowledged and welcomed his religious experience, but he interpreted it to involve God's personal will, thereby going beyond what we have called a "core religious experience." Given the reality of nontheistic religions, we will acknowledge religious experiences that are not interpreted as theistic, in addition to religious experiences interpreted as theistic. It would be implausibly narrow to confine religious experiences to those interpreted as theistic. In doing so, we would neglect or distort some of the major world religions, including some prominent versions of Buddhism and Confucianism, as we shall see in Chapter 2.

Tolstoy's talk of "the single most important purpose" in his life *can* be interpreted coherently as theistic, as involving God, and this would agree with Tolstoy's own preferred understanding. This is not, however, the only option for understanding the talk of "the single most important purpose" of a life. According to some religious and philosophical traditions, including some versions of Confucianism, Buddhism, Daoism, and Neoplatonism, values and purposes emerge from reality without depending on a God who is personal. These traditions hold that reality is ultimately value-laden and purposive even if God does not exist. They affirm that reality is ordered, structured, or law-governed in a way that sustains values and purposes, even though there is no ultimate personal law-giver, such as God.

The view of value and purpose independent of an intentional agent is foreign to many theists who take values and purposes to depend ultimately on God. Even so, the view in question is a historical reality, and it looms large in various nontheistic religions, including some of the major world religions (some versions of which are characterized in Chapters 2–5, in connection with religious experience and life's meaning). We therefore will acknowledge this view's existence and its bearing on a core religious experience. We can maintain a distinction between *personal purposes*, depending on the intentions of a personal agent, and *quasi-personal purposes*, which do not depend on such intentions. Some religions recognize only quasi-personal purposes for ultimate reality. (For some recent Neoplatonic approaches to value and purpose, without dependence on personal agents, see Leslie 1979 and Rescher 2010.)

In many cases, people understand or interpret the life goal, suggested by Tolstoy, of one's becoming *better* in different preferred ways. We see this diversity in the varying, and sometimes conflicting, conceptions in circulation of one's *moral improvement*, although we should not limit becoming better to moral improvement. Some people, for instance, think that moral improvement is compatible with hating some (evil) people (see Murphy and Hampton 1988), whereas others oppose this. In addition, some people hold that becoming morally better can include the military killing of some people who are not an immediate threat, whereas others deny this. So, a core religious experience can leave people with different preferred understandings of a person's becoming better. This consideration, however, does not support *substantive* moral relativism, the view that moral facts and truths vary among people. It supports only diversity in *preferred concepts* or *notions* of moral improvement for imagining or interpreting situations. Evidence of such diversity comes from empirical indicators of how people variously prefer to understand the relevant notion of moral improvement in their imagining or interpreting some situations. Such variation applies as well to the broader notion of becoming better.

Variation in preferred concepts bears on religions as well as persons. Various religions, in addition to various religious experiences as well as various nonreligious traditions, are accompanied by different preferred understandings of the relevant notion of moral improvement for a person. For instance, some but not all religions show preference for a pacifist understanding of the relevant notion of moral improvement, in their opposing the use of violence toward people. Other religions show preference for a nonpacifist understanding in recommending at least self-protective violence in the face of violent threats. We find such variation regarding violence, in relation to a preferred understanding of moral improvement, even within certain single religions, including Christianity (see Niebuhr 1940). Religions, then, do not manifest a singular preferred concept of moral improvement for a person. Instead, they exhibit varying preferred understandings of the relevant notion of one's becoming morally better. This consideration complicates our understanding of the relevant notion of religion, but it fits with the actual character of the diverse religions in circulation.

William James has characterized Tolstoy's religious experience as his overcoming a "divided self" or a "heterogenous personality." He explains:

[Tolstoy's] crisis was the getting of his soul in order, the discovery of its genuine habitat and vocation, the escape from falsehoods into what for him were ways of truth. It was a case of heterogenous personality tardily and slowly finding its unity and level. And though not many of us can imitate Tolstoy, . . . most of us may at least feel as if it might be better for us if we could. (1902, p. 183)

James suggests that Tolstoy's self, or his personality, is unified by the religious life's meaning grounded in his religious experience with conviction. This life's meaning, in James's perspective, yields a personal identity for Tolstoy with unity, self-integration, and inner harmony.

Tolstoy's personal identity had suffered previously from being pulled in different directions, at least regarding its goals. This made his personality disintegrated or disunified in its focus. His religious life's meaning, as experienced with conviction, replaced his divided self with singularity of life focus and thus with a unified self. Such a transformation of Tolstoy's personality prompts James's remark that "most of us may at least feel as if it might be better for us if we could" imitate Tolstoy. A divided self yields a divided life, at least in its purposes, and such a life thus entails inadequate unity of goodness in life. A core religious experience can figure in self-integration and life-integration as a cure for a divided self and a divided life. We shall return to illustrations of this lesson in connection with sensemaking for persons and their lives.

James introduces a common but disputable subjectivist view regarding the kind of meaning suitable to a religious experience: "Whatever of value, interest, or meaning our respective worlds may appear endued with are pure gifts of the spectator's mind" (1902, p. 147). Perhaps this is true of some human *passions*, and James does mention "the passion of love": "The passion of love is the most familiar and extreme example of this fact.... It sets the whole world to a new tune for the lover and gives a new issue to his life" (pp. 147–48). Even so, we should hesitate to identify (the sensed value underlying) the meaning for one's life, such as Tolstoy's life's meaning, with a purely subjective human passion.

Tolstoy appears to have experienced (the sensed value underlying) life's meaning in a way that exceeds a purely subjective human passion. It seems to be something non-subjective, at least in part, to which a human passion can respond, either with love or with something else. It appears to be something, as suggested by Tolstoy, by which one can be convicted toward a life-transformation, perhaps even toward one's becoming better. We should not preclude, then, the option that (the sensed value underlying) religious life's meaning for a person is irreducible to purely subjective human passions. This topic will recur in due course.

The kind of life's meaning under consideration is not an *explanation* of the world at large. So, it is not an explanatory "worldview" offering a satisfactory account of the world. For instance, this meaning does not yield a satisfactory explanation of the unjust suffering in the world at large, even though this suffering prompts a direct challenge to God's moral character and existence. A religious experience can give overarching meaning to one's life without giving one a satisfactory explanation of the world at large, if only because it does not adequately account for unjust suffering in the world. One could lack a satisfactory explanation of the larger world despite having a religious experience transform one's life with overarching meaning. (The book of Job arguably illustrates this point.) Denial of this consideration would leave us with an excessively rationalist or explanationist approach to religious experience and its corresponding meaning for one's life.

The approach to religious experience under consideration fits well with a portrait of a typical human as *Homo teleologicus*, as one who needs and wants meaning or purpose in life. Typical humans fulfill this portrait consciously or unconsciously, and in various specific ways, but we still can think of *Homo religiosus* as *Homo teleologicus*. Famously, Plato recommended that the meaning or purpose for human life should include preparation for dying, at least for philosophers: "Those who practice philosophy in the right way are in training for dying" (Phaedo 67e; 1997, p. 59). Philosophers have largely ignored Plato's view on preparation for dying, but it merits serious consideration, and not just by philosophers. Dying is an undeniable part of human life, and it deserves attention regarding questions about life's meaning. We thus shall attend to it as the opportunity arises.

In many cases, humans vary in how they pursue meaning for their lives. Some people look for meaning as a kind of *control* over their situation and even over certain humans.

Other people look for meaning that does not require their having control over their situation or certain humans. Some of the latter people hold that life's meaning must be *given* to us ultimately, whereas others hold that we can create or otherwise *achieve* life's meaning. These differences rest on big, complicated questions about human life, and they resist quick and easy explanations. We need not answer them now, but they will recur. One big question will be whether we should expect life's meaning to be *earned* or *achieved with self-credit* by humans rather than to be received as *gift-like*, without being thus earned or achieved. Religious traditions, we shall see, differ on this issue.

Some of the variation regarding (pursuit of) life's meaning stems from differing human experiences, including religious experiences. The fact, if it is a fact, that some people have a religious experience does not entail that *other* people likewise have a religious experience, let alone a similar religious experience. Religious experiences are not *inherently* socially shared, at least if our relevant evidence about such experiences points in the right direction. For instance, Tolstoy's religious experience of (value underlying) overarching meaning for his life was not socially shared, at least initially. A religious experience, then, can be relative to an individual agent without being socially shared. In addition, a religious experience need not depend on a social religious institution. Social and institutional religion may or may not be involved in a religious experience.

The person-variability of religious experiences suggests an important lesson for agnosticism about either the actuality or the veridicality (or reality-capturing) of such experiences. We should not generalize such agnosticism to bear on all people on the basis of *some* people lacking religious experience or questioning its veridicality. The experiential basis for the agnosticism of one person does not extend automatically to all other people. The latter people may have a different experience, and this would give them different evidence. Relevant evidence thus can vary among people, and this applies beyond a religious context. Caution about generalization, then, is fitting when religious experience and its corresponding life's meaning are under scrutiny.

William James has offered a rationale for being attentive to religious experience (at least of one kind), even if such experience is not universal. He explains:

Religious experience [of a sort acknowledged by the apostle Paul and Martin Luther, among others] brings all our naturalistic standards to bankruptcy. You are strong only by being weak, it shows. You cannot live on pride or self – sufficingness.... Sincerely to give up one's conceit or hope of being good in one's own right is the only door to the universe's deeper reaches.... There are ... possibilities that take our breath away, of another kind of happiness and power, based on giving up our own will and letting something higher work for us, and these seem to show a world wider than either physics or philistine ethics can imagine.... Reason, operating on our other experiences, even our psychological experiences, would never have inferred these specifically religious experiences in advance of their actual coming. She could not suspect their existence, for they are discontinuous with the "natural" experiences they succeed upon and invert their values.... They suggest that our natural experience ... may be only a fragment of real human experience.... So religious experience ... needs, in my opinion, to be carefully considered and interpreted by everyone who aspires to reason out a more complete philosophy. (1909, pp. 304–7)

If James is right, religious experience, at least of some kinds, merits our careful attention as an avenue to otherwise neglected power and reality. We will direct our attention accordingly, with special consideration of the role of religious experience in the overarching meaning of human life.

3 CONCEPTS AND DIVERSITY

The plot thickens now. We have diversity not only in preferred concepts of religion, but also in preferred concepts of the things that provide life's meaning in the various religions. Indeed, some might find *logical* incompatibility between some religions, including between what they offer as providing life's meaning. So, we do well to start at the beginning, with an understanding of what a *concept* of religion is, and how it figures in our inquiry.

A concept (or a notion or an idea) is a mental means of representing or portraying something, including a situation. An *object* represented by a concept, however, need not exist. We have a concept of a unicorn, for instance, and a concept of the tooth fairy. Both concepts represent or portray "something," broadly speaking, and their doing so does not suffer from their having purely fictional objects. Human imagination, underlying human concepts, is like that: It projects, or imagines, coherent objects or situations that may or may not correspond to actual, or factual, objects or situations. Without correspondence to actual objects or situations, we have *mere* imagination; with such correspondence, we have imagination agreeing with what is factual. When we want truth, we want correspondence with what is factual, because we want to identify factuality, that is, what actually is the case. Whether we actually get what we want is, of course, a separate matter.

Strictly speaking, concepts are neither correct nor incorrect, because they do not make *claims* that are either correct or incorrect. They are not statements, judgments, or propositions, because they do not predicate something of a subject *term*. Concepts can have applications that are correct or incorrect, and they can be constituents of propositions that are either true or false. They themselves, however, lack the full predication of a proposition that, bearing a truth-value, is either true or false. A concept can be either *satisfied* or *not satisfied* by a real object or situation. For instance, there is no real tooth fairy to satisfy our familiar concept of a tooth fairy, but this does not threaten the existence or the informative value of that *concept*. Only the reality of the *object* imagined is thereby threatened.

In some cases, we are hard put to *tell* whether a concept is satisfied by a real object, but this difficulty in our "telling" does not hinder a concept's actually *being satisfied* (or not being satisfied) by a real object. Some people hold that our general concept of God, used as an honorific title for one worthy of worship, illustrates this consideration: It is hard to tell whether God exists, but our general concept of God is, nonetheless, either satisfied or not satisfied by a real object. Our cognitive limitation in "telling" would not block an ontological reality of satisfaction (that may be unknown to us). Reality need not yield to our intellectual life. It has its own features, as we should learn early in life, if only by being frustrated and bruised by aspects of reality.

A concept of religion is a mental representation of *what it is to be* a religion. There is no such singular thing as "the concept" of religion, because there are many concepts of religion in circulation. For instance, there are concepts of religion that are theistic, and there are concepts of religion that are nontheistic. A notion of God figures in some concepts of religion (the theistic concepts), but not in others (the nontheistic concepts), and notions of God typically vary in theistic religions. What is the significance of such conceptual diversity? At least this: It would be surprising if such diversity did not exist, given the diversity in the output of human imagination, especially in the area of religion.

Conceptual diversity, as suggested, does not entail or otherwise support substantive relativism about what is factual or true in religion. In particular, it does not recommend that what is true in religion for some people is not true for other people. Some people prefer to use or actually do use different concepts of religion in imagining or interpreting situations, but this does not entail or otherwise support that some *facts* of religion vary among those people. Without variation in religious facts (and such variation would go beyond variation in religious experiences among people), religious truths will not vary among the people in question. So, substantive relativism about truth does not result from diversity or variation regarding preferred concepts of religion. In addition, the people in question are not barred from understanding each other regarding their differing preferred notions of religion. *Using* different preferred concepts for imagining or interpreting situations does not entail *understanding* different concepts. So, communication about religion among the relevant people is a live option.

Preferred concepts of religion vary at a level of specificity among many people. Even so, a large group of people can share a *general* preferred concept of religion. We need to ask whether we can identify such a general concept. I hold that we can, and I will offer a case in support. We can allow a general preferred concept of religion to be linked to a notion of meaning for human life, and we can allow notions of meaning for human life to vary at a level of specificity among people. For instance, some notions of life's meaning involve a notion of God, whereas others do not. In addition, some notions of such meaning involve a notion of lasting meaning, whereas others do not. We shall illustrate such variation in due course.

How people get their understood and preferred concepts is an empirically complex matter, and we need not give a comprehensive account now. Some concepts, such as familiar visual or auditory concepts, arise in connection with perceptual experience or at least sensory experience, and others apparently do not. Some concepts, such as those of subatomic physics, seem to arise for theoretical purposes, to aid in *explaining* why or how something is the case, and others seem not to have such an explanatory role. Some concepts, such as color concepts, seem to have more of a *descriptive* or at least a *categorizing* role than an explanatory role. In either case, however, concepts serve an organizing role of some sort for humans, whether in terms of mere categories or in relation to explanations. Human understanding of the world depends on unifying organization, whether descriptive or explanatory, and concepts are important components of such organization. Variation in their preferred use fits with variation in human interpretation and understanding of the world.

4 WHITHER RELIGION?

This book explains how religious experience and meaning are *integrative* for human selves, experiences, beliefs, practices, and lives in a way that gives *overarching transformative meaning* to various human lives. They bring a broad coherence of life-directedness to a human life. The relevant meaning is practical, and not just reflective, as a result of accompanying intentions regarding the direction of a life. Religious meaning is thus sensemaking, or meaning-making, for various human persons and their lives, and it is practical for them, too. It does not follow, however, that the relevant meaning explains the world at large, including its unjust suffering.

The book's methodology recommends evaluating a religion internally, by its own reported experiences relative to its general religious criteria, before introducing external criteria. The book gives due attention to formative *religious experience* as a distinctive kind of direct awareness, or direct attention-attraction, related to overarching practical meaning for human life. Even so, we will attend to the plausible skeptical view that a veridical religious experience should meet a standard for evidentially trustworthy experience and thereby avoid a charge of evidential illusion or prejudice. The book will use cases of religious experience from various religions, including Buddhism, Confucianism, Hinduism, Judaism, Christianity, and Islam, to illustrate many of its points.

The book's standard for evidentially trustworthy religious experience includes an explanatory, or "abductive," consideration. Does the experience, including its apparent object, figure in a *best available explanation* of what is actually occurring in the life of the religious person having that experience? Alternatively, is the experience equally or better explained as being illusory by psychology or some other discipline? Such questions will help to clarify what various religious experiences include and what best accounts for them and their apparent objects. So, the book's method for religious inquiry is descriptive (or phenomenological) *and* explanatory (or abductive) for religious experiences. It thus enables religious inquirers to distinguish what is abductively grounded in their experience from what is grounded *only* in tradition, testimony, or speculation. This distinction is important for identifying misplaced dogmatism, authoritarianism, and wishful thinking in religion. It thereby can protect against some of the dangers in religion.

I offer here a new taxonomy to explain the relevant meanings of "religion" and thus of "religious experience" and "religious meaning." The *Oxford English Dictionary* (OED), 2nd edition, comments on the term "religion": "Latin *religiōn-religiō*: supernatural feeling of constraint, usually having the force of a prohibition or impediment, ... manifestation of divine sanction, ... quality evoking awe or reverence." These terms merit attention: supernatural feeling of constraint, manifestation of divine sanction, quality evoking awe or reverence. Such terms point to *experiences* of special kinds, and not (just) to beliefs, creeds, theories, or rituals.

An account of religion in general must avoid two extremes: reducing religion to ethical theory or philosophy and reducing religion to theistic religion (i.e., making religion acknowledge a personal God). Socrates and Plato, for instance, offered a distinctive approach to ethical theory and philosophy, but they did not formulate a distinctive religion on the basis of religious experience (even though they had religious commitments of their own). Religion offers a person transformation with experienced existential value and meaning, via convicting one toward life's meaning while bearing on all of one's life in a practical, intentional way (a way different from ethical theory and philosophy). Ethical theory and philosophy can give one general principles of various sorts, but they fall short of the experiential convicting of one toward life's meaning while bearing in a practical way on all of one's life. We shall uncover some of the details of this contrast.

To be adequately informative, an account of religion in general should seek to identify what is common to religions. Given the significant diversity of religions, William James remarked with pessimism: "The very fact that they [definitions of 'religion'] are so many and so different from one another is enough to prove that the word 'religion' cannot stand for any single principle or essence, but is rather a collective name" (1902, p. 27). This negative response to the complex data is understandable, but we shall see that it is misleading. Contrary to James, I shall defend a common core for religion in general.

Famously, Rudolf Otto has suggested a unifying approach to religions. Regarding "the holy" (*das Heilige*), he has claimed: "There is no religion in which it does not live as the real inner most core, and without it no religion would be worthy of the name" (1923, p. 6). (Following Otto, Mircea Eliade (1959) has offered a similar view, while contrasting "the holy" with "the profane.") The English translation of Otto's book (p. 5) suggests that the term "sacred" is interchangeable with the word "holy" in translating *heilig*, and this fits with broader German use of the term. Otto remarks that "moral significance is contained in the word *holy*, but it includes in addition as even we cannot but feel a clear overplus of meaning [beyond moral significance]" (p. 5). We shall see, however, that the approach of Otto and Eliade misses the mark regarding the nature of religion, if "the holy" must be morally good.

The OED offers this definition of "sacred": "dedicated, set apart, exclusively appropriated *to* some person or some special purpose." This definition needs refinement to distinguish what is sacred from what is merely an object of ethical or philosophical commitment, such as a Platonic Idea. We should follow Otto's suggestion that the relevant notion of "sacred reality" does not reduce to the idea of moral goodness, even if it includes the latter idea. Otherwise, we would risk the collapse of some religions into ethical theory, and these religions then would lose their distinctiveness as religions.

We should allow for the reality of a religion, such as a religion supporting murderous evil, that lacks a genuinely sacred object (with actual moral goodness), even if it is directed by religious commitment to a counterfeit sacred object. A commitment to something as sacred does not make it actually sacred. The murderous and genocidal religion of ISIS (aka ISIL or Daesh) offers a clear example, with its practice of slavery, rape, jihad, and suicide bombing for avowed religious purposes. (Easy examples come as well from Christian and other religious traditions.) It would be ad hoc and misleading to claim that ISIS does not have religion as part of its motivation and doctrine. More generally, there is no good reason to exclude *evil* religion from the general category of religion. Ideally, a religion would be morally good, but the ideal, of course, is not always met in reality. As a result, we should not understand religion in terms of what is genuinely holy or sacred.

I propose that what is sacred is *what is worthy of worship-like reverential awe and commitment*. I speak of "worship-like," instead of "worshipful," to allow for a religion that relates to what is sacred but does not acknowledge a personal God worthy of worship. The Gautama Buddha, as Chapter 2 will explain, did not recommend worship of a personal God, but he had worship-like reverential awe and commitment toward Enlightenment or Nirvana. An analogous point holds for Confucius regarding his recommendation for a life of religious meaning in social virtue, as Chapter 2 will document. A religion, then, need not recommend actual worship toward a personal agent worthy of worship. That is, it need not endorse worship of God, but it still can include and promote *worship-like* awe and commitment toward something *deemed* sacred.

Religion requires a human's offering worship-like reverential awe and commitment *to something*. When that thing is a sacred reality, the religion in question has a *sound object*, an object *worthy* of the corresponding awe and commitment. Not all religion, however, has a sound object. A religion with an unsound object can involve worship-like reverential awe and commitment toward a false god, such as the evil, genocidal god of ISIS. An unsound object of religion is not worthy of worship-like reverential awe and commitment, given its failure in moral goodness. So, we should dissent from Otto and Eliade on the matter of the sacred in religion, if they have in mind what is actually sacred. A religion can fail to have what is sacred as its core, but still have religious awe and commitment toward something that is not sacred (such as the evil god of ISIS). As suggested, *commitment* toward something as sacred does not entail that it is sacred. A contrary view results in crass relativism about what is sacred.

Preferred human understandings of the objects of *religious* awe and commitment diverge among many people, and we can capture a key part of the divergence with a descriptive–normative distinction. A merely *descriptive* understanding of the objects of religious awe and commitment allows that *any* object can qualify as an object of religious awe and commitment. Setting no normative requirement for the object, a merely descriptive understanding makes a religious *attitude* of awe and commitment sufficient for an object to be religious. So, such mundane objects as cars, coins, and clothing can be objects of religious awe and commitment from a person. Ordinary use of the term "religious" sometimes follows this kind of merely descriptive, "anything goes" understanding of religious objects, but such use does not exhaust the options.

A *normative* understanding of the objects of religious awe and commitment conflicts with an anything-goes descriptive understanding. It treats such objects as cars, coins, and clothing as insufficiently powerful, valuable, or meaningful, religiously, to serve as the objects in question. Such objects lack the kind of power or value that can contribute to transforming a human life by integrating it with overarching, all-pervasive *value* and *meaning* for living and dying. Such integrating is religiously empowering for a life, owing to its investing a life with powerful, transformative meaning that has overarching breadth, with no part of the life excluded. Religion is thus sensemaking for a human life overall. In addition, when accompanied by a person's intention to conform to the relevant meaning, it is practical in its life-directing importance for that person.

The transformative, existential value and meaning in question are fitting objects of religious experience and devotion. They can supply meaning for humans not only for living but also for dying, whereas a coin collection, a car, and clothing fail here. So, religious meaning is broadly self-integrating and life-integrating in an existential and experiential way. It bears on *all* of one's life, including one's identity as an integrated person, as one is committed to live and to die for it. A coin collection, in contrast, lacks the value and meaning needed to cover the breadth of a human life, such as the psychological and moral life of even a full-time coin collector. Some things are too thin on value and meaning, too sketchy in sensemaking, to provide religious meaning in the relevant sense. A human context of interpretation will not change this fact. We shall use the term "religion" accordingly.

A normative approach to religious objects does not require that a religious object actually be sacred. It does enable, however, a distinction in religious significance between something experienced that can integrate a life with overarching existential meaning and something that cannot, such as a coin collection, a car, or clothing. This book supports a normative understanding of the objects of religious awe and commitment. It does not assume, however, that all religions are positively related to what is sacred. Religious awe and commitment can be *mis*directed regarding what is sacred, while still being related to a normative object that yields overarching meaning for a life. ISIS offers a clear example, to the detriment of many of its victims and followers.

We should distinguish *life-enhancing* overarching meaning from *life-diminishing* overarching meaning. The former kind of meaning can bring one into positive relation to what is sacred, but the latter kind of meaning fails to do so. The religion of ISIS gives overarching meaning to its followers and their lives; it thus structures, in a comprehensive way, how they live their lives. Even so, its overall meaning is life-diminishing, owing to its approval of murder, genocide, and various other destructive evils. In contrast, a religion consistently favoring a sacred object (i.e., an object worthy of worship-like reverential awe and commitment) offers overarching *life-enhancing* meaning. We shall see that a source of such meaning for a person is a sacred object for that person's religious commitment.

The book's new taxonomy for something's being a religion is represented by the following chart:

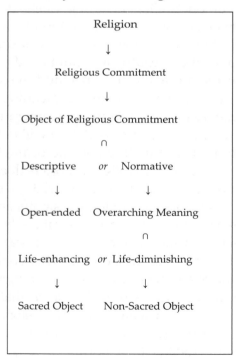

This taxonomy enables us to clarify why some things qualify as a religion while others do not. It also avoids the implausible view that all religion is sacred and hence morally good. The taxonomy thus accommodates a familiar understanding of religion.

The proposed taxonomy encourages us to explore the existential experienced value and meaning central to a religious commitment and to ask how exactly they are sensemaking for some humans and their lives. It also prompts us to ask whether a religious commitment or its object is part of a best available explanation of one's overall experience. Worship-like reverential awe and commitment require more than thinking or reflection. They require *self*-commitment, the giving of *oneself*, to the overarching existential value and meaning for one's life, one's personality, and one's identity as a person. This kind of self-commitment should be *merited* or *deserved* by the religious value and meaning on offer, but this requirement can be violated. We shall explore how self-commitment can be thus merited by something *worthy* of it, and how we thereby can avoid normative inadequacy in religious life's meaning.

We need a distinction between *direct* religious commitment and *indirect* religious commitment. Direct religious commitment is *immediately related* to its religious object or practice, without any needed religious explanation or theory on the part of the religious person. It allows that a person can have a religious commitment, experience, or practice without *conceiving* of the commitment, experience, or practice *as religious*, let alone as involving a supernatural agent such as God. This distinction is important, because it allows one's religious commitment, experience, or practice to be genuine without one's having a *theory* about the commitment, experience, or practice. Such a theory could be valuable in relation to an explanation, but we should not confuse it with first-order religious commitment, experience, or practice. Otherwise, we risk over-intellectualizing religion in its basic commitments, experiences, and practices.

Religious commitment, experience, or practice need not be explanatory for a person in the way a *theory* about religion is. Indirect religious commitment, however, is intellectual, consisting of one's believing that some religious claim, such as a doctrine, is true. One can believe that a religious claim is true (say, that God exists) even if one lacks a corresponding religious experience and practice. Such a religious belief does not depend on a supporting experience or practice for its existence, even if religious beliefs are typically grounded in experiences or practices. We shall honor the distinction between direct and indirect religious commitment in order to avoid an unduly intellectual or theoretical approach to religion for religious people.

From a cognitive or epistemic point of view, a religion should be *responsible to reality*, at least in virtue of its explanatory considerations bearing on a person's overall experience concerning reality. Specifically, one's religion, from a cognitive or epistemic viewpoint, should have unsurpassed explanatory power relative both to the whole range of one's experience and to one's available explanations of one's experience. The range of experience includes any religious experience that is not better explained as being illusory, say, *just* by human psychological considerations. Without such explanatory power, a religion would be open to a charge of ungrounded dogmatism, authoritarianism, or traditionalism, if not wishful thinking. It thus would be vulnerable to many of the familiar dangers of religion.

Religious as well as nonreligious assumptions about reality should earn their keep, from a cognitive point of view, in a way that avoids arbitrariness and irrationality. Explanatory power, at least relative to explanatory competitors and one's overall experience, can serve here. We shall see, in this connection, how a religion should be integrative of a human self and life in virtue of supplying overarching existential meaning for that self and life. This meaning, overall, should be life-enhancing rather than life-diminishing, in order to be morally sustainable. Religious commitment, like nonreligious commitment, can and should be resilient and nonarbitrary on the basis of its explanatory power and experienced meaning. So, it need not seek to escape cognitive assessment (as in the case of many fideist perspectives of religion indifferent to evidence) or to minimize its importance in human commitment.

5 WHY BE RELIGIOUS?

Philosophers and others often ask: Why be moral? In doing so, they have in mind this question: Why *should* one be moral (i.e., morally good)? A key issue then is: What do inquirers mean by "should" in the previous question? If they mean "morally should," we have this question: Why *morally* should one be moral? If that is the pertinent question, we may proceed to this question: In virtue of what consideration does a morality recommend that one should be moral? One might answer: A person's being morally good requires that person to be moral. This answer could prompt another question: Why should one be morally good at all? If it does, we need to identify the sense of "should" in the previous question. We will not have real progress if the sense is that of "morally should." In that case, we will not have gone deeper than the previous questions. We then will be left with the view that one morally should be morally good. Some people, however, are apparently looking for a different kind of answer to the question, "Why should one be moral?" In any case, the question itself requires careful attention, including clarification of its key terms, before a fitting answer will apply.

Inquiring beyond morality, many people will ask: Why be religious? Their question amounts to this: Why *should* one be religious? So, we end up, again, with an issue about "should": What sense of "should" figures in the question? Some people, opting for a moral sense, offer: Why morally should one be religious? Given my taxonomy for religion, we should not assume that one morally should be religious, because some religions are immoral. (ISIS is a clear example of an immoral religion, if any religion is.) We need to distinguish between morally good and morally bad religions, and only the former will be advisable candidates for people seeking a morally good life. One morally should be religious, not in the case of just any religion, but *at most* in the case of a *morally good* religion. Why not settle, however, for a morally good life, and let religion go – including morally good religion? Many inquirers will wonder what, if anything, a religion, including a morally good religion, would add, in such a way that it is required of a person.

We can clarify our question for anyone who proposes a particular religious way of life, including any of the Buddhist, Confucian, Hindu, Jewish, Christian, and Islamic perspectives introduced in Chapter 2. Why should a person be religious *in that particular way* rather than in a different way or in no way at all? Advocates of a religious perspective might respond by saying that this is just what they *mean* by "being religious," as if an analytic or quasi-definitional truth is being offered. Even so, we can raise a follow-up question: Why should one accept and follow (in action) *that* proposed truth regarding "being religious" rather than some different proposed truth or no such truth at all? The latter question suggests that an adequate answer needs a more developed rationale.

We can give the relevant sense of "should" in our question an overriding value relative to other uses of "should" (prudential, economic, legal, aesthetic, and other senses), and then restate the question. Why should one, *all things considered*, accept or practice what is being proposed (if as an analytic truth) regarding "being religious" in the sense indicated rather than in a different sense or in no sense at all? Now the latter question can be understood to include this question: Why suppose that it is responsible, all things considered, for a person to accept or practice the proposal for "being religious" in the sense indicated?

An *epistemically* responsible decision by a person will conform to that person's readily available evidence regarding what is real, including all such evidence from the person's overall experience. Such an epistemically responsible decision may not fully determine what is responsible *all things considered* for a person, but it can set a constraint on the latter. It will be accountable to a person's readily available evidence, where being "readily" available does not require anything intolerable in getting the evidence. (We can proceed now with some vagueness in the relevant notion.) One need not be aware of all of one's readily available evidence, but such evidence will be retrievable by one on the basis of one's recognized evidence.

Given that experience and available evidence can and do vary among persons, "all things considered" responsible decisions about being religious (among other things) likewise can and do vary among persons. In this regard, such decisions differ from mere truths about reality but conform to responsible decisions in general. If, in addition, one's evidence supports the reality of God and gives access to divine priorities, one can have a basis in those priorities for responsible decisions all things considered. (Chapters 7 and 8 return to this topic.)

We have considered a distinctive contribution of religion, including a morally good religion, to a human life: namely, its offering practical, overarching, and self-integrating experiential meaning that saves one from a significantly divided self and life. We have noted the experience of being convicted of such meaning in Tolstoy's life, and we have seen how it differs from what ethical theory and philosophy offer. We also have observed that in contributing meaning for a human life, a religion need not be morally good. The overarching and self-integrating meaning contributed by a religion, even if experienced or perceived by a person, can be bad overall, as in the case of ISIS. Even so, such meaning can remove division and fragmentation in purpose from a self and a life. A morally bad purpose can unify a self and

life, at least considerably if not perfectly, despite its lack of
moral goodness. This consideration blocks any attempt to
reduce religion to considerations of moral goodness.

Religion contributes to a human life an overarching
experiential meaning for that life in a way that has definite
practical value. Many people find a compelling reason for
religion, that is, for being religious, in that regard. If they
have a reason to adopt unifying practical meaning for their
lives, they have a reason to embrace a religion that supplies
such life's meaning, on the assumption that no alternative
to a religion offers such a meaning and they have no good
reason to avoid a religion. More specifically, a religious
conviction can bear on one's moral life in a unifying, practical way. Socrates and Plato suggested that if one knows
what is good or virtuous, then one will do what is good or
virtuous. This position is dubious at best, as Aristotle noted
in connection with *akrasia*, or weakness of will. A person can
know what is good, but, owing to an inadequacy in his or
her exercise of will, fail to do what is good. The same
applies to what a person *believes* to be good: An inadequacy
in one's exercise of will can result in one's failing to do what
one believes to be good.

The apostle Paul remarks: "I do not do what I want, but
I do the very thing I hate.... I can will what is right, but
I cannot do it. For I do not do the good I want, but the evil
I do not want is what I do" (Rom. 7:15, 18–19, NRSV, here
and in subsequent Biblical translations). He thus acknowledges the failure, in some cases, of one's performing the
desired actions one deems good. Receiving a religious conviction can enable some people to overcome such failure,
because it can empower them to (resolve to) carry out the
desired actions they consider good. They may be wrong
about what is actually good, but their religious conviction,
having causal influence, can give them motivating power,
via their intentions, to perform the actions they regard as
good. In doing so, the religious conviction can contribute to
the integrating of their beliefs and practices. When such

integrating is morally good for a person, a religious conviction can figure centrally in something morally good for a
person. Even so, other religious convictions, however
motivating and integrating, can be antithetical to what is
morally good. Religion and moral goodness, then, are not
co-extensive and hence not interchangeable. In addition,
even when it is morally good, religion takes us beyond
moral theory to its own domain of religious life's meaning
for a person.

6 TWO EXTREMES ON RELIGIOUS EXPERIENCE

In some religious traditions, we find religious theorists who
display fear, if not antipathy, toward a significant role for
religious experience in religious life. This is an extreme
that distorts the character of religious life and offers no
corresponding gain. We find this extreme in various religious traditions, but a recent clear illustration comes from
the Protestant Christian theology of Karl Barth and some of
his followers. We can apply a lesson about his neglect
of religious experience to a number of other religious
traditions.

Barth reacted negatively to the role of felt dependence in
religious experience proposed by Schleiermacher. He asks
concerning the alleged support for religion in experience:

What if [the] attempt to fill up the yawning gulf of religion's
unprovability by means of the "individual experience" should
also be abandoned like the rest in the knowledge that to *this*
entity, *autopistis*, no one can possibly assert a claim? What if
faith can only be a sign pointing toward that basis, founded in
itself, which is never in any sense "object," but is always
unchangeably subject? How would it be if the datum with
which dogmatics [or religious inquiry] has to begin were not
man – in his experience as little as in his thinking – but again
God himself in *his* Word? (1925 [1962], p. 260)

Barth allows such questions to guide his perspective on religion, departing from Schleiermacher and others who include human experience at the foundations of religious commitment. As a replacement for human experience in one's starting point for religious inquiry, Barth proposes starting with God, or what he calls "the Word of God." He states: "Here no other 'way' whatever exists except the road from above [i.e., from God] downwards [to anything human, such as human experience]" (p. 265). This perspective abandons a guiding role for religious experience in a religious life.

The mistake in Barth's approach stems from the assumption that "the datum with which [religious inquiry] has to begin ... [is] God himself in his Word" (p. 260). Barth's similar language for his proposed starting point is "God giving himself to be known through his Word" (p. 260). This language leaves us with an unanswered key question: Giving himself *to whom*? Thus far we have no specification of "God giving himself" to anyone at all or relating to humans at all, such as in their experience. So, Barth's talk of a starting point in "God himself in his Word" and in "God giving himself" is *non*relational concerning any humans and their experiential or psychological perspective. It is akin to one's speaking of an offer of friendship but failing to mention to whom the offer was made. Such talk would be unacceptably indeterminate in content, at least for any notion of an actual offer of friendship.

Barth claims that "through the Word of God, God himself will let himself be revealed" (p. 263). We see the indeterminacy in this claim's semantic content relative to this inevitable question: Revealed *where*, and *to whom*? Barth has no basis for an answer. At best, the revelation is in the abstract and to no one at all. So, Barth lacks a basis for (a claim to) determinate, actual revelation to actual humans. We thus find that he has offered a semantically indeterminate approach to a starting point for religious inquiry. If Barth answers the key questions at hand in order to gain semantic determinacy, he will introduce the experiential or psychological perspective of a human being. This will involve a human perspective in the starting point, including a human as a personal, psychological agent with experiences whose perspective bears on a proposed starting point for religious inquiry.

Barth's fear of the role of experience in religious commitment and life influenced many of his followers, including Emil Brunner. Despite Brunner's dissent from Barth on some important matters, he did not fully escape Barth's influence against a definite role of religious experience in religious commitment. In a late work, Brunner remarks: "Faith [in God] really and exclusively is dependent on the Word [of God], which against all empirical reality, supported by no experience, is in itself enough; the Word ... is only to be grasped in the event in which that affirmation is uttered" (1962, p. 201).

The misleading language is: "supported by no experience," and this language yields Barth's kind of exclusive contrast between the Word of God and human experience. It thus divorces human experience from religious inquiry, as if such experience were irrelevant. This extreme position devalues human experience and psychology in a way that makes them negligible by religious inquiry and commitment. It thus does not fit with familiar religious inquiry and life, and it opens the door to a misleading kind of dogmatism. Brunner's full position does not fit with this extreme position, but he did make some troublesome claims, such as the previously quoted claim, that stem from Barth's fear of giving human experience a role in religious inquiry and commitment.

The second extreme regarding religious experience portrays it as irresistible or coercive toward human agents who are religious. This extreme is found across religious traditions, but we find it widespread in the Christian tradition. For instance, H. R. Mackintosh has suggested that in Christian religious experience, people gain a religious conviction "because the influence of Christ upon us leaves us no option" (1929, p. 53). This is a strong claim, and one should ask whether it fits with the actual evidence regarding religious experience. This strong view does not fit with Mackintosh's more cautiously stated view that "faith [in God] is equally a gift or bestowal of [God] and an independent venture of our own," or with his view, in keeping with John 7:17, of the positive role of human willing in human knowledge of truths regarding God (Mackintosh 1921, p. 65; 1929, p. 59).

The strong view in question has received support from Edgar P. Dickie, who has endorsed a kind of conviction in religious experience that omits a cooperative component. Such conviction allegedly arises from a coercive part of reality, and it does not wait on the will of a human. Dickie states his position: "We believe because we must, and we also believe that the coercion comes from God" (1954, p. 37). Similarly, he claims: "[Divine] revelation produces conviction and the conviction so produced may be characterized by the sense that all is of God; that it is the divine truth itself which comes to the human heart to exercise a sway that cannot be challenged or gainsaid" (p. 19).

If "to gainsay" means "to deny, oppose, or contradict," as many dictionaries indicate, the conviction from a God who respects human agency in this area *could* be gainsaid. Indeed, a lament from numerous Biblical writers is that God's effort to convict God's people is opposed and resisted by them. This lesson is a large part of the story of the later prophets in ancient Israel, and it has a painful psychological realism about it. We evidently have in religious experience and its history no good reason to deny that humans can oppose and resist a divine effort of conviction toward moral improvement. This holds true for the kind of religious experience and conviction reported by Tolstoy.

Willem Zuurdeeg has endorsed the strong view explicitly: "People are convinced because a Good, a Cause, or a God has taken hold of them. They cannot help themselves; for they are drawn irresistibly" (1958, p. 30). (A similar view is found in Brown 1930.) In this perspective, God brings about religious experiences that are humanly irresistible in their power to draw people to God. God's power to convict people regarding God and God's will thus has no threat of resistance from any human power. God's power in religious experience always prevails against human power, according to the strong view.

In general, being convicted by God does not require that God be irresistible in a way entailing that people "cannot help themselves" in yielding to God. A religious experience involving a divine challenge or intrusion in human conscience can allow for human resistance and rejection toward God and God's will, thus preserving a role for genuine human agency in an experience of religious conviction. The same point applies to a religious experience of "being led" by God. Human resistance and rejection are genuine options for typical humans. Omission of this role for human agency will result in an implausibly mechanical approach to divine convicting and leading of humans, because it will omit the key role for human agency and cooperation.

An account of religious experience and life's meaning will be more resilient if it avoids commitment to the two extremes just noted. Regardless of where these two extremes occur, in theistic or nontheistic religious traditions, they misrepresent the nature of religious experience as central to responsible religious commitment. We will obscure such commitment if we omit the crucial role of either religious experience or responsible human agency in religion. We turn now to the role of interpretation in responding to religious experience with a view toward life's meaning. (Chapters 7 and 8 return to the role of conviction in religious experience.)

Religious Experience Interpreted

Chapter 1 characterized a core religious experience as an experience of a sensed overarching value and meaning for a human life, regardless of the actual sacredness or moral goodness of that value or meaning. It also allowed the value and meaning experienced, after the example of Tolstoy, to be related to an *individual* human agent, apart from a social or institutional setting. In doing so, it allows for individual reformers in religion who, on the basis of their unshared religious experiences, go against the grain of social or institutional religion. Still, interpretations from religious reformers must earn their keep somehow, and this consideration calls for our attending to the interpretation of religious experience. We shall see that interpretation looms large in religion, even if it does not constitute the nature of religious experience itself.

1 EXPERIENCE BEYOND INTERPRETATION

Seeking understanding of our world, we humans ask questions about ourselves and our surroundings. Our questions range far and wide, in the hope of finding answers that illuminate or at least describe something we deem worthy of our effort. In this context, a human is *Homo interrogatus*, formulating and using questions to make some sense of something under consideration. Given a purpose to make some sense of things, a human is a *senseseeker*, one who aims for sense as meaning or significance of some sort. This observation offers no support, however, to the controversial view that, apart from language, our experience is what William James (1890) called a "blooming, buzzing confusion."

Typically, we humans do not stop with our questions, as if interrogation is an end in itself. We move on to *interpretation* of ourselves or at least our surroundings. *Homo interrogatus* becomes *Homo hermeneuticus*: one who is interpreting, or at least seeking interpretation of something under question. Perhaps one's question is only: What actually is *this*? The relevant *this* could be mysterious to an inquirer, only vaguely grasped. In any case, it need not be just further interpretation being interpreted. A human experience thus need not be interpretation "all the way down," with no additional, qualitative residue of something independent of interpretation. One could have, in addition, salient evidence of something independent of experience, on the basis of the felt reality of corresponding bumps, bruises, and the like – no mere interpretation there. In any case, an external world of physical objects and events, accompanied by persons, would enable human experience to be something other than interpretation without residue.

Interpreters favor a range of familiar questions about their experiences, such as: What? Why? How? Who? Where? and When? They may work with different preferred understandings of such questions in the details, but they share a general aim for interpretation via description and explanation of various sorts. If the results of their interpretations are incomplete and fragmentary, those results still can aid human understanding of experience and the larger world. Incomplete human understanding is nonetheless human *understanding*, as it can illuminate *to some extent* human experience and the broader world. The sciences, for instance, do not lose their interpretive value for being incomplete and fragmentary. Their value does not depend on their being complete, as their history shows.

Individual people can interpret their own experience from a first-person, egocentric perspective, without relying on input from other people. This option would not make an interpretation inherently private, but it would allow for contingently private interpretation. For instance, a particular interpretation of a religious experience of overarching value and meaning for life (say, a particular theistic interpretation) can be private for a person. Even so, in typical cases, it *could* be shared with other people, perhaps if the person with the experience so desired. Sharing, however, is optional in this context. So, if the word "I" did not exist, we would have to invent it to capture the first-person perspective of an individual interpreter. It picks out something distinctive and important in human experience, although its referent can be elusive at times.

Even doubts about the importance of "I" presuppose an egocentric perspective from which those doubts arise (e.g., "my" doubts). It matters that "I" is indispensable in our world, and it makes for some mysteries in the mix. Eliminativists about the selves behind "I" omit something that we are well advised to acknowledge: the distinctive *intentional* features of individual selves. Persons as selves intend to do things, and these things include their interpreting various aspects of the world. In neglecting an egocentric perspective, we would overlook what sets the intentional context for much interpretation, including the interpretation of religious experience. We thus shall give this perspective its due.

Persons as interpreters often seek truth in interpretation, among other things, but seeking truth does not entail acquiring truth. Human interpreters manifest fallibility, that is, the real potential of going wrong in interpretation. When they do go wrong, they miss the truth, because they miss the relevant facts that are truth-makers for correct claims. Beyond beliefs, facts matter, because they can frustrate or enhance a human life, regardless of human intentions and hopes. In representing facts aright, truths can portray reality for us, thus saving us from distorted interpretations of reality. The issue of how we come to *know* truths is a separate matter, with abundant complexities of its own. Even so, the complexities do not challenge the value of truth itself in interpretation.

Many of our interpretations offer a causal story of some aspect of our experience, such as its origin or its continuation. In the case of religious experience, for instance, some people offer an interpretation that assigns a causal role to a God of some sort. The God proposed thus figures in a causal story of the origin or the continuation of a religious experience. In a noteworthy story, one's experiencing a challenge to care for one's resolute enemy arises, at least in part, from God's convicting power for a human to do what is morally good. In a related story, offered by Tolstoy in Chapter 1, one's experience of life's value and meaning as becoming a better person originates from God's intervention in one's experience. The causal stories offered throughout human history for religious experience are highly diverse, and they attract and sustain ongoing controversy among interpreters and theorists of religion.

Alister Hardy has commented on the interpretation of religious experience by British economist Beatrice Webb:

[She] was conscious of experiencing a sense of reverence or awe – an apprehension of a power and purpose outside herself – which she called "feeling" and which was sometimes induced by appreciation of great music or corporate worship. But the experience went further than this nebulous, fleeting "feeling" – because as a result of it she achieved a religious interpretation of the universe which satisfied and upheld her and enabled her to seek continuous guidance in prayer – and this without compromising her intellectual integrity. (1979, p. 18)

In Hardy's language, the religious interpretation arose "as a result of" the religious experience. So, the two are not the same thing. The religious experience, in this case, *grounds* a religious interpretation in a manner that saves one from "compromising intellectual integrity," at least according to Hardy. The latter claim, however, is controversial among theorists of religion, and therefore we need to examine how a religious experience can ground a religious interpretation, if it can. The important point now is that we not conflate the category of "religious experience" with the category of "religious interpretation," even though many people do so.

The interpretation of an alleged experience does not guarantee the reality of the experienced object, particularly *as interpreted*. It can miss the mark regarding the actual features and causes of an experience, and thus be misleading and mistaken regarding the experienced object. Interpreting an actual experience, in any case, is not creating that experience or its qualitative content. Interpretation can obscure the qualitative content of an actual experience for a person, but it does not constitute that content. So, there is room for error in such interpretation, given the independence of the content of an experience.

We can benefit from a distinction between *de re* and *de dicto* features relevant to experiences. The *de re* features of the content of an experience are qualitative features that do not include such human interpretation as judgment or conception (even if the latter are accompaniments). Some philosophers have called such features "what is given" or "what is present" directly to one in experience. The qualitative redness in a direct experience of such redness, for instance, does not include and is not constituted by human judgment or conception regarding redness or any other qualitative feature of experience. In this respect, the redness is a qualitative reality that does not depend for its existence on human judgment or conception, that is, on *de dicto* activity. In addition, human *de dicto* activity in judgment or conception can fail to represent and can even misrepresent the *de re* content of an experience. Human error in the interpretation of an experience is thus a live option and, as it happens, is often an actual option (as our experience often indicates).

A person's having an experience, given its *de re* character, does not require that person's interpreting the experience. So, it does not require one's knowing or even believing that one has the experience. One could have a direct experience of redness, for instance, without formulating any judgment about it. If the qualitative content of an experience *directly attracts one's attention,* even apart from one's *selective focus* of attention on it, one has an experience of it. This is a matter of something (understood broadly) being *present directly to one's awareness,* and it does not depend logically on an inference or a judgment. One may or may not take or have the time to proceed to an interpretation of the experienced content. A person's experiences can be too abundant to give that person an opportunity to interpret all of them in the time available. So, an experience can have a reality of its own, including in its qualitative content, apart from its being interpreted. Given this kind of reality, we have realism about (some) experience and its content, in contrast with various kinds of idealism and subjectivism about experience.

For any experience, we can ask whether its qualitative content is *altogether subjective,* that is, not indicative at all of the objective world. An affirmative answer is not automatic. The content of an experience *can,* in principle, indicate or represent something objective, and it can do this even when inquirers are undecided or confused about the matter. Some religious experiences, among other kinds of experiences, are candidates for having content indicative of the objective world. They may present special problems for our *confirming* that they indicate something objective, but that matter is separate from the factual issue of whether they actually indicate something objective. We do well not to confuse epistemology and ontology in this area.

In general, an experience's indicating something objective, courtesy of its qualitative content, does not depend on one's confirming that it does so. It would give human confirming too much world-making and experience-constraining power to assume otherwise. Tolstoy's religious experience of life's meaning, for instance, is not automatically a case where he created, constituted, or even confirmed (the reality of) the relevant meaning. The object of his experience can have a reality of its own, apart from human constitution or confirmation of it. This is typical of human experiences with regard to any such human activity.

Experiences are not true or false in the way interpretations in their judgments are, because they do not consist in judgments, that is, in affirmations that something is the case. Experiences, nonetheless, can be *veridical* or *unveridical*. That is, they can accurately portray reality or fail to do so. In failing to do so, they can be illusions, hallucinations, or distortions of reality in other ways. Religious experiences, in particular, can be unveridical. An apparent experience of God, for instance, can be *merely* apparent and thus fail to be a genuine experience of *God*. Some critics of religions have suggested that all religious experiences are unveridical, but the relevant data do not yield easily to such a sweeping judgment. A responsible approach would attend to the actual religious experiences in question, giving them due careful attention. It is at least a live option that some religious experiences relate one to features of objective reality. A mere contrary assumption or claim will not preclude this option. The hard work of careful assessment needs to be done, if inquiry is to be responsible.

The fact that an experience has *de re* content does not entail that the experience is veridical regarding the objective world. The qualitative content of an experience can be real and definite but still unveridical in relation to objective reality. A salient apparent experience of God, for instance, can have real and definite content but fail to portray reality (if reality does not include God's existence). So, we can ask coherently whether the qualitative content of an experience, including a religious experience, accurately portrays reality.

This option stems from a logically coherent *appearance–reality* distinction that applies to the qualitative content of experience. It makes skepticism about objective representation from experience a logically coherent option. A logically coherent option, however, is not the same as a correct option or even a reasonable option. Matters of correctness and reasonableness call for separate assessment, beyond matters of mere logical coherence.

The independence of experience relative to human interpretation stems from the independent causal status of experience and its *de re* content. It is hard to account for human experience if we disregard such independence. Even so, interpretation matters, despite its not constituting an experience or its content. One prominent way that it matters concerns sensemaking, that is, the formulating of meaning for human experience. We shall explore sensemaking in this regard.

2 INTERPRETATION AND SENSEMAKING

Inquirers tend to value their making sense of their experience, even when the result is fragmentary and not complete. They often value sensemaking of at least two kinds: *descriptive* sensemaking that answers, if only partially, the question of *what* something is, and *explanatory* sensemaking that answers, if incompletely, the question of either *why* or *how* something is as it is. So, an inquirer who has an apparent experience of God will tend to ask what it really is, in terms of its constituents and objects, and why or how this experience is occurring when it is. Such asking would seek to illuminate the experience in a way that makes it *understandable* to some extent. Inquirers tend to value such understanding, because it familiarizes their experience and world for them to some extent, and it can help them to relate new experiences in important ways to some prior experiences.

An attempt at sensemaking occurs in the New Testament book of Acts, when Jews with different languages from various nations hear some early Jewish Christian disciples from Galilee speaking in those languages. "Amazed and astonished, they asked, 'Are not all these who are speaking Galileans? And how is it that we hear, each of us, in our own native language?'" (Acts 2:7–8). Their general response, according to Acts 2:12, is: "All were amazed and perplexed, saying to one another, 'What does this mean?'" A literal translation of the original Greek statement of the question is: "What can this be?" Whichever translation we prefer, the question seeks a kind of meaning, either descriptive or explanatory.

The formulation of meaning for experience can be a matter of *discovering* meaning, but it also can be a matter of *ascribing* meaning. Ascribed meaning can differ from actual meaning that resides, somehow, in an experience. Discovered meaning, in contrast, would be actual meaning residing in an experience. For instance, a member of the terrorist religion ISIS could have an apparent experience of God, and he could ascribe its explanatory meaning to God's wanting him to destroy some innocent civilians. Given that this meaning contradicts moral decency, many of us would be inclined to regard it as *merely* ascribed and not actual, that is, as not representing God. So, we would tend not to think of this meaning as something discovered about God. Of course, a member of ISIS would not link God to moral decency in the way many of us would, and hence controversy could arise about the relevant meaning. Such controversy is common in the case of interpreting religious experiences, but it does not undermine the veridical character of every religious experience.

Inquirers attempt to make sense of their experiences by using concepts, words, judgments, sentences, and theories of various sorts. The latter sense-making instruments, however, do not fully determine the sense made of experiences. The qualitative features of experiences figure in the actual meaning, and they are irreducible to the instruments in question. Qualitative redness, for instance, is not exhausted in its content by a concept, word, judgment, sentence, or theory. Even when described correctly, such content has features that are not reducible to correct description. This qualitative content, as suggested, is not a judgment or a concept of any kind.

Correct judgment about the qualitative content of an experience will have terms that *refer* to that content. Otherwise, the judgment would not be correct. Successful reference to objective, mind-independent reality, however, need not occur for sensemaking. The meaning one ascribes to an experience can misrepresent the features of objective reality, despite the value of that meaning for subjective matters. The sensemaking in interpreting experience, then, differs from capturing objective truth. Capturing such truth is a common goal in sensemaking, but it is not a necessary condition of it. Sensemaking can go wrong, and often does go wrong, relative to objective reality.

Sensemaking of a religious experience can depend on a particular religious tradition, but it need not. It can have a breadth that applies across various religious traditions. The case of Tolstoy's experience in Chapter 1 can be interpreted with a breadth that goes beyond any particular religious tradition, even though Tolstoy himself offered a Christian theistic interpretation. We can and will benefit from attention to some additional experiences and interpretations. Our topic is religious experience and its significance for the meaning of human life, rather than the wide range of world religions and their amazing diversity. So, we can be highly selective in our focus on some religious experiences and their corresponding interpretations of life's meaning. We will do so by attending to six seminal figures in the history of religion. We need not cover the remarkable breadth and diversity of the world religions in our focus. Such coverage, if done with adequate detail, would call for a multivolume project.

3 NONTHEISTIC RELIGIOUS INTERPRETATION

We cannot adequately understand religious experience and its interpretation apart from acknowledging the diversity of such experiences and interpretations. Even if religious experience is inherently an experience of a special kind of overarching value and meaning for life, it comes in diverse forms and with diverse interpretations. Neglect of this diversity leaves an unduly narrow understanding of religious experience and its interpretation. We see this in, for instance, an exclusively theistic approach to religious experience and interpretation. Even if theism of some kind looms large in traditional religious interpretations, it does not have a monopoly on those interpretations. Nontheistic approaches to religious experience and interpretation merit a fair hearing in attempts to understand religion and its contribution to life's meaning.

Chapter 1 proposed that a core religious experience is a direct experience of a sensed value and meaning for human life that is practical, overarching, primary, and self-engaging for that life. Tolstoy's experience of that sort, we saw, does not require an appeal to God, but it does allow for such an appeal, in keeping with Tolstoy's own Christian interpretation. We can find nontheistic interpretations of religious experience within most of the world religions, even if they have a minority position in some of them. I say "within," because some self-avowed practitioners of those religions opt for nontheistic interpretations of their religion, even in such traditionally theistic religions as Judaism and Christianity. We need to consider some actual religious experiences relevant to our topic.

The Buddhist Path of Gautama: Self-Practice in Awakened Life

We shall consider a wide-ranging religious perspective that is nontheistic in its practical focus: the Buddhism of

Siddhārtha Gautama, or the Buddha (c. 558–c. 491 BCE). This nontheistic focus has not blocked some other variations on Buddhism from being theistic in their focal interpretations of religious experience. Much of the history of Gautama Buddha is shrouded in myth and a shortage of definite evidence and hence in controversy among scholars. Even his dates of birth and death, as well as his historical reality, attract debates among historical scholars. Fortunately, we need not take up the historical debates for our purposes. Instead, we shall consider some relevant texts in an early collection of Buddhist writings, the Pāli Canon (written in the Pāli language).

Gautama, as an adult, had a meaningful transformative experience called his "Awakening" (also called "Enlightenment" or "Nirvana"). His experience fits with what we have called a "core religious experience," because its significance is practical, overarching, primary, and self-engaging for his life. Having experienced the luxuries of his father's wealth in eastern India, Gautama came to feel, as one of his biographers puts it, that his life was "meaningless" (Armstrong 2001, p. 50). This feeling led to his search for an alternative, for something that could give overarching practical meaning to his life as well as to the lives of others. He thus sought a new path for his life, a new method of living, beyond the ultimate emptiness of wealth and luxury.

Gautama proceeded in the context of prior Indian enlightenment traditions, while seeking an alternative to debilitating human suffering and frustration. His acquaintance with such suffering and frustration motivated his search for a meaningful path for human life. This path would not eliminate suffering and frustration, but it would identify a self-insulating method for avoiding their turbulent and destructive psychological consequences in one's life.

Gautama identifies a motivating realization behind his quest for meaningful life in the face of suffering: "Before my

Awakening, . . . the realization came to me: How this world has fallen on difficulty! It is born, it ages, it dies, it falls away and rearises, but it does not discern the escape from this stress, from this aging-and-death. O when will it discern the escape from this stress, from this aging-and-death?" (*Samyutta Nikaya* 12:65). Many people have settled on despair or hopelessness about any such escape or relief, but Gautama recommends a disciplined practical path as an alternative to despair. His path offers freedom and relief from a familiar but pain-producing chain of dependence in human life.

Gautama presents his experience of Awakening to include relief via "cessation" in a chain of dependence bearing on humans. He uses this broad notion of "name-and-form": "Feeling, perception, intention, contact, and attention: This is called *name*. The four great elements [the earth element, the water element, the fire element, the wind element], and the form [of materiality] dependent on the four great elements: This is called *form*. This name and this form are called *name-and-form*" (*Samyutta Nikaya* 12:2). The name-and-form thus encompasses *the mental* and *the material* domains, in more familiar terms. A key question for Gautama is whether there is any relief via cessation in the troubling vicissitudes of the mental and material domains as they contribute to human suffering and frustration.

Beginning with various psychological tendencies in humans, Gautama identifies the relief via cessation involved in his Awakening:

I have attained the following path to Awakening: From the cessation of name-and-form [the mental and the material] comes the cessation of consciousness [eye-consciousness, ear-consciousness, nose-consciousness, tongue-consciousness, body-consciousness, intellect-consciousness], from the cessation of consciousness comes the cessation of name-and-form. From the cessation of name-and-form comes the cessation of the six sense [i.e., sensory]-media [the eye-medium, the ear-medium, the nose-medium, the tongue-medium, the body-medium, the intellect-medium]. From the cessation of the six sense-media comes the cessation of contact [eye-contact, ear-contact, nose-contact, tongue-contact, body-contact, intellect-contact]. From the cessation of contact comes the cessation of feeling [feeling born from eye-contact, feeling born from ear-contact, feeling born from nose-contact, feeling born from tongue-contact, feeling born from body-contact, feeling born from intellect-contact]. From the cessation of feeling comes the cessation of craving [craving for forms, craving for sounds, craving for smells, craving for tastes, craving for tactile sensations, craving for ideas]. From the cessation of craving comes the cessation of clinging/sustenance [sensuality-clinging, view-clinging, habit-and-practice-clinging, and doctrine-of-self-clinging]. (*Samyutta Nikaya* 12:65; additions in brackets are from *Samyutta Nikaya* 12:2)

The general path of relief via cessation in Gautama's Awakening moves from relief via cessation of certain kinds of consciousness to relief via cessation of certain kinds of clinging to some features of ordinary life. This includes letting go of those features as one is released or relieved from certain kinds of consciousness. The relief via cessation, however, does not end there.

Gautama continues his report of his Awakening:

From the cessation of clinging/sustenance comes the cessation of becoming [sensual becoming, form becoming, and formless becoming]. From the cessation of becoming comes the cessation of birth [taking birth, descent, coming-to-be, coming-forth, appearance of aggregates, and acquisition of (sense) media of the various beings]. From the cessation of birth, then aging-and-death, sorrow, lamentation, pain, distress, and despair all cease. Thus is the cessation of this entire mass of stress [and suffering]. Cessation, cessation. Vision arose, clear knowing arose, discernment arose, knowledge arose, illumination arose within me with regard to things never heard before. (*Samyutta Nikaya* 12:65)

Gautama's key claim is: "From the cessation of birth [as the change of "coming-to-be"], aging-and-death, sorrow, lamentation, pain, distress, and despair all cease." The alleged culprit is *change* of certain kinds, and its antidote is in *relief via cessation* of change of those kinds. Gautama regards his illumination regarding relief via cessation as central to his Awakening, and he describes it as something that "arose within" him, as an experience of overarching meaning for his life and human life in general.

Gautama credits his awakened predecessors with pointing him to the path of his Awakening, but he reports his own discovery of a special truth about the path.

I saw an ancient path traveled by the Rightly Self-Awakened Ones of former times. And what is that ancient path, that ancient road, traveled by the Rightly Self-Awakened Ones of former times? Just this noble eightfold path: right view, right resolve, right speech, right action, right livelihood, right effort, right mindfulness, right concentration. That is the ancient path traveled by the Rightly Self-Awakened Ones of former times. I followed that path. Following it, I came to direct knowledge of aging-and-death, direct knowledge of the origination of aging-and-death, direct knowledge of the cessation of aging-and-death, direct knowledge of the path leading to the cessation of aging-and-death. I followed that path. Following it, I came to direct knowledge of birth ... becoming ... clinging ... craving ... feeling ... contact ... the six sense-media ... name-and-form ... consciousness, direct knowledge of the origination of consciousness, direct knowledge of the cessation of consciousness, direct knowledge of the path leading to the cessation of consciousness. I followed that path. (*Samyutta Nikaya* 12:65)

Gautama's breakthrough to Awakening came in his *following* the path to relief via cessation of the consciousness in question, not just in his reflecting on truths about the path. So, there is a *practical*, participatory component to his distinctive contribution and his Awakening. His participatory "following" led to his "direct knowledge" of the desired relief via cessation, and this knowledge is experiential and not abstract.

Gautama credits his following the path to relief via cessation for bringing about his liberation from fabrication and ignorance: "Following it [the path to relief via cessation], I came to direct knowledge of fabrications [bodily fabrications, verbal fabrications, mental fabrications], direct knowledge of the origination of fabrications, direct knowledge of the cessation of fabrications, direct knowledge of the path leading to the cessation of fabrications." He adds: "Not knowing stress, not knowing the origination of stress, not knowing the cessation of stress, not knowing the way of practice leading to the cessation of stress: This is called ignorance" (*Samyutta Nikaya* 12:2). His distinctive way or path is thus "the way of practice" aimed at relief via cessation of the stress of suffering and frustration. It is a matter of practicing the path to relief via cessation for the sake of avoiding the kinds of corrosive change that empty a life of its meaning.

We can call Gautama's path for life a "method" so long as we portray it as a practical method, and not purely intellectual or reflective. We might call it "the threefold practical method" of right conduct, right concentration, and right commitment, all for the sake of being liberated or relieved in practical effect from life's destructive changes. The method focuses not on an "external world," but on the practical means to insulating one psychologically *from* the corrosive effects of the world and *within* stable conduct, concentration, and commitment. Gautama considered this method to be central to "the holy life," and he proclaimed it to a wide audience.

We have a summary of Gautama's method toward Awakening in the following terms:

When the mind was concentrated, purified, bright, unblemished, rid of defilement, pliant, malleable, steady, and attained
to imperturbability, I directed it to the knowledge of the
ending of the mental effluents [or pollutants]. I discerned, as it
had come to be, that: This is stress.... This is the origination of
stress.... This is the cessation of stress.... This is the way leading
to the cessation of stress.... These are effluents [pollutants]....
This is the origination of effluents.... This is the cessation of
effluents.... This is the way leading to the cessation of effluents.
My heart, thus knowing, thus seeing, was released [or relieved]
from the effluent of sensuality, released from the effluent of
becoming, released from the effluent of ignorance. With release
[or relief], there was the knowledge, "Released." I discerned
that Birth is ended, the holy life fulfilled, the task done. There
is nothing further for this world. (*Majjhima Nikaya* 36)

Mental effluents are pollutants or toxins that stem from
harmful mental activities and lead to destructive changes
in human life. Here, again, Gautama focuses on relief via
cessation. This is relief or release from certain kinds of
change or "becoming," for the sake of a special knowledge
of "the holy life," the life that saves one from destruction by
stress and suffering.

The special knowledge arises from an experience of *relief*
or *release* from destructive becoming, and this experience is
described in such language as "darkness was destroyed;
light arose" (*Majjhima Nikaya* 36). This relief via cessation
yields "imperturbability," a psychological insulation
against being downtrodden by one's circumstances in life.
Such an insulation includes a kind of calm in the storms of
life, a calm that can save one from succumbing to despair
over suffering and frustration. It counters meaning-
threatening changes with an attitude of perseverance in
"the holy life," the life resistant to giving up on right conduct, right concentration, or right commitment.

The experience of Awakening in question is religious,
because it includes an experience of meaning that is

practical, overarching, primary, and self-engaging for a life. This practical meaning for a human life includes one's living for "the holiness" of right conduct, right concentration, and right commitment. It is overarching because it bears on one's dying as well as living, in all of the relevant aspects. In addition, it is akin to the meaning for life that Chapter 1 attributed to Tolstoy as a result of his core religious experience: the quest to become better. In both cases, the quest to become better includes an aim to become morally better, in a way that bears on all of one's life. The paths to realizing the quest differ, but in broad terms there is a similarity in practical meaning for human life. Gautama focuses more than Tolstoy on a practical method of life, but they share a broad moral goal for human life: the goal to become morally better.

While Tolstoy interprets his religious experience to have a central role for God, Gautama does not. Gautama focuses on a practical human method for life on the basis of a key assumption about human self-purification. Even so, Gautama was a theist, specifically a polytheist, as the following exchange indicates:

Then the Brahmin Sangārava said: "The great efforts of good Gautama have become profitable. They are the efforts of a Great Man, as it happens to the perfect rightfully enlightened one. Good Gautama, are there gods?"

"Bhāradvāja, it should be known with reasons, whether there are gods," Gautama replied.

"Good Gautama, when asked, are there gods, it was said, it should be known with reasons, whether there are gods. Are not these words useless lies?"

"Bhāradvāja, when asked are there gods, whether told there are gods, or told it should be known with reasons, a wise man should conclude that there are gods," Gautama replied.

"Why did good Gautama not declare this to me earlier?"

"Bhāradvāja, it is taken for granted, that there are gods in the world," Gautama replied. (*Majjhima Nikaya* 100)

The key claim from Gautama is: "A wise man should conclude that there are gods." This is not monotheism from
Gautama, but it is a polytheistic variation on theism, an
acknowledgment of the existence of gods. The nontheism
of many later Buddhists thus departs from the evident
position of Gautama himself.

Despite his avowed polytheism, Gautama does not give
any god a central role in his practical path to Awakening or
to a holy life. This explains why I have called Gautama's
publicly and practically significant interpretation of his religious experience of Awakening "nontheistic." His being a
theist does not make his publicly or practically significant
interpretation of his Awakening theistic. Various factors
may account for his nontheistic interpretation, but one
factor dominates. It emerges in his following remarks:
"Evil is left undone by oneself, by oneself is one cleansed.
Purity and impurity are one's own doing. No one purifies
another. No other purifies one" (*Dhammapada* 12:165).
Gautama thus holds that the practical path to one's
Awakening must be taken, if it is taken, *by oneself.*

A god, in Gautama's perspective, cannot take the path to
Awakening for one or even empower one's taking it. Otherwise, *self*-purification would be lost. Gautama's path to
Awakening depends on self-purification in self-conduct,
self-concentration, and self-commitment. It admits of no
Awakening by proxy for a person or even empowerment
by another agent, such as a god. The crucial responsibility for
following or practicing the path is altogether one's own, in
Gautama's message, even if other people can point one to the
path. Such individualism is central to Gautama's path, and it
calls for each person's discovering in Awakening the overarching practical meaning for his or her life. It thus calls for
each person's finding in Awakening an insular self-antidote
to this world's suffering and frustration. The self-antidote
brings relief via cessation of corrosive changes for a life.

Contrary to some popular suggestions, Gautama's interpretation of following the path to Awakening does not

allow for dispensing altogether with one's selfhood, even if it permits considerable flexibility or fluidity in selfhood. His positive, explicit role for *oneself* in following the path to a holy life is too prominent to allow for omitting selfhood altogether. His misgivings about individual selfhood concern various understandings and tendencies of the self that hinder one's following the path to Awakening. So, what Gautama calls a "doctrine-of-self-clinging" can be an obstruction to a holy life, but it does not follow that selfhood itself is dispensable.

Gautama emphasizes a central role for a *self in action* in following his path to Awakening: "Purity and impurity are *one's own doing*." Neglect of this role for a self will result in Gautama's path to a holy meaningful life being obscure, incoherent, and impracticable. Although a prominent interpretation of Gautama Buddha includes a goal of dispensing with individual selves, I recommend the less extreme interpretation just suggested. (For some controversy among Buddhists over the role of a self in Buddhist Awakening, see Conze 1959, pp. 190–97.)

By way of analogy from the Jewish religious tradition, consider the following remark from the author of Psalm 23: "The Lord is my shepherd, I shall not want" (Psalm 23:1). On the surface, the claim appears to prohibit wants, all wants. Clearly, however, this is not the author's intention. Later in the psalm, the author expresses an important want, his desire "to dwell in the house of the Lord" forever. In literary religious expression, a person sometimes speaks without stating assumed restrictions or qualifications on a statement, but they are implicit nonetheless. When we need such restrictions to make good sense of what is being expressed, we should acknowledge them, in keeping with a principle of interpretive charity. One can make a good case that this applies to some of the unrestricted claims by Gautama about the self. The very notion of relief via cessation involved in Gautama's understanding of an Awakening experience assumes a self who is getting such relief. At least, a plausible case can be made to that end.

We should ask whether we actually have access to self-provided psychological insulation from life's suffering and frustration, and whether God actually has no role to play in the desired insulation. We now need, however, to identify another prominent nontheistic interpretation of religious experience, that of Confucius.

The Way of Confucius: Self-Cultivation for Relational Virtue

Like Gautama Buddha, Confucius (c. 551–c. 479 BCE) presents difficulties for historical reconstruction. Once again, many historical details are shrouded in myth and inadequate evidence. We can proceed, however, with his teachings summarized by some of his Chinese followers in the *Analects of Confucius*, which became a main document of Confucianism for the Way (*dao*) of Confucius.

As in the case of Gautama, Confucius was a theist of a sort, even though many later followers have not shared his theism. We shall see that he did not give his theism a central role in interpreting his life-guiding religious experience or in his recommended Way of life. Even so, his theism is clear in the *Analects.* Here is one aspect of his religious experience he deems to be theistic:

The Master said: When I was fifteen I set my heart on learning. At thirty I took my stand. At forty I was without confusion. At fifty I knew the command of Tian [Heaven, or Supreme Deity]. At sixty I heard it with a compliant ear. At seventy I follow the desires of my heart and do not overstep the bounds. (*Analects* 2.4)

Confucius reports his *hearing* and *knowing* the command of Heaven, that is, of God. If Heaven were altogether non-personal (say, just a set of moral principles), it would be unable to issue a command, let alone a command heard by a human. Hearing God's command would be an *experience* of God's action, and not just a thought or a reflection. In this respect, Confucius acknowledges and testifies to a religious experience, however much some later followers sought to reject his theism.

We find a second kind of religious experience for Confucius in prayer:

The Master fell ill. Zilu requested permission to offer prayers. The Master said, "Is there precedent for this?" Zilu answered, "There is. In the liturgy it says, 'Pray to the spirits above and below.'" The Master said, "My prayers are longstanding." (*Analects* 7.35)

If the "spirits above" include God, we have Confucius testifying to his praying to God. In any case, given this passage, we may consider that his "hearing the command of Heaven" (*Analects* 2.4, just above) included his praying to God. At a minimum, his praying would have involved some kind of religious experience, and he would have acknowledged a role for the spirits and Heaven above.

A third area of acknowledgment of God by Confucius arises as follows:

The Master said, "No one recognizes me!" Zigong said, "How is it that this is so?" The Master said, "I do not complain against Tian [Heaven], nor do I blame men. I study what is lowly and so get through to what is exalted. Is it not Tian who recognizes me?" (*Analects* 14.35)

If Heaven "recognizes" Confucius, it must include an *agent* capable of recognition, beyond abstract entities or principles. Confucius seems to have valued such recognition for his personal life, quite aside from its lack of a role in his public life of teaching.

The evidence from the *Analects* indicates that Confucius was familiar with religious experience, including such experience of Heaven as (including) God. He was, in short, a theist of some sort. Perhaps his theology was not valued widely by many of his subsequent followers in the way his religious, moral, and social instruction was and therefore was largely omitted from edited collections of his advice. It may be, too, that his theological reflections did not include much practical advice and therefore did not merit focal attention in compilations devoted to his counsel for others.

Whatever the fate of the theology of Confucius, he does not give theology a central role in his practical interpretation of his religious experience, including his Way of self-cultivating a human life. He does say: "Tian [Heaven] has engendered virtue in me" (*Analects* 7.23), but this theological view remains in the ontic background in his public teaching. Like Gautama Buddha, he omits theology from his practical wisdom and thus from the center of his religious, moral, and social influence. We shall see why this is so, in connection with the importance of *self*-cultivation in his religious Way of life.

Confucius identifies a kind of interpersonal relationality, or "loyal reciprocity," as the center of his religious experience and advice for human life. For instance:

The Master said, "Shen, a single thread runs through my *dao* [Way for human life]." Master Zeng said, "Yes." The Master went out, and the other disciples asked, "What did he mean?" Master Zeng said, "The Master's *dao* is nothing other than loyalty and reciprocity." (*Analects* 4.15)

Zigong asked, "Is there a single saying that one may put into practice all one's life?" The Master said, "That would be 'reciprocity': That which you do not desire, do not do to others." (*Analects* 15.24)

Confucius finds practical, overarching, primary, and self-engaging meaning for human life in a certain kind of loyal reciprocity in virtuous human relationships. We thus may think of his experience of such reciprocity as central to his core religious experience and as grounding a religious (rather than a merely ethical) perspective for him.

Here is another endorsement from Confucius of the reciprocity in question:

Zhonggong asked about *ren* [goodness, including benevolence]. The Master said, "When you go out your front gate, continue to treat each person as though receiving an honored guest. When directing the actions of subordinates, do so as though officiating at a great ritual sacrifice. Do not do to others what you would not wish done to you. Then there can be no complaint against you, in your state or in your household." (*Analects* 12.2)

Confucius endorses the primary value of his *dao* for human life focused on virtuous reciprocity: "The Master said, 'Set your heart on the *dao*, base yourself in virtue, rely on *ren*'" (*Analects* 7.6). The relevant virtue is to be reciprocal in human relationships: "Someone said, 'To employ virtue to repay resentment, how would that be?' The Master said, 'What, then, would you employ to repay virtue? Employ straightforwardness to repay resentment; employ virtue to repay virtue'" (*Analects* 14.34). Relational virtue, then, is to multiply relational virtue, for the good of all concerned.

Like Gautama, Confucius emphasizes a kind of self-control in his Way for human life, that is, self-control as the *self*-cultivation of virtuous reciprocity.

Zilu asked about the *junzi* [ideal person]. The Master said, "Cultivate in yourself respectful attentiveness." Zilu asked: "Is that all there is to it?" The Master replied: "Cultivate yourself to bring comfort to others." Zilu asked: "Is that all there is to it?" The Master replied: "Cultivate yourself to bring comfort to the people." (*Analects* 14.42)

The central advice here is: *"Cultivate yourself* to bring comfort to others." This is benevolent *self-cultivation* for the sake of others, and it serves at the center of what Confucius offers as his religious Way of human life.

Confucius endorses a strict approach to self-cultivation in his perspective on human goodness:

Yan Yuan asked about *ren*. The Master said, "Conquer yourself and return to *li* [proper, fitting conduct]: that is *ren*. If a person could conquer himself and return to *li* for a single day, the world would respond to him with *ren*. Being *ren* proceeds from oneself, how could it come from others?" Yan Yuan said, "May I ask for details of this?" The Master said, "If it is not *li*, don't look at it; if it is not *li*, don't listen to it; if it is not *li*, don't say it; if it is not *li*, don't do it." (*Analects* 12.1)

Confucius thus denies that a person can have the desired relational virtue by proxy or by the power of other people. In short: "Being *ren* proceeds from oneself, how could it come from others?" If it cannot "come from others," it cannot come from God. So, Confucius assigns strict self-cultivation of virtue to humans and therefore leaves no place for God to cultivate or to empower virtue for them. God thus has no salient or practical function in the religious Way of life offered by Confucius.

We now can make sense of the absence of theology in Confucius' practical interpretation of his central religious experience and his Way for human life. In addition, we can see a direct parallel to the nontheistic approach of Gautama Buddha. Neither religious leader finds a practical role for divine involvement in their paths to a meaningful religious life for humans. They both require *self*-determination and *self*-empowerment, rather than external determination or empowerment, in following their recommended paths. As a result, in their perspectives, humans have no practical need to invoke God or God's power. Even if one accepts theism of some sort, as Gautama and Confucius do, one does not have a practical need to involve God in achieving a holy meaningful life. One's practical life can be religious with experienced value and meaning that is overarching, primary, and self-engaging, but this will not make it theological for one in any practical way. This consideration underlies the nontheistic religious approaches to life's meaning offered by Gautama Buddha and Confucius.

Nontheistic religious interpretations are not limited to certain variations on Buddhism or Confucianism. As suggested, they can be found across most of the world's major religions, if with a minority role in many cases. It would be a mistake to try to reduce such interpretations to ethical theory or philosophy, because they involve a core religious experience of overarching value and practical meaning for human life that does not reduce to ethical theory or philosophy. The cases of Gautama Buddha and Confucius illustrate this lesson, even though they endorse theism of a sort among their personal beliefs. Endorsing theism, however, does not entail giving it a practical role, or any central role, in one's religious Way of life. Our evidence regarding Gautama and Confucius illustrates two actual, influential cases of this separation of theology from religion. Whatever one thinks of the merits of this separation, it is a religious reality in human history. In addition, it provides a distinctive alternative to theistic interpretations of religion, to which we now turn.

4 THEISTIC RELIGIOUS INTERPRETATION

We have noted a role for theism in the personal thought of Gautama and Confucius but an absence of any practical role for it in their religious life and advice. Many other religious figures offer a practical role for theistic interpretation of some kind in relation to religious experience, meaning, life, and advice. We shall consider four such prominent figures: Krishna, Moses, the apostle Paul, and Muhammad.

Our focus will be on their distinctive roles for religious experience, and not on their theologies in general.

Hindu Theology in Krishna: Constant-Adoration Theism

Fortunately, we need not undertake a quest for the historical Krishna; that would be a massive undertaking. Our focus now is on his religious perspective found in the *Bhagavad-Gita*, rather than on his reported life in northern India (c. 3227–c. 3102 BCE). We would have no easy time sifting through myths and legends to reach confirmable, evidence-based history regarding Krishna's life. Even so, we can identify some important features of an ancient theistic (but not monotheistic) perspective on religious experience and life attributed to him. This perspective, found in certain variations on Vaishnavism within Hinduism, represents him as an incarnation of the supreme God (namely, Vishnu) in visible human form. It also portrays him, in the *Bhagavad-Gita*, as befriending and advising an Indian warrior and inquirer, Arjuna.

Krishna offers a short description of his own "divine work" in chapter 4 of the *Bhagavad-Gita:*

> I come, and go, and come. When Righteousness
> Declines, O Bharata! when Wickedness
> Is strong, I rise, from age to age, and take
> Visible shape, and move a man with men,
> Succouring the good, thrusting the evil back,
> And setting Virtue on her seat again.
> Who knows the truth touching my births on earth
> And my divine work, when he quits the flesh
> Puts on its load no more, falls no more down
> To earthly birth: to Me he comes, dear Prince!
> Many there be who come! from fear set free,
> From anger, from desire; keeping their hearts
> Fixed upon me – my Faithful – purified

By sacred flame of Knowledge. Such as these
Mix with my being. Whoso worship me,
Them I exalt; but all men everywhere
Shall fall into my path.

(Bhagavad-Gita 4.6–11)

Krishna aims for humans' being "purified by sacred flame of knowledge" of him, and this evidently includes humans' "mixing with his being" in some manner. The purification and mixing would be experiential and not just reflective for humans. They would include humans who "keep their hearts fixed upon [Krishna]," and they thus call for human devotion to Krishna. Such devotion, however, needs a ground in human experience of some kind, because it is not offered as blind commitment or just wishful thinking.

The ground suggested for Arjuna's devotion to Krishna is the latter's unique "manifesting" to him. Arjuna asks to see the divine Self, and Krishna replies:

Gaze, then, thou Son of Pritha! I manifest for thee
Those hundred thousand shapes that clothe my Mystery:
I show thee all my semblances, infinite, rich, divine,
My changeful hues, my countless forms. See! in this
    face of mine,
Adityas, Vasus, Rudras, Aswins, and Maruts; see
Wonders unnumbered, Indian Prince! revealed to none
    save thee.
Behold! this is the universe! – Look! what is live and dead
I gather all in one – in Me! Gaze, as thy lips have said,
On God eternal, very God! See Me! See what thou prayest!
Thou canst not! – nor, with human eyes, Arjuna! ever
    mayest!
Therefore I give thee sense divine. Have other eyes,
    new light!
And, look! This is My glory, unveiled to mortal sight!

(Bhagavad-Gita 11.5–8)

This self-manifesting by Krishna is distinctive to Arjuna, courtesy of Krishna's special love for him, and it is enabled by divine perception given to Arjuna by Krishna.

Krishna reaffirms the special character of his divine manifesting to Arjuna:

> Yea! thou hast seen, Arjuna! because I loved thee well,
> The secret countenance of Me, revealed by mystic spell,
> Shining, and wonderful, and vast, majestic, manifold,
> Which none save thou in all the years had favour to
>   behold;
> For not by Vedas cometh this, nor sacrifice, nor alms,
> Nor works well-done, nor penance long, nor prayers,
>   nor chanted psalms,
> That mortal eyes should bear to view the Immortal
>   Soul unclad,
> Prince of the Kurus! This was kept for thee alone!
>   Be glad!
> Let no more trouble shake thy heart, because thine eyes
>   have seen
> My terror with My glory. As I before have been
> So will I be again for thee; with lightened heart behold!
> Once more I am thy Krishna, the form thou knew'st
>   of old!
>
> (*Bhagavad-Gita* 11.53–54)

Krishna intends his divine manifesting to Arjuna to have a practical consequence for a religious life: "Let no more trouble shake thy heart, because thine eyes have seen My terror with My glory." Such intended insulation from trouble parallels Gautama's goal of an imperturbable holy life in relief via cessation from corrosive change. In Krishna's perspective, however, this depends on *divine* aid and power for humans, beyond any human self-production or self-empowerment. As a result, we find a theistic interpretation of practically relevant religious experience in Krishna, in contrast with Gautama and Confucius.

Krishna's self-manifesting in human experience is not limited to Arjuna but supposedly extends widely among humans. Krishna's followers report his manifesting to people more generally, to those who experience with suitable discernment the divine power of Krishna. Where an older translation speaks of those "who comprehend My [Krishna's] reign of mystic majesty," a contemporary translation is a bit more explicit for present purposes: "Those who know in truth my glories and divine powers become united with me through unwavering *bhakti yog*. Of this there is no doubt" (*Bhagavad-Gita* 10:7). One of Krishna's "glories and divine powers" is described by him as follows: "Out of compassion for them, I, who dwell within their hearts, destroy the darkness born of ignorance, with the luminous lamp of knowledge" (*Bhagavad-Gita* 10.11). The older, more poetic translation has Krishna say:

And, all for love of them, within their darkened souls
  I dwell,
And, with bright rays of wisdom's lamp, their
  ignorance dispel.

Is there, however, an experienced manifestation of divine power more basic than removing ignorance by gaining knowledge? The latter phenomenon seems too close to an intellectual process to be a salient experience of divine power. In addition, Krishna reports that he does not manifest himself to everyone: "I am not manifest to everyone, being veiled by my divine *Yogmaya* energy. Hence, those without knowledge do not know that I am without birth and changeless" (*Bhagavad-Gita* 7.25).

We may think of Krishna as manifesting the divine power of God's character of "perfect bliss" (the "divine *Yogmaya* energy") to people willing to receive, and thus manifest, that divine character in their own lives. Such people would experience that power, if temporarily or intermittently in their lives, and they thus would face the

call of responding to it. A *yogi* is a person willing to participate cooperatively in that divine power in human life.

Krishna describes the process of response toward divine
bliss by a *yogi*:

> Steadfastly the will
> Must toil thereto, till efforts end in ease,
> And thought has passed from thinking. Shaking off
> All longings bred by dreams of fame and gain,
> Shutting the doorways of the senses close
> With watchful ward; so, step by step, it comes
> To gift of peace assured and heart assuaged,
> When the mind dwells self-wrapped, and the
>   soul broods
> Cumberless. But, as often as the heart
> Breaks – wild and wavering – from control, so oft
> Let him re-curb it, let him rein it back
> To the soul's governance; for perfect bliss
> Grows only in the bosom tranquillised,
> The spirit passionless, purged from offence,
> Vowed to the Infinite. He who thus vows
> His soul to the Supreme Soul, quitting sin,
> Passes unhindered to the endless bliss
> Of unity with Brahma [a supreme God, according to
>   some Hindus].
>
> (*Bhagavad-Gita* 6.25–28)

Even if "perfect bliss grows only in the bosom tranquil-
lised," it still could be manifested by God, in God's perfect
character, to receptive humans, and this could be a basis for
human response to God. This makes good sense of the
value of divine self-manifestation reported by Krishna. It
involves the kind of religious experience of God that can
anchor a meaningful religious life for people receptive to
such a life.

Moving beyond an initial experience of divine bliss,
Krishna identifies the importance of "being united" with

him "through unwavering *bhakti yog*" (*Bhagavad-Gita* 10.7, in a contemporary translation). One's becoming thus united is the practical, overarching, primary, and self-engaging value and meaning of human life in Krishna's theistic interpretation of religion. Its core is ongoing devotional union with a personal God, in this case, Krishna. So, Krishna commands: "Always think of me, be devoted to me, worship me, and offer obeisance to me. Doing so, you will certainly come to me. This is my pledge to you, for you are very dear to me" (*Bhagavad-Gita* 18.65, contemporary translation). The properly devoted response to Krishna is to be constant, "always" thinking of him, with worship and obedience.

Krishna characterizes the desired human response of ongoing obedient worship, conformed to the divine will:

> Whoso performeth – diligent, content –
> The work allotted him, whate'er it be,
> Lays hold of perfectness! Hear how a man
> Findeth perfection, being so content:
> He findeth it through worship – wrought by work –
> Of Him that is the Source of all which lives,
> Of Him by Whom the universe was stretched.
> (Bhagavad-Gita 18.46)

Humans will find perfection in relation to God only through their obedient worship of God, and this requires doing the work assigned by God to them. This is Krishna's theistic path to contentment and satisfaction in meaningful human life.

Krishna commands, above all else, singularity of focus and devotion toward himself:

> Nay! but once more
> Take My last word, My utmost meaning have!
> Precious thou art to Me; right well-beloved!
> Listen! I tell thee for thy comfort this.
> Give Me thy heart! adore Me! serve Me! cling

> In faith and love and reverence to Me!
> So shalt thou come to Me! I promise true,
> For thou art sweet to Me!
> And let go those –
> Rites and writ duties! Fly to Me alone!
> Make Me thy single refuge! I will free
> Thy soul from all its sins! Be of good cheer!
> (*Bhagavad-Gita* 18.64–66)

Above religious rites and practices, *God* becomes through human devotion one's singular focus for a good, meaningful life. We have noted this contemporary translation of *Bhagavad-Gita* 18.65: "Always think of me, be devoted to me, worship me, and offer obeisance to me." The singularity of devotion is to be constant, "always" in place as ongoing obedient worship. This path of devotion is mandatory for proper knowledge of God: "Only by loving devotion to me does one come to know who I am in truth. Then, having come to know me, my devotee enters into full consciousness of me" (*Bhagavad-Gita* 18.55). I thus have named Krishna's religious position *Constant-Adoration Theism.*

In Krishna's theology, obedient adoration of him is the primary value and the all-encompassing meaning for a human life. Krishna thus calls people to renounce anything that interferes with such adoration (*Bhagavad-Gita* 18.51–53). He does not offer this adoration as optional for humans, because he regards it as what enables the empowerment of humans to obey and please him and thereby enter his perfect bliss. At this point we find a sharp contrast between the position of Krishna and the perspectives of Gautama and Confucius on the meaning of human life. According to Krishna, humans need God in practical ways for a meaningful life, particularly in constant devotion to God, but Gautama and Confucius do not agree.

The disagreement at hand concerns the kind of power available to humans without their devotion to God. Krishna

denies that humans have the power to flourish in a meaningful life without their receiving divine power in devotion
to God. Gautama and Confucius hold that human *self*-deter-
mination, without their adoration of God, can deliver the
needed power. We shall return to this topic after identifying
some other theistic interpretations of religious experience
and life.

Jewish Theology in Moses: Law-Based Atonement Theism

The life of Moses (c. 1391–c. 1271 BCE) attracts ongoing
controversy from historical scholars, to such an extent that
many scholars deny the existence of the historical Moses.
Even so, as the leading prophet and lawgiver of Judaism,
Moses is immortalized (if only as a symbol) for his guiding
role in bringing Israel out of slavery in Egypt to the Promised Land of Canaan. According to the Hebrew Bible, the
liberated Jews were promised the land of Canaan by God,
and God played an active role in the liberation of Israel and
in the broader life of Moses. We need not digress to historical controversies for our purposes of illustrating the Mosaic
perspective on religious experience and its overarching
meaning for human life.

Moses's religious experience includes God's self-
manifesting to him with direct pronouncements and commands. For instance:

God called to [Moses] out of the bush, "Moses, Moses!" And
he said, "Here I am." Then he said, "Come no closer! Remove
the sandals from your feet, for the place on which you are
standing is holy ground." He said further, "I am the God of
your father, the God of Abraham, the God of Isaac, and the
God of Jacob." And Moses hid his face, for he was afraid to
look at God. (Exod. 3:4–6)

This seminal passage for ancient Judaism reports a religious
experience of God by Moses. It thus takes us beyond

thinking, reflecting, or theorizing about God to a divine intervention in the experience of Moses. God attracts his attention directly, and Moses responds with fear and hiding. His religious experience thus differs from any merely intellectual process.

God offers a grand promise to Moses in the context of his religious experience:

"The cry of the Israelites has now come to me; I have also seen how the Egyptians oppress them. So come, I will send you to Pharaoh to bring my people, the Israelites, out of Egypt." But Moses said to God, "Who am I that I should go to Pharaoh, and bring the Israelites out of Egypt?" He said, "I will be with you; and this shall be the sign for you that it is I who sent you: when you have brought the people out of Egypt, you shall worship God on this mountain." (Exod. 3:9–12)

God promises to "be with" Moses in the liberation of Israel. So, the process will not be a human self-help program, as if Moses and the people of Israel had the power of their own to accomplish God's plan of liberation. Human resolve is needed in the people of Israel, but that is not the full story of the power behind their liberation.

God plays an indispensable role in supplying needed power and guidance for the liberation of Israel. Here is one reported statement by God of this recurring lesson: "I know that the king of Egypt will not let you go unless compelled by a mighty hand. So, I will stretch out my hand and strike Egypt with all my wonders that I will perform in it; after that he will let you go" (Exod. 3:19–20). This lesson figures centrally in Moses's broader theology for a meaningful human life pleasing to God, and it stands in sharp contrast with the religious perspectives of Gautama and Confucius that emphasize human self-determination without God.

God's guidance of Moses and Israel to freedom in Canaan is anything but smooth and easy. In fact, the divine presence and power seem to be altogether absent at times, to the detriment and consternation of Moses and Israel. As a result, the people of Israel are tempted to revolt, with a return to slavery in Egypt: "The whole congregation of the Israelites complained against Moses and Aaron in the wilderness. The Israelites said to them, 'If only we had died by the hand of the Lord in the land of Egypt, when we sat by the fleshpots and ate our fill of bread; for you have brought us out into this wilderness to kill this whole assembly with hunger'" (Exod. 16:2–3). The trials in the wilderness brought the people of Israel to their limits of patience, trust, and obedience toward God. Those trials represent, as it turned out, not only that particular time period, but also the future of Israel's struggles with their God.

The exodus or liberation story of Israel gives us a promise-and-conflict model of relationship between God and Israel. A key lesson is that humans, even God's people, need *atonement* as reconciliation with God, owing to human moral failures that conflict with God's character and commands. Humans, however, either cannot or will not exercise the power needed for such atonement, and therefore God would need to undertake a special redemptive effort toward them, beyond promises of benefits. We thus find the role of a divine *covenant* in Jewish history, including in the theology of Moses. A divine covenant is not a simple contract between God and humans. Instead, it is *God's* specifying terms for human life with God in the light of God's promises for humans, and those terms can call for an obedient response from humans.

A divine covenant announced through Moses begins with God's calling Israel to obey what God commands:

You [Moses] shall say to the Israelites: You have seen what I did to the Egyptians, and how I bore you on eagles' wings and brought you to myself. Now therefore, if you obey my voice and keep my covenant, you shall be my treasured possession out of all the peoples. Indeed, the whole earth is mine, but you shall be for me a priestly kingdom and a holy nation.

These are the words that you shall speak to the Israelites. (Ex. 19:3–6)

The divine covenant via Moses includes a system of laws of various sorts that God commands the people of Israel to obey. God seeks Israel's conformity to the covenant to make it unique among all nations, a distinctively "holy nation" that reflects God's morally righteous character.

Moses serves as the primary human representative for God and the divine covenant for ancient Israel, including its laws, and he experiences good and bad consequences in this role. The Jewish Torah (five "books of Moses") containing the divine covenants and the Mosaic Law thus is integral to Judaism. According to Abraham Joshua Heschel: "If other religions can be characterized as a relation between man and God, Judaism must be described as a relation between *man with Torah and God*" (1996, p. 185). The role of divine law is central in the religious experience and the theology of Moses.

Aware of human moral shortcomings, God formulates the Mosaic Law to include atoning sacrifices and a special Day of Atonement (Yom Kippur). We thus find these rigorous commands to the priests of Israel:

Every day you shall offer a bull as a sin offering for atonement. Also you shall offer a sin offering for the altar, when you make atonement for it, and shall anoint it, to consecrate it. Seven days you shall make atonement for the altar, and consecrate it, and the altar shall be most holy; whatever touches the altar shall become holy. (Ex. 29:36–37)

The altar has a special status of divine holiness, because it is an assigned meeting place for God and humans. It is a specified place of human approach to God in worship, and therefore it must represent the holy character of the God being worshipped. As a result, the altar is to be set apart in ongoing consecration to God. The priests are to use it as a regular place of divine atonement for humans through animal sacrifices to God: "The priest shall make atonement on your behalf for the sin that you have committed, and you shall be forgiven" (Lev. 5:10). The needed forgiveness is a means to the desired atonement of divine–human reconciliation.

The importance of atonement for humans before God merits a special day:

The Lord spoke to Moses, saying: Now, the tenth day of this seventh month is the day of atonement; it shall be a holy convocation for you: you shall deny yourselves and present the Lord's offering by fire; and you shall do no work during that entire day; for it is a day of atonement, to make atonement on your behalf before the Lord your God. (Lev. 23:26–28)

This day under the Mosaic Law highlights the significance of divine–human atonement in the Jewish theology of Moses. It focuses on the importance of humans' being reconciled to God despite their past conflicts with God's character and commands. The reconciliation is law-centered atonement, because it requires observance of the Mosaic Law, including a renewed commitment to such observance.

God views humans as having a definite choice and thus personal responsibility in their reply to the commandments of the Mosaic Law:

See, I am setting before you today a blessing and a curse: the blessing, if you obey the commandments of the Lord your God that I am commanding you today; and the curse, if you do not obey the commandments of the Lord your God, but turn from the way that I am commanding you today, to follow other gods that you have not known. (Deut. 11:26–28)

On the same theme, we have:

Surely, this commandment that I am commanding you today is not too hard for you, nor is it too far away.... I call heaven and earth to witness against you today that I have set before you life and death, blessings and curses. Choose life so that you and your descendants may live, loving the Lord your God, obeying him, and holding fast to him; for that means life to you and length of days, so that you may live in the land that the Lord swore to give to your ancestors, to Abraham, to Isaac, and to Jacob. (Deut. 30:11, 19–20)

We should not confuse *personal responsibility to obey* commandments and *personal self-sufficiency to live* a meaningful life without God or God's power. Moses endorses the former personal responsibility but rejects the latter self-sufficiency. In rejecting that self-sufficiency, he stands in sharp contrast to the religious perspectives of Gautama and Confucius.

We should avoid two distortions of the atonement theism of Moses. The first distortion is that the required obedience toward the Mosaic Law is *merely* behavioral, without an internal psychological center. Here is a clear internalizing antidote to that distortion: "The Lord your God will circumcise your heart and the heart of your descendants, so that you will love the Lord your God with all your heart and with all your soul, in order that you may live" (Deut. 30:6). God's power is portrayed here as able to affect a person's deepest motivational center, the "heart," and thus as able to move a person to something deeper than mere behavior or "external" obedience. This point holds even if we lack an explanation of exactly how God "circumcises" a human heart. It also allows for God's accommodating human freedom of decision in the process.

The second distortion is that the required obedience of the Mosaic Law is a matter of *earning* or *meriting* one's approval by God by obligating God, on one's own merits, to approve oneself. That would be a matter of *earning-legalism* contrary to the theology of Moses. In his theology, as suggested, the Mosaic Law resides in a broader covenant wherein God has freely chosen to redeem humans from their various conflicts and failures in relation to God and God's will. God takes the initiative in launching this covenant and its terms, and humans are not in a position to have their own terms or merits obligate God to approve them. Their chosen conduct has definite consequences, according to the terms of the covenant, but that does not entail earning-legalism. Instead, it entails the importance of *obedience*, which does not entail such legalism.

The theology of Moses relies on a future-fulfillment theme that acknowledges the imperfection of present life, including life now obedient to God. We find a hint of this theme in an acknowledged restriction on Moses's experience of God:

[God] said [to Moses], "You cannot see my face; for no one shall see me and live." And the Lord continued, "See, there is a place by me where you shall stand on the rock; and while my glory passes by I will put you in a cleft of the rock, and I will cover you with my hand until I have passed by; then I will take away my hand, and you shall see my back; but my face shall not be seen." (Ex. 33:20–23)

This is metaphorical language for Moses's seeing not the fullness of God but only something partial or fragmentary regarding God. As a result, there is room for a better experience of God, perhaps in the fullness of time. For now, however, the experience is incomplete and thus susceptible to expansion and improvement in the future. One's experience of God now, then, is not a perfect experience of God.

We find a more explicit role for the future-fulfillment theme in a reflection from Moses:

[Moses said:] "The Lord your God will raise up for you a prophet like me from among your own people; you shall heed such a prophet. This is what you requested of the Lord your God at Horeb on the day of the assembly when you said: 'If I hear the voice of the Lord my God any more, or ever again see this great fire, I will die.'" Then the Lord replied to me: "They are right in what they have said. I will raise up for them a prophet like you from among their own people; I will put my words in the mouth of the prophet, who shall speak to them everything that I command." (Deut. 18:15–18)

This means that the prophet Moses is not the end of the story for Judaism. God's work begun in Moses extends into the future, including the future after the life of Moses. Some interpreters find the prophecy of Moses to concern the fullness of time and thus to be eschatological in intent. In this approach, the Mosaic meaning of life is not complete now but finds completion only in the future, at God's time of completion or fulfillment of human history.

According to the theism of Moses, the meaning of human life stems from God's plan for divine–human atonement in accordance with the Mosaic Law. The focus is on human reconciliation to God, including deepening reconciliation via obeying the Mosaic Law. The process of obedience includes human resolve and cooperation, but it is not just human self-determination. *God's* power enables people to cooperate effectively in the redemptive process. God seeks full cooperation from humans, but that goal awaits future fulfillment, given ongoing human shortcomings and failures. Even so, God self-manifests to receptive humans in their ongoing experiences, for the sake of law-governed covenant relationships central to divine–human reconciliation.

If the meaning of human life is goal-directed toward God's future fulfillment, it will not be fulfilled yet for humans. They will have to endure incomplete meaning for now, and in that regard their explanation of their lives will be fragmentary. Perfection for humans will await God's future, and it calls for trust in God now regarding the promised realization in the future. The unsettled future recommends against our assuming that we have full meaning for our lives now, even if we have meaning adequate for enduring life's challenges. We turn to a version of theism that stems from Jewish theism and shares its hope for fulfillment in the future.

Christian Theology in Paul: Christ-Based Atonement Theism

As a Jew, Paul (formerly Saul) of Tarsus (c. 5–c. 65 CE) was raised with Mosaic theism and the Mosaic Law. He became, however, an apostle to the Gentiles for his Jewish Messiah, Jesus of Nazareth (c. 4 BCE–c. 33 CE), the founder of what became the "Christian" religious movement. Paul is known for his life-changing religious experience of the resurrected Jesus on the road to Damascus. As a Jewish Pharisee, Paul persecuted some of the earliest followers of Jesus, and he intended to arrest some Christians in Damascus for their teaching contrary to his Judaism. His intention was not realized, in the end.

Paul's plan was interrupted by a religious experience of Jesus:

Now as he [Saul = Paul] was going along and approaching Damascus, suddenly a light from heaven flashed around him. He fell to the ground and heard a voice saying to him, "Saul, Saul, why do you persecute me?" He asked, "Who are you, Lord?" The reply came, "I am Jesus, whom you are persecuting. But get up and enter the city, and you will be told what you are to do." The men who were traveling with him stood speechless because they heard the voice but saw no one. (Acts 9:3–7)

This experience was the beginning of a new life-direction for Paul, a departure from his Pharisaic Judaism to become a follower of Jesus. He thought of it as his becoming a "new creation," courtesy of God (2 Cor. 5:17).

Paul became not only a follower of Jesus but also a missionary for Jesus and his message:

For several days he was with the disciples [of Jesus] in Damascus, and immediately he began to proclaim Jesus in the synagogues, saying, "He is the Son of God." All who heard him were amazed and said, "Is not this the man who made havoc in Jerusalem among those who invoked this name? And has he not come here for the purpose of bringing them bound before the chief priests?" Saul became increasingly more powerful and confounded the Jews who lived in Damascus by proving that Jesus was the Messiah. (Acts 9:20–22)

The Messiah (= the Christ), in Paul's message, is God's specially assigned agent for calling humans to God and God's righteous ways. A complication for Paul's message is that Jesus underwent a criminal's death by crucifixion on a Roman cross. As a Pharisaic Jew, Paul could not have accepted God's Messiah, or Christ, dying on a criminal's cross, because this would have left him "cursed" (Gal. 3:13; cf. Deut. 21:23). Paul's earlier, pre-Christian conception of God conflicted with the idea of the crucifixion of God's Messiah, and this resulted in his initially opposing and persecuting the earliest Christians.

As a Christian, after his experience of Jesus on the road to Damascus, Paul reconceived God as having a special redemptive purpose in the crucified Christ, that is, Jesus. The purpose was God's provision of righteous atonement as divine–human reconciliation for humans, courtesy of the death of God's special agent, Jesus. Echoing the exodus story of the Hebrew Bible, Paul thought of Jesus as "Christ our Passover" lamb from God (1 Cor. 5:7), that is, as God's person for reconciling humans to God through his death and resurrection from death. Jesus himself suggested this approach to atonement in his enacted parable of the Last (Passover) Supper, where he implicates himself as an agent in divine atonement (see Mark 14:12–25; cf. Matt. 26:26–29). The resurrection of Jesus, according to Paul, was God's way of vindicating Jesus for his perfect obedience to God for the sake of redeeming humans (Phil. 2:8–11).

Paul thought of Jesus as the divine son of God who, being divine, merits human worship (see Phil. 2:5-6, 10–11). Jesus, in Paul's language, is divine "Lord" over humans, and hence worthy of their full obedience and worship. Paul thus updates the "Shema" of the Hebrew Bible as follows: "For us there is one God, the Father, from whom are all things and for whom we exist, and one Lord, Jesus Christ, through whom are all things and through whom we exist" (1 Cor. 8:6). Paul does not digress, however, to an exact explanation of the ontological relation between Jesus and his divine Father. His missionary aim did not leave him the opportunity to pursue such an explanation, and he considered the former aim to be more urgent than philosophical explanation.

The role of *God's* providing the atonement for humans is crucial to Paul's theology. It secures what Paul deems central to God's moral character in human redemption: divine righteous *grace*. In Paul's theology, God sends Jesus to die for humans in order to enact and to display God's righteous response to human opposition to God. He explains: "[Humans] are now justified by [God's] grace as a gift, through the redemption that is in Christ Jesus, whom God put forward as a sacrifice of atonement by his blood, effective through faith. He did this to show his righteousness, because in his divine forbearance he had passed over the sins previously committed" (Rom. 3:24–25). God's approval, or justification, of humans comes as a costly divine gift, via the costly atoning death of Jesus, and it calls for human faith, including trust, in God as the way to receive the gift on offer. This prospect contrasts with any kind of human earning or meriting of divine approval.

Paul sometimes sets faith (in God) in opposition to "works" (of the Mosaic Law) as an intended avenue to righteousness and approval by God. In the relevant cases, "works" has a technical sense for Paul, and it does *not* mean "obedience to God's commands." Paul thus can say: "Circumcision is nothing, and uncircumcision is nothing;

but obeying the commandments of God is everything"
(1 Cor. 7:19). So, the kind of "works" that stand in opposition to faith, in Paul's thinking, should not be confused
with obeying God. Many commentators miss this important
lesson about obedience in Paul's thought. (For discussion,
see Moser 2013, chap. 4.)

We find Paul's occasional technical sense of "works" in
his discussion of Abraham in his letter to the Romans.
He explains:

If Abraham was justified by works, he has something to boast
about, but not before God. For what does the scripture say?
"Abraham believed God, and it was reckoned to him as
righteousness." Now to one who *works*, wages are not
reckoned as a gift but as something due. But to one who
without works trusts him who justifies the ungodly, such faith
is reckoned as righteousness. (Rom. 4:2–5, emphasis added)

Paul's technical sense of "works" here requires (intended)
earning or meriting and thus "something due" to a person
from God. It thus contrasts with God's giving humans an
unearned *gift* of righteousness or approval, that is, by divine
grace. *Obeying* God need not include (intended) earning of
God's approval; so, it should not be confused with "works"
in Paul's technical sense. Actions qualify as "works," in this
sense, only if they involve (intended) earning of something
due to one. Neither divine grace nor human faith excludes
human action or obedience; instead, (intended) human
earning of divine approval is excluded by Paul's approach
to grace and faith.

Paul criticizes some of his fellow-Jews for neglecting the
role of divine grace and faith in the divine atonement of
humans. He writes:

What then are we to say? Gentiles, who did not strive for
righteousness, have attained it, that is, righteousness through
faith; but Israel, who did strive for the righteousness that is

based on the law, did not succeed in fulfilling that law. Why not? Because they did not strive for it on the basis of faith, but as if it were based on works. (Rom. 9:30–32; cf. Rom. 10:3)

Paul raises the same theme in another letter: "I have suffered the loss of all things, and I regard them as rubbish, in order that I may gain Christ and be found in him, not having a righteousness of my own that comes from the law, but one that comes through faith in Christ, the righteousness from God based on faith" (Phil. 3:8–9).

Paul is not saying that all Jews seek to earn divine approval by obeying the Mosaic Law. Instead, he is commenting on some Jews who shared his own earlier mindset of seeking to earn God's approval by "works" of the law. His opposition to such intended earning arises from his aim to protect the central role of divine grace and human faith in redemption (see Rom. 11:6). Paul identifies God's intention to undermine all human self-boasting and self-crediting before God, in order to make room for human boasting in God (1 Cor. 1:26–31).

Faith in God is a kind of obedience in Paul's thinking, and thus he can talk of the two interchangeably (Rom. 10:16–17). Even so, it is a special kind of obedience irreducible to obeying the Mosaic Law. Paul identifies a need to "die to" the Mosaic Law in order to relate properly *to God*. He thus says: "Through the law I died to the law, so that I might live to God" (Gal. 2:19). This suggests a kind of directness in living to God that is not provided by the Mosaic Law. He understands the directness as one's "dying and rising" with Christ in relation to God (Rom. 6:1–14). A summary statement is: "I want to know Christ and the power of his resurrection and the sharing of his sufferings by becoming like him in his death, if somehow I may attain the resurrection from the dead" (Phil. 3:10–11). Paul thus thinks of the crucifixion and resurrection of Christ as something to be willingly shared in by Christians, as part of God's redemptive plan for the world.

The cross of Christ looms large in Paul's thought, because it has this costly significance: "God proves his love for us in that while we still were sinners Christ died for us" (Rom. 5:8). This divine self-giving love has an interpersonal relational goal of reconciliation in Paul's message:

In Christ God was reconciling the world to himself, not counting their trespasses against them, and entrusting the message of reconciliation to us. So, we are ambassadors for Christ, since God is making his appeal through us; we entreat you on behalf of Christ, be reconciled to God. For our sake he made him to be sin who knew no sin, so that in him we might become the righteousness of God. (2 Cor. 5:19–21)

The relational goal is reconciliation to God through Christ, the one who, in obedience to God, died for humans. The overarching meaning of human life, in Paul's approach, is to enter into this interpersonal reconciliation, ever more deeply, with trust in God and fellowship (koinōnia) with God. The risen Christ vindicated by God supplies the personal guidance and power for this redemptive process; the Mosaic Law does not. The process is future-directed toward God's goals, and it is thus eschatological in its fulfillment by God's future. Even so, it has begun in human history and now awaits, through hope, future fulfillment by God (Rom. 8:18–24).

Paul's religious experiences extend beyond the road to Damascus, and he expects some of them to be shared by other people. For example, he speaks of God's *self-manifestation* to some humans (Rom. 10:20), and he has in mind God's manifesting his unique personal character to certain humans, with the goal of their being reconciled to God. He also identifies what this unique character includes: "We boast in our sufferings, knowing that suffering produces endurance, and endurance produces character, and character produces hope, and hope does not disappoint us, because God's love (agapē) has been poured into our hearts through the Holy Spirit that has been given to us" (Rom. 5:3–5). The intervention of God's personal character of righteous love in one's experience serves as personal evidence of God's reality and goodness for one, in Paul's thought. Paul does not portray God, however, as coercing such an experience against the will of a person. He assumes volitional receptivity on the part of some humans toward God's intervening Spirit, which Paul identifies with the Spirit of the risen Christ (Rom. 8:9–10).

The reconciliation announced by Paul includes membership, via adoption, in God's family and personal assurance from God's own Spirit. He writes:

All who are led by the Spirit of God are children of God. For you did not receive a spirit of slavery to fall back into fear, but you have received a spirit of adoption. When we cry, "Abba! Father!" it is that very Spirit bearing witness with our spirit that we are children of God. (Rom. 8:14–16)

The key evidence for God's reality, in Paul's perspective, is thus inherently person-centered, being based in the personal character, self-manifestation, and assurance of a personal God who is worthy of worship. This is not the kind of abstract evidence for God's reality typically offered by philosophical theists advocating natural theology. Instead, it is the kind of evidence, arising in human experience, that brings a person directly before God in interpersonal interaction. Paul thinks of the human conscience as a place where such an interpersonal meeting can occur (Rom. 9:1; see also Forsyth 1912 and Robinson 1956).

Paul's atonement theism is person-oriented throughout, including in its role for a personal Messiah (or Christ) as God's atoning sacrifice. Its approach to divine atonement contrasts with the Constant-Adoration theism of Krishna and the Law-Based theism of Moses, although it explicitly acknowledges and promotes the God of Moses. In Paul's perspective, God planned for a change in the Mosaic redemptive plan with the emergence of the Messiah, Jesus, in human history. The central features of the change included the atoning death and vindicating resurrection of Jesus for the sake of all humans, without their reliance on the Mosaic Law.

The experience and the power of God's intervention through Jesus Christ are, in Paul's message, to form all aspects of a human life, as people become, after the unsurpassed model of Jesus, living sacrifices for God (Rom. 12:1). Paul's religious meaning of human life is thus practical, overarching, of primary value, and self-engaging for humans, and it is based on religious experience widely available to receptive people. (Chapters 7 and 8 will develop a perspective inspired by Paul's approach.) We turn now to an influential development of theism after Paul's time.

Islamic Theology in Muhammad: Absolute-Submission Theism

Islam is the religion of absolute submission to Allah, or God, and its final prophet, Muhammad (c. 570–632 CE), is the messenger of absolute submission to God. A *Muslim*, according to the term's original meaning, is one who submits or surrenders (to God). We find this meaning represented in the *Qur'an*: "Our Lord, ... make us submissive to You, and from our descendants a community submissive to You" (*Qur'an* 2:128). Likewise: "Who is better in religion than he who submits himself wholly to God, and is a doer of good, and follows the faith of Abraham the Monotheist?" (*Qur'an* 4:125; cf. 31:22, 72:14).

Islam claims to be the original monotheism of which Abraham was a proponent: "Abraham was neither a Jew nor a Christian, but he was a Monotheist, a Muslim. And he was not of the Polytheists" (*Qur'an* 3:67). It also aims to include Moses and Jesus under the religion of Allah:

"He [Allah] prescribed for you the same religion He enjoined upon Noah, and what We inspired to you, and what We enjoined upon Abraham, and Moses, and Jesus: 'You shall uphold the religion, and be not divided therein'" (*Qur'an* 42:13).

The *Qur'an* portrays one of Muhammad's formative religious experiences as follows:

4. It is but a revelation revealed.
5. Taught to him by the Extremely Powerful.
6. The one of vigor. He settled.
7. While he was at the highest horizon.
8. Then he came near and hovered around.
9. He was within two bows' length, or closer.
10. Then He revealed to His servant what He revealed.
11. The heart did not lie about what it saw.
12. Will you dispute with him concerning what he saw?

(Qur'an 53:4–12)

This kind of experience led to Muhammad's conveying the contents of the *Qur'an* as the word of God, as a communication from God through him. It anchored his conviction that he was called to be God's final prophet to humans. It thus grounded his religious message of the overarching meaning for human life.

The *Qur'an* elaborates on the divine revelation to Muhammad as follows:

1. Read [or: Proclaim]: In the Name of your Lord who created.
2. Created man from a clot.
3. Read [or: Proclaim]: And your Lord is the Most Generous.
4. He who taught by the pen.
5. Taught man what he never knew.

(Qur'an 96:1–5)

The report here is that God the Creator is using Muhammad and his pen, as a prophetic messenger, to reveal divine things previously unknown to humans. This report accompanies the religious experience of Muhammad, and it led to the formation of Islam as a religious way of life.

The *Qur'an* gives the angel Gabriel credit as an intermediary in Allah's revelation to Muhammad:

97. Say, "Whoever is hostile to Gabriel – it is he who revealed it to your heart by Allah's leave, confirming what preceded it, and guidance and good news for the believers."

98. Whoever is hostile to Allah, and His angels, and His messengers, and Gabriel, and Michael – Allah is hostile to the faithless.

99. We have revealed to you clear signs, and none rejects them except the sinners. (*Qur'an* 2:97–99)

Neither Muhammad nor any other messenger is to be regarded as the author of the revelation in the *Qur'an*: "This *Qur'an* could not have been produced by anyone other than God; . . . it is from the Lord of the universe" (*Qur'an* 10:37). Allah's revelation to Muhammad, according to the *Qur'an*, came with "clear signs" of divine involvement in the process, but these signs were rejected by some people. We should ask what kind of "sign" of God was central to Muhammad's religious experience.

The experience of *being commanded (by Allah)* is at the center of Muhammad's formative religious experience. Here is a summary statement that identifies this center: "The guidance of Allah is the guidance, and we are *commanded to surrender* [or submit] to the Lord of the universe" (*Qur'an* 6:71, emphasis added). The *Qur'an* places Allah's status as the one who commands on equal footing with Allah's status as the one who creates: "Your Lord is Allah; He who created the heavens and the earth in six days, then established Himself on the Throne. The night overtakes the day, as it pursues it persistently; and the sun, and the moon, and the stars are subservient by His command. His is the creation, and His is the command. Blessed is Allah, Lord of all beings" (*Qur'an* 7:54). This is a strong sense of "command," because it involves a kind of divine control over the objects of the command. A command need not have such control, but Allah's command does, at least in some cases, according to the *Qur'an*.

The signs of Allah to humans are "within yourselves," and they should be clear to those who pay attention:

> 20. And on earth are signs for the convinced.
> 21. And within yourselves. Do you not see?
> 22. And in the heaven is your livelihood, and what you are promised.
> 23. By the Lord of the heaven and the earth, it is as true as the fact that you speak.
>
> (Qur'an 51:20–21)

A key question is: How are the signs of Allah "within yourselves"? An answer will guide one in where to look for the intervention of Allah in human experience.

One way of having signs "within yourselves" involves Allah's "calling" people to himself through his Messenger, the Prophet Muhammad, who represents "clear revelations" from Allah:

> 7. Believe in Allah and His Messenger, and spend from what He made you inherit. Those among you who believe and give will have a great reward.
> 8. What is the matter with you that you do not believe in Allah, when the Messenger calls you to believe in your Lord, and He has received a pledge from you, if you are believers?
> 9. It is He who sends down upon His servant clear revelations, to bring you out of darkness into the light. Allah is Gentle toward you, Most Compassionate. (*Qur'an* 57:7–9)

Allah's commanding people to submit in obedience and worship is an experience that many people report to have or feel, and it motivates their commitment to an Islamic way of life. It was front and center in Muhammad's life, and it accounted for his carrying the message of the *Qur'an* to a wide audience.

The *Qur'an* goes beyond the view that God hides from some people to the stronger view that God "leads astray" or "misguides" some people:

We have appointed only angels to be wardens of the Fire, and caused their number to be a stumbling block for those who disbelieve; so that those given the Scripture may attain certainty; and those who believe may increase in faith; and those given the Scripture and the believers may not doubt; and those in whose hearts is sickness and the unbelievers may say, "What did Allah intend by this parable?" Thus Allah leads astray whom He wills, and guides whom He wills. (*Qur'an* 74:31)

In the same vein: "Whomever Allah desires to guide, He spreads open his heart to Islam; and whomever He desires to misguide, He makes his heart narrow, constricted, as though he were climbing up the sky. Allah thus lays defilement upon those who do not believe" (*Qur'an* 6:125). This is a kind of divine judgment, and it raises the question of who wills unbelief first, Allah or humans. The matter is controversial, but we may assume that the Islamic missionary movement depends on the view that individual people need to make a responsible decision about the message offered.

The central role of *divine command* in the *Qur'an*'s religious message involves a conception of the law of God. Thus: "We revealed to you the Book, with truth, confirming the Scripture that preceded it, and superseding it. So, judge between them according to what Allah revealed, and do not follow their desires if they differ from the truth that has come to you. For each of you We have assigned a law and a method" (Qur'an 5:48). The relevant divine law is the updated, clarified version (relative to past versions, such as the Mosaic Law) based in the commands of the Qur'an.

The meaning of human life, in Muhammad's Islamic perspective, focuses on submitting completely to Allah by obeying the divine law based in the Qur'an. Submitting to Allah is thus law-based, and it is a law dependent on Allah's unique revelation to Muhammad. The Qur'an endorses "earning," "reward," and "wages" from God on the basis of its law and human submission to God. For instance: "Whoever submits himself to God, and is a doer of good, will have his reward with his Lord – they have nothing to fear, nor shall they grieve" (Qur'an 2:112). This kind of submission includes active striving on the part of humans: "The human being attains only what he strives for. And . . . his efforts will be witnessed. Then he will be rewarded for it the fullest reward. And that to your Lord is the finality" (Qur'an 53:39–42). This suggests that humans are not mere pawns of the will of God, but they have an active role in responding to God's will in their lives.

The idea of God's crediting humans on the basis of what they "earn" arises as follows: "God does not burden any soul beyond its capacity. To its credit is what it earns, and against it is what it commits" (Qur'an 2:286). Similarly: "How about when We gather them for a Day in which there is no doubt, and each soul will be paid in full for what it has earned, and they will not be wronged?" (Qur'an 3:25). Such language suggests payment from God for human merit.

Talk of God's paying *wages* to humans on the basis of their good works arises in the Qur'an:

As for those who believe and do good works, He will pay them their wages in full, and will increase His grace for them. But as for those who disdain and are too proud, He will punish them with an agonizing punishment. And they will find for themselves, apart from God, no lord and no savior. (*Qur'an* 4:173)

In the same vein: "He [Allah] will pay them their dues in full, and will increase them from His bounty" (*Qur'an* 35:30). This talk of "dues" involves a notion of human earning or meriting something from God.

The *Qur'an's* wages-earning approach to submission to God differs from the two versions of atonement theism in Moses and Paul (even though Moses and Paul portray God as giving rewards to humans). A law-based theism need not include human earning of God's approval, because it can offer human obedience as simply a fitting human response to God's goodness toward humans. In Muhammad's approach, however, the meaning of human life will require human earning toward God, on the basis of human submission to God in obedience. This kind of theistic interpretation of religious experience adds special rigors to the meaning of human life, but it is genuinely religious in being practical, overarching, primary in value offered, and self-engaging. It thus serves as a distinctive religious perspective that offers to integrate a human life under absolute submission to God's commanding will.

5 PROSPECTS AND QUESTIONS

We have identified some religious experiences of six seminal figures in religious history and their distinctive interpretations of their experiences with regard to the meaning of human life. In sum, the distinctive positions are:

a. The Buddhist Path of Gautama: Self-Practice in Awakened Life
b. The Way of Confucius: Self-Cultivation for Relational Virtue

c. Hindu Theology in Krishna: Constant-Adoration Theism

d. Jewish Theology in Moses: Law-Based Atonement Theism

e. Christian Theology in Paul: Christ-Based Atonement Theism

f. Islamic Theology in Muhammad: Absolute-Submission Theism

Gautama and Confucius, we have seen, offer nontheistic interpretations of their formative religious experiences bearing on their understandings of life's meaning. In contrast, Krishna, Moses, Paul, and Muhammad offer corresponding theistic interpretations that give God a central practical role in life's meaning. As a result, we have contrary positions about the role of God in the meaning of human life; they cannot all be true. This poses a problem for any simple "unity of religions" thesis that implies agreement among the religions in question about the specific features of the meaning of human life.

We can benefit by formulating some questions to clarify and to begin to assess the religious perspectives identified. A question facing all of the perspectives is this: If a person lacks the kind of religious experience described, is that person at a disadvantage for assessing the perspective? If so, can that person still be a responsible evaluator? If that is a viable option, how does the person proceed? Clearly, I should not assume that *my* lacking a specific religious experience entails, or otherwise indicates, that *everyone* lacks it. No single human's experience is the benchmark for the religious experiences of all people. The same holds true for experiences in general, including ordinary perceptual experiences. Human experiences, including veridical experiences, vary in a way that goes beyond the experience of any single human. So, general skepticism about religious experiences should not rest on the experience of a single human or even a special subset of humans. A more representative base for evidence would be needed.

In general, we can ask the following questions of the nontheistic interpretations of life's meaning offered by Gautama and Confucius. (1) Is human self-determination adequate to achieve either the kind of Awakening or the kind of interrelational virtue recommended by Gautama and Confucius? If so, why is the kind of achievement recommended so rare among humans? (2) Can life's meaning be sufficiently enduring, if not lastingly valuable, in the absence of a *caring* and *intentional enduring supervisor* for it, given the many ways life can go from bad to worse, from trouble to futility? Are human self-determination and guidance adequate to sustain a meaningful human life without humans being sufficiently guided, encouraged, and loved toward what is good in life? Without a superhuman intentional agent involved in the supervision of human life, will there be a shortage of guidance, encouragement, and love toward humans? (3) Does human growth toward needed moral awakening or enlightenment depend on acquaintance with a personal moral character superior to any merely human moral character? If so, how does this consideration bear on the need for a superhuman agent in the meaning of human life?

We can raise some important questions for the theistic interpretations of religious experience offered by Krishna, Moses, Paul, and Muhammad. (1) Given the vast diversity of conceptions of God, how should we settle on a conception of God for interpreting religious experience and life's meaning? In casual language: *Which* god, from the large roster of gods, should have priority in that area? (2) How does a theistic approach bear on the many people who report not having an experience of God? Are they excluded from having a meaningful life? If so, are they somehow culpable for this? (3) If God is to have a central role in the meaning of human life, why does God tend to be elusive, if not altogether hidden, at least at many times and for many people? How does this consideration about human access to God bear on God's character and purposes? Does it reflect badly on God's character, or is there some subtle factor that makes some sense of divine elusiveness? In addition, does this factor illuminate the difficult problem of evil regarding unjust suffering, often of extreme sorts, in many human lives?

A question from Chapter 1 bears on each of the nontheistic and the theistic interpretations offered. Why should a person, all things considered, accept or practice what is being proposed regarding "being religious" in the sense indicated rather than in a different sense or in no sense at all? Chapter 1 suggested that we understand this question to include the following question: Why suppose that it is responsible, all things considered, for a person to accept or practice the proposal for "being religious" in the relevant sense? A decision that is *epistemically* responsible for a person will conform to that person's relevant experience and available evidence concerning what is real. The responsible decision need not be the same for all people, however, because different people can and do have different experiences and available evidence. This result is acceptable as long as our approach to responsible decision-making depends on one's available evidence, and not mere factuality or truth. We can avoid a kind of personal arbitrariness by maintaining epistemic responsibility in "all things considered" responsibility.

We are not in a position now to answer our questions raised for nontheistic and theist interpretations of religious experience. We need further elaboration of such interpretations in connection with the effects, including the practical effects, of religious experience and meaning in human lives. To this we now turn. (Chapters 7 and 8 return to the main questions just raised.)

3

∾

Religious Experience Practiced

If world religions are known for anything, they are known for their various religious practices. When, however, is a practice *religious* rather than nonreligious, and what, if anything, has religious experience to do with religious practice? Chapter 1 characterized a core religious experience as relating one directly to sensed value and meaning for human life that are overarching, primary in value for one, and self-engaging in a transformative manner. We shall explore how religious experience bears on religious practice in a normative way. The six prominent positions on life's meaning in Chapter 2 will illustrate the normative significance of religious experience. They will enable us to clarify how religious experience is action-guiding for the people having such experience along with a corresponding intention to act.

1 PRACTICE IN ACTION

When is something a practice? One familiar definition of "practice" offered by the *Oxford English Dictionary* is: "the customary, habitual, or expected procedure or way of doing of something." We can subsume typical talk of a religious practice under this definition as long as we allow the customary, habitual, and expected procedures in question to vary among people and religious groups. The relevant talk of "procedures" or "ways of doing something" is talk of actions, that is, intentional actions. We thus can think of a practice as a customary intentional action. We also can think of a religious practice as a customary religious intentional action. When, however, is an action intentional and religious?

Intentional *states*, like belief states, are psychological attitudes that are not episodic (in being exhausted by events), but they may be causally based in episodic events. So, I can have an intentional state to buy a new car even while I am asleep and "doing" nothing, just as I can believe while asleep that new cars have a distinctive odor. We may think of intentional states as decision-based settled commitments to act.

My intention to buy a new car stems from my (perhaps past) decision to buy a new car, but the episodic event(s) of deciding may have ceased, leaving me nonetheless in a dispositional intentional state. My action of buying the new car, in that case, would be intentional as a result of its causal basis in my decision-based intentional state. We sometimes use the terms "decision" and "intention" interchangeably, but we should not confuse an intentional *state* with a discrete *episode* of decision. A state can exist at a time when no episode is occurring at that time.

The basing-role of intentional states accounts for the difference between intentional actions and mere bodily movements. My bodily movement of blinking my eyes, for instance, is not an intentional action, because it is not based in an intentional state to blink. We typically do not intend or decide to blink our eyes, but we still manifest the bodily movement of blinking, without its being an intentional action. As a customary intentional action, a religious practice is not just bodily movement. It has a basis in an intentional state and thus in a decision, even when it is habitual.

Blaise Pascal has suggested that behaving in a certain way can diminish human passions that obstruct religious belief. He advises:

Concentrate then not on convincing yourself by multiplying proofs of God's existence but by diminishing your passions.

You want to find faith and you do now know the road. You want to be cured of unbelief and you ask for the remedy: learn from those who were once bound like you.... They behaved just as if they did believe, taking holy water, having masses said, and so on. That will make you believe quite naturally, and will make you more docile. (1658 [1966], p. 152)

It is an empirical matter whether behaving as if you believe in God will "make you believe quite naturally" in God. The evidence on balance does not favor an affirmative response, and thus it is doubtful that Pascal gives us a reliable recipe for natural belief in God. Mere behavior involving religious customs can leave a person's intentions short of agreement with the religious meaning involved in those customs. It thus can fail to bring one into agreement with that meaning. So, natural religious belief need not arise from the mere behavior. Such behavior does not go deep enough into a person's intentions to yield religious belief in the "natural" manner suggested by Pascal.

An intentional action or practice is goal-directed and thus future-oriented. It proceeds typically on the assumption of an open future that will allow for the undertaking of the action or practice in question. If undertaken, the action or practice will close off what were previously some open options in the future. In this regard, an undertaken action or practice is reality-forming and thus reality-changing in excluding many action-options and realizing one option at a particular time. An intentional action or practice thus takes one beyond reflection to a manner of forming and changing reality, if in a small way. Part of the importance of religious action or practice is its contribution to the formation and change of reality in some area.

Intentional action is religious when it stems, in its motive, from religious meaning of the kind that Chapter 1 characterized in terms of being practical, overarching, of primary value, and self-engaging. (We will consider some examples below.) Our talk of *practicing* religious experience is talk of undertaking an intentional action or practice motivated by a religious experience, and this may be done to achieve or to maintain a religious experience. Religious commitment based on religious experience is inherently practical, because its defining meaning is practical as a result of one's intention to conform to it. It includes not just reflections but also practical intentions, based on religious experience, to achieve goals.

Some theorists of religion have endorsed the primacy of religious practice over any religious belief or commitment with representational content. Commenting on religion in some premodern cultures, Karen Armstrong states: "Religion was not primarily something that people thought but something they did" (2009, p. 15). It is unclear how to understand "primarily" here, but we should be cautious about this kind of contrast between thought and action, even given my claim that religious commitment is inherently practical. A similar point applies to a possibility noted by Masao Abe: "It could be claimed that though Buddhism dispenses with orthodoxy . . ., it replaces orthodoxy with orthopraxy. It replaces the right word with the right deed, so that in the beginning was the deed, not the word" (1993, p. 78).

If an action or practice is intentional, as in the case of religious action or practice, it is goal-directed (and not haphazard) toward what one intends with the action or practice. It thus depends on reflective guidance from a standard or norm (perhaps of a minimal sort) to reach the goal in question. The standard or norm can come from a judgment, but it also can come from something that is not a judgment, such as a qualitative image in experience, or present to awareness. Without reflective guidance from a standard of some kind, the behavior in question would be blind rather than intentional as goal-directed.

Dependence on a standard or norm for guidance excludes any contrast that makes religious action devoid of reflection or thought in guidance of the action. Even if the standard or norm is just a *de re* image in experience, we would not have *mere* behavior as religious practice. In that case, one would be reflecting on *the fit* or *congruence* of behavior with the content of the image. Reflective comparison for fit or congruence between the image as norm and the behavior would be needed for goal-*directed* action. The behavior in question would not be suitably *directed* in the absence of such reflective comparison. Without direction toward the goal intended, the intentional character of the behavior would be omitted.

A coherent goal, being determinate in content, sets a satisfaction condition for its being actualized or realized, and that condition is a norm for its satisfaction. Reflective norm-fitting for intentional action includes measuring congruence between a norm (such as that set by a goal in action) and behavior. It thus goes beyond mere behavior in a way that precludes intentional religious practice as mere behavior or as occurring without a reflective component of norm-fitting. If behavior is directed toward a goal, as in the case of intentional action, it will not be mere behavior, devoid of reflective fitting of behavior with a norm. So, it would be a mistake to endorse the primacy of religious practice in the absence of reflective norm-fitting. That kind of endorsement would undermine the intentional character of religious action and practice.

If humans are intentional agents as well as thinkers, their actions as well as their thoughts will be important for their self-expression and self-realization. In that case, they will adequately express and realize themselves only through their intentional actions. In doing so, they will self-manifest what they take to be meaningful for their lives, and this self-manifesting can include religious practice and meaning. We shall consider the perspectives on religious practice offered by the religious figures introduced in Chapter 2.

2 PRACTICING RELIGION

Chapter 2 identified significant divisions in religious interpretation among Gautama, Confucius, Krishna, Moses,

Paul, and Muhammad. Gautama and Confucius propose a nontheistic interpretation of their religious experience that anchors their recommended practical meaning for human life. Krishna, Moses, Paul, and Muhammad, in contrast, offer a theistic interpretation of their corresponding religious experience. Even so, these six religious figures share the view that their relevant religious experiences serve as a basis for practical religious meaning for human life. They all think of religion as something to be practiced by humans in a way that goes beyond mere reflection. We shall consider their distinctive approaches to religious practice as a response to religious experience and its corresponding meaning for human life.

Gautama on Religious Practice for Self-Awakening

The religious practice of meditation (*Dhyāna*), or concentration, is crucial to the religious goal of Awakening, or "self-Awakening," promoted by the Gautama Buddha. In what some take to be his first message after his own Awakening, Gautama advises people to avoid the following two extremes in human life, for the sake of a "middle way":

That which is devoted to sensual pleasure in connection with sensuality: base, vulgar, common, ignoble, unprofitable; and that which is devoted to self-affliction: painful, ignoble, unprofitable. Avoiding both of these extremes, the middle way realized by the Tathāgata [i.e., the Buddha] – producing vision, producing knowledge – leads to stilling, to direct knowledge, to self-awakening, to unbinding. (*Dhammacakkappavattana Sutta* 56:11)

Gautama reports that he realized a middle way to "self-Awakening," going between the extremes of sensuality and asceticism. The "unbinding" is the relief via cessation of corrosive changes in a human life. It is noteworthy that the Awakening is "self-Awakening," thus being an

Awakening of the self. This fits with the positive role for the self that Chapter 2 attributed to Gautama, against a prominent interpretation that omits a positive role.

Gautama offers a distinctive practical way to "self-Awakening":

And what is the middle way realized by the Tathāgata that – producing vision, producing knowledge – leads to stilling, to direct knowledge, to self-awakening, to unbinding? Precisely this noble eightfold path: right view, right resolve, right speech, right action, right livelihood, right effort, right mindfulness, right concentration. This is the middle way realized by the Tathāgata that – producing vision, producing knowledge – leads to stilling, to direct knowledge, to self-awakening, to unbinding. (*Dhammacakkappavattana Sutta* 56:11)

Gautama's eightfold path as the middle way is inherently practical, depending on a practice of right view, resolve, speech, action, livelihood, effort, mindfulness, and concentration. He thus refers to "the noble truth of the way of practice" found in his eightfold path.

Gautama's "way of practice" is a way of *guided* practice, and not haphazard behavior. It is inherently intentional in action, *self*-guided toward "self-Awakening." Gautama thus calls it "the way of practice leading to the cessation of stress," the kind of stress in conflict with self-Awakening. His "way of practice" is intended to counter the kind of stress or change at odds with self-Awakening, for the purpose of either achieving or maintaining self-Awakening. This consideration indicates that Gautama's central religious practice is intentional action, and not haphazard or blind behavior. His goal of self-Awakening guides the practices that make up the eightfold path, in a way that makes them goal-directed and thus intentional. In addition, his goal of relief via "the cessation of stress" depends on *self*-Awakening and thus on a central role for the self as liberated or relieved from stressors.

Gautama has clear advice about practice for people aiming for self-Awakening:

When asked, "What are you?" you claim that "We are contemplatives." So, with this being your designation and this your claim, this is how you should train yourselves: We will undertake and practice those qualities that make one a contemplative, ... so that our designation will be true and our claim accurate; so that the services of those whose robes, alms-food, lodging, and medicinal requisites we use will bring them great fruit and great reward; and so that our going forth will not be barren, but fruitful and fertile. (*Mahā Assapura Sutta* 39)

Gautama thus recommends the practice of things inherent to the goal of being a contemplative, that is, a person aiming at self-Awakening. He remarks: "Don't let those of you who seek the contemplative state fall away from the goal of the contemplative state when there is more to be done." So, the role of a *goal* is central to his advice, and he recommends what will "direct and incline" one's mind toward the goal of self-Awakening (*Mahā Assapura Sutta* 39). His path for a meaningful life is thus inherently intentional and goal-directed.

Gautama offers practical advice in terms of a "practice for restraint" from sensual and intellectual evil:

We will guard the doors to our sense faculties. On seeing a form with the eye, we will not grasp at any theme or variations by which – if we were to dwell without restraint over the faculty of the eye – evil, unskillful qualities such as greed or distress might assail us. We will practice for its restraint. We will protect the faculty of the eye. We will achieve restraint with regard to the faculty of the eye. On hearing a sound with the ear ... On smelling an aroma with the nose ... On tasting a flavor with the tongue ... On feeling a tactile sensation with the body ... On cognizing an idea with the intellect, we will not grasp at any theme or variations by which – if we were to dwell without restraint over the faculty of the intellect – evil, unskillful qualities such as greed or distress might assail us. We will practice for its restraint. We will protect the faculty of the intellect. We will achieve restraint with regard to the faculty of the intellect. That's how you should train yourselves. (*Mahā Assapura Sutta* 39)

Gautama's talk of "practice for its restraint" is talk of intentional action, of action directed toward a goal: restraint. The intended restraint itself has a higher goal: self-Awakening that insulates one(self) from suffering and frustration. This higher goal is normative for intentional action aimed at such Awakening. It sets a standard for action that enables and calls for norm-fitting on the part of people aiming at self-Awakening. Such norm-fitting, being reflective for these people, does not admit of mere behavior as what leads one to self-Awakening.

The normative goal of self-Awakening bears for Gautama on the practice of any religious rite, ritual, or action, such as burning incense, ringing a bell, lighting a candle, sprinkling water, maintaining silence, or regulating breathing. Religious actions gain their religious value in relation to the primary religious goal of self-Awakening. In the absence of the latter goal, they will fall short of pointing or contributing to human liberation or relief via cessation from the corrosive effects of suffering and frustration. So, goal-directed action is inherent to Gautama's path for meaningful life.

Gautama's advice assumes a self that discerns what the goal of self-Awakening requires as that self proceeds, intentionally, toward that goal. The omission of such a self will undermine the goal-directed process toward life's ultimate meaning recommended by Gautama. If one "kicks away" the "raft" of the self *altogether* (and not just bad variations) as one reaches the shore of Awakening, no personal agent will be left to enter the *self*-Awakening achieved by one (self) through self-restraint and self-concentration. In that respect, one will not have *self*-Awakening in any literal sense.

Confucius on Religious Practice for Interpersonal Virtue

Chapter 2 explained how Confucius put interpersonal relationality as "loyal reciprocity" at the center of his religious experience and his advice for a meaningful human life. He thus found practical, overarching, primary, and self-engaging meaning for human life in loyal reciprocity in virtuous human relationships. His central advice, as noted, is: "Cultivate yourself to bring comfort to others" (*Analects* 14.42). Such benevolent self-cultivation for the sake of others occupies the center of the religious Way of human life taught by Confucius.

Tu Wei-ming has captured the general religious goal of Confucius as follows: "The Confucian self . . . seeks to generate its inner resources for self-transformation. Self-transformation, the result of self-cultivation, signifies a process of self-realization" (1993, p. 142). Chapter 2 illustrated that the desired self-transformation for Confucius is inherently relational as interpersonal, and not just inward or subjective for a person. The "inner resources for self-transformation" are directed toward interpersonal virtue, that is, virtue in relationships with people. So, the goal is self-transformation toward interpersonal virtuous relationships.

Confucius sets a clear goal for practicing ritual (*li*), and the goal is internal as well as external. For instance, according to *The Junzi Practices Ritual*: "The Master said, 'Hui, the *junzi* [ideal person] practices ritual in order to cleave to *ren* [goodness, including benevolence].'" The kind of goodness (*ren*) serving as the goal of ritual is inward as well as outward; it includes goodness in one's psychological states and in one's outward actions, in relation to other people.

Confucius identifies the importance of inner self-possessed goodness in the following context:

The Master said, If a man can recite from memory the three hundred odes of the *Poetry* but, when you entrust him with governance, he is unable to express his meaning, or, when you send him to the four quarters on diplomatic missions, he is unable to make replies on his own initiative, though he may have learned much, of what use is he? The Master said, If he is upright in his person, he will perform without orders. If he is not upright in his person, though you give him orders, he will not carry them out. (*Analects* 13.5–6)

Confucius thus values being "upright in one's person," which exceeds just going through the motions in a way that neglects inward self-possessed goodness.

Reliance on inner resources of goodness, according to Confucius, can benefit interpersonal relationships by creating virtuous habits for those relationships:

Zhonggong asked about *ren* [goodness, including benevolence]. The Master said, "When you go out your front gate, continue to treat each person as though receiving an honored guest. When directing the actions of subordinates, do so as though officiating at a great ritual sacrifice. Do not do to others what you would not wish done to you. Then there can be no complaint against you, in your state or in your household." (*Analects* 12.2)

Confucius thus likens his version of the Golden Rule, the core of virtuous relationships, to the ritualized conduct of a public sacrifice. He aims to make one's actions beneficial to all concerned, in a way that is caring and respectful toward others.

Parts of the *Analects* portray Confucius as choreographing his public behavior in a ritualized way that offers a model for others. For instance:

When the ruler was present, he walked with quick step, yet evenly. When the ruler ordered him to greet a guest to court, he changed expression, as if flushing. His step became hurried. When he stood beside the guests, he bowed to them, putting first his left or right hand, as appropriate. His robes remained even in front and back. When stepping with them towards the throne, he walked with quickened step, his arms bent wing-like. (*Analects* 10.2–3)

The goal of Confucius is to accommodate others with care and respect, with the aid of ritualized action when helpful. This is a feature of his benevolent interaction with others, aimed at loyal reciprocity in his relationships.

Ritualized conduct is not an end in itself, according to Confucius, but finds its value in its contribution to interpersonal virtue. He promotes the self-cultivation of such virtue in social (including political) interactions, and ritualized conduct can serve that end by contributing to virtuous habits in interpersonal relations. Confucius recommends the self-cultivation of interpersonal virtue over political coercion:

Is it not so that when distribution is even, there is no poverty; when there is harmony, there is no underpopulation; when there is peace, there is no danger the ruler will topple? It is just in this spirit that if those who are distant do not submit, one must cultivate patterns and virtue to attract them. Once they have come, one must comfort them. (*Analects* 16.1)

The self-cultivation of "patterns and virtue" aims at interpersonal relationships that are good for all involved. It is thus an antidote to selfishness with help from cultivated virtuous habits. The practice of rituals, according to Confucius, can contribute to the formation and maintenance of such habits.

Ritual serves for Confucius as a goal-directed feature toward his ultimate religious goal of "loyal reciprocity" among people. Tu Wei-ming has characterized his goal-directed approach to ritual as follows:

Ritual, in the Confucian context, is closely related to the social vision of human communication. Ritual is not the concern of external form; rather, ritual is a concern for both verbal and nonverbal communication within the human community. Children must be taught ritual behavior, because adult behavior, after all, derives from habits learned as children. (1993, p. 195)

The habits in question are not blind, or devoid of a reflective component. Instead, they arise from intentional conformity to ritualized practices, and that conformity includes one's willingness to have the practices serve as one's patterns for action. We thus may call them "intentional habits." Such habits, coupled with ritualized actions, also serve to communicate intentional religious practices to others. They offer a model for others to assess and to follow in practice. They thus can have social religious value in a community of religious people.

We have seen that Gautama made his practice of religious experience inherently goal-directed and thus intentional, rather than a matter of mere behavior. We now see that Confucius did the same. His experience of interpersonal virtue was his basis for goal-directed action toward realizing more such virtue in human relationships. That is, his experience of "loyal reciprocity" grounded his intentional actions to actualize more loyal reciprocity among humans. This experience also grounded his religious advice that recommended such reciprocity for a meaningful human life. (Chapter 8 considers how a kind of relativism bears on such a position, with regard to its responsible acceptance.)

Krishna on Religious Practice for Obedient Adoration

Unlike Gautama and Confucius, as Chapter 2 noted, Krishna gives commitment to God a central role in his practical religious perspective on life's meaning. He intends to protect some of his followers from the trouble of this world: "Let no more trouble shake thy heart, because thine eyes have seen My terror with My glory" (*Bhagavad-Gita* 11.53–54). His intended psychological insulation from the world's trouble is analogous to Gautama's goal of a constant holy life, but Krishna invokes *divine* help for humans, beyond human self-protection or self-empowerment. So, Krishna offers a theistic interpretation of practically relevant religious experience and its corresponding meaning for human life.

We saw in Chapter 2 that Krishna values the self-manifesting of God's powerful character of "perfect bliss" (the "divine *Yogmaya* energy") to some receptive people. People who have that experience confront a divine call to respond cooperatively. This is a call to "be united" with God "through unwavering *bhakti yog*" (*Bhagavad-Gita* 10.7, in a contemporary translation). Becoming thus united in devotion is the practical, overarching, and primary value and meaning of human life according to Krishna. Krishna therefore demands: "Always think of me, be devoted to me, worship me, and offer obeisance to me. Doing so, you will certainly come to me. This is my pledge to you, for you are very dear to me" (*Bhagavad-Gita* 18.65, contemporary translation). One's devotion to Krishna should be constant, "always" thinking of him, with worship and obedience.

Religious ritual contributes value only in a subsidiary way, as an aid to constant devotion to Krishna, who says:

And let go those –
Rites and writ duties! Fly to Me alone!
Make Me thy single refuge! I will free
Thy soul from all its sins! Be of good cheer! (*Bhagavad-Gita* 18.65–66)

Obedient and constant adoration of Krishna is the primary value and meaning for a human life, and therefore Krishna commands people to renounce anything that interferes with such adoration (*Bhagavad-Gita* 18.51–53). This kind of singularity of focus is to guide a meaningful human life.

A contemporary translation of our passage has: "Abandoning all forms of rites and duties, take refuge in Me alone." Krishna is not, however, dispensing with all rites and duties. His point is that one should set aside any rites and duties that conflict with or otherwise challenge one's primary duty to be devoted to Krishna. Abandoning all rites and duties would be to abandon morality, but Krishna insists on a rigorous morality for humans, in the context of obedient worship of him.

In remarks on the performance of sacrificial offerings (*yajnas*) to God and on other ritualized actions, Krishna endorses regulated activities as being crucial to a holy life. For instance, he states: "Those who do not accept their responsibility in the cycle of sacrifice established by the Vedas [the scriptures] are sinful" (*Bhagavad-Gita* 3.16). Krishna's endorsement does not assume the intrinsic value of the various rituals; instead, it depends on his presumed role of God in sacrifices and other human rituals. He states: "The duties for human beings are described in the Vedas, and the Vedas are manifested by God himself. Therefore, the all-pervading Lord is eternally present in acts of sacrifice" (*Bhagavad-Gita* 3.15). We find here Krishna's main motive for religious rituals, such as acts of sacrifice to God: They include the presence of God, who merits obedient worship, including constant adoration, from humans.

Krishna's statements on meditation confirm the priority of God and divine presence in religious practices. He remarks: "The yogis [those practicing yoga for worship] who have conquered the mind rise above the dualities of cold and heat, joy and sorrow, honor and dishonor. Such yogis remain peaceful and steadfast in their devotion to God" (*Bhagavad-Gita* 6.7). He adds: "The yogi should strive to purify the mind by focusing it in meditation with one pointed concentration, controlling all thoughts and activities. He must hold the body, neck, and head firmly in a straight line, and gaze at the tip of the nose, without allowing the eyes to wander" (*Bhagavad-Gita* 6.12–13). This instruction regarding one's posture and gaze in meditation may seem puzzling at first, but it has a definite goal regarding one's relating to God.

Krishna elaborates as follows: "With a serene, fearless, and unwavering mind, and staunch in the vow of celibacy, the vigilant yogi should meditate on me [Krishna], having me alone as the supreme goal. Thus, constantly keeping the mind absorbed in me, the yogi of disciplined mind attains *nirvāṇ* [awareness of true self in God] and abides in me in supreme peace" (*Bhagavad-Gita* 6.14–15). In such meditation, God becomes the focal center of all things for a person. Krishna adds: "The self-controlled yogi, thus uniting the self with God, becomes free from material contamination, and being in constant touch with the Supreme [God], achieves the highest state of perfect happiness. The true yogis, uniting their consciousness with God, see with equal eye, all living beings in God and God in all living beings" (*Bhagavad-Gita* 6.28–29).

We now see that religious rites, rituals, and practices serve a higher goal for Krishna, the goal of constant adoration of God. Their value is thus instrumental to that goal. As a result, there should be an intentionality about the practice of religious rites and rituals: a goal-directedness to obedient worship of God. Such worship is at the heart of human life's overarching meaning, according to Krishna, and, as such, it merits a guiding status above rites and rituals. Religious rites and rituals can become formulaic in the absence of suitable inwardness, but it does not follow that they are dispensable in a religious life. The needed inwardness, according to Krishna, is personal directedness toward worship or adoration of God. It thus is intentional inwardness, with a goal in need of satisfaction for a holy and meaningful life, a life approved by God.

Krishna's commands in favor of religious practices are typically straightforward, but they prompt consideration of our recurring question for any religious perspective. Why suppose that it is responsible, all things considered, for a person to adopt and to follow the religious interpretation and advice of Krishna rather than some alternative religious position or none at all? It would be irresponsible simply to assume, without due support, that one would be thus responsible. Perhaps some of the competing alternatives serve as well as, if not better than, what Krishna offers for a meaningful human life. A key question, we shall see in Chapters 7 and 8, is whether one's available evidence supports a religious interpretation regarding its bearing on reality.

Moses on Religious Practice for Law-Based Atonement

As Chapter 2 noted, Moses taught that humans need atonement as reconciliation with God. This need stems from human moral conflicts with, including sin against, God's moral character and commands. He also taught that humans on their own will not exercise the power needed for such atonement; so, God would need to undertake a special redemptive effort toward them. God undertakes that effort in a covenant specifying God's terms for reconciled, coopera-tive human life with God. This covenant comes through Moses, and it includes laws of various sorts that God com-mands the Jewish people to obey. People are to practice religion through obedience to God's laws (the Mosaic Law) as the way to atonement or reconciliation with God. As a social group, they are thus to reflect God's morally righteous character for the benefit of others as well as themselves.

God's laws for atonement include the sacrificial system developed through Moses. Here is an explicit connection between the two:

If the offering is a burnt offering from the herd, you shall offer a male without blemish; you shall bring it to the entrance of the tent of meeting, for acceptance in your behalf before the

Lord. You shall lay your hand on the head of th
offering, and it shall be acceptable in your behalf as at
for you. (Lev. 1:3–4)

The atonement mentioned is at least for humans in relation
to God, to counter the damage from human sin to the
divine–human relationship. Sacrifices demanded by the
Mosaic Law are to serve that end, at least.

The sacrificial system for atonement applies to a group of
people as well as to individuals. Thus:

[The priest] shall do with the bull just as is done with the bull
of sin offering; he shall do the same with this. The priest shall
make atonement for them, and they shall be forgiven. He shall
carry the bull outside the camp, and burn it as he burned the
first bull; it is the sin offering for the assembly. (Lev. 4:20–21)

In addition: "The guilt offering is like the sin offering, there
is the same ritual for them; the priest who makes atonement
with it shall have it" (Lev. 7:7). The desired atonement
responds to human guilt as well as human sin, because full
human reconciliation to God requires attention to both, for
groups of people as well as for individuals.

The Mosaic sacrificial system is not limited to human sin
and guilt. It recognizes a positive side to divine–human
reconciliation:

This is the ritual of the sacrifice of the offering of well-being
that one may offer to the Lord. If you offer it for thanksgiving,
you shall offer with the thank offering unleavened cakes
mixed with oil, unleavened wafers spread with oil, and cakes
of choice flour well soaked in oil. With your thanksgiving
sacrifice of well-being, you shall bring your offering with cakes
of leavened bread. (Lev. 7:11–13)

The Mosaic Law thus acknowledges that divine–human
reconciliation involves human gratitude. It thereby

acknowledges that suitable human inwardness, beyond merely behavioral rituals, figures in the genuine reconciliation of humans to God. An inward intentional component, then, is central to the redemptive process of divine–human reconciliation.

The following passage, noted in Chapter 2, captures the heart of Mosaic religion, including its valuing human inwardness in love toward God:

Surely, this commandment that I am commanding you today is not too hard for you, nor is it too far away ... I call heaven and earth to witness against you today that I have set before you life and death, blessings and curses. Choose life so that you and your descendants may live, loving the Lord your God, obeying him, and holding fast to him; for that means life to you and length of days, so that you may live in the land that the Lord swore to give to your ancestors, to Abraham, to Isaac, and to Jacob. (Deut. 30:11, 19–20)

The commanded obedience to the Mosaic Law is thus not merely external; it is to be coupled with "loving the Lord your God" and "holding fast to him." This fits with the explicit command of Deuteronomy 6:5: "You shall love the Lord your God with all your heart, and with all your soul, and with all your might."

Moses sums up the law he received from God, identifying its core:

So now, O Israel, what does the Lord your God require of you? Only to fear the Lord your God, to walk in all his ways, to love him, to serve the Lord your God with all your heart and with all your soul, and to keep the commandments of the Lord your God and his decrees that I am commanding you today, for your own well-being. (Deut. 10:12–13; cf. 11:1)

The desired atonement via the Mosaic Law requires a certain fullness and singularity in human cooperative response.

It thus demands love, obedience, and service toward God "with all your heart and with all your soul," leaving no place for half-heartedness in commitment to God. The relevant talk of "heart" concerns the psychological center of a person, involving mind, volition, and emotion – the whole person as responsible agent in the presence of God.

Atonement with God via the Mosaic Law does not end with a Godward direction for human reconciliation to God. It requires analogous attention to other humans for the sake of human–human reconciliation. One clear command is: "You shall not take vengeance or bear a grudge against any of your people, but you shall love your neighbor as yourself: I am the Lord" (Lev. 19:18). The command regarding others is not limited to others as *similar* neighbors, let alone as ethnic or religious Jews. Even aliens in Israel qualify: "The alien who resides with you shall be to you as the citizen among you; you shall love the alien as yourself, for you were aliens in the land of Egypt: I am the Lord your God" (Lev. 19:34). Likewise, strangers are to be included: "You shall also love the stranger, for you were strangers in the land of Egypt" (Deut. 10:19). These commands illustrate the broad social concern for reconciliation illustrated by the Mosaic Law.

Walther Eichrodt has identified the importance of the command to love in the Mosaic Law according to the book of Deuteronomy:

By the derivation of the whole law from the command to love, the basic demand of the divine will for the surrender of the whole person to the divine Thou was brought within the comprehension of the simplest citizen. In this way, even the commandment whose meaning is not immediately transparent – apart from the fact that it comes from the sovereign will of God, and is therefore valid as such – can still touch heart and conscience, because it derives from the counsel of the love of God, who has ordered all things for the sake of his people's salvation, and who accepts no keeping of the commandment just for the commandment's sake, desiring rather to see in each fulfilment of the law the living effect of a single-minded profession of love for God. (1967, p. 372)

The relation of the Mosaic Law to divine and human love is often neglected, but it bears on moral as well as ritual commands. Eichrodt thus adds: "The moral demands, too, are emphatically included in the prevenient act of God's love, inasmuch as they are seen to be the obvious logical consequence of his beneficent will revealed in the covenant-making" (1967, p. 372; see also Levenson 2016, chap. 1). The book of Deuteronomy is particularly concerned to highlight the role of love in the Mosaic Law. As a socially shared legal system, the Mosaic Law can prompt and encourage a social group toward cooperation with God's will, for the sake of interpersonal reconciliation.

The Mosaic Law enables God to be relevant to all of a human life rather than just to some narrow areas of life. Jacob Neusner explains:

The human condition takes on heightened intensity when God cares what you eat for lunch, on the one side, but will reward you for having a boiled egg, on the other. For a small, uncertain people, captured by a vision of distant horizons, behind and ahead, a mere speck on the crowded plain of humanity, such a message bore its powerful and immediate message as a map of meaning. (1993, p. 318)

We do indeed find "a map of meaning" in the Mosaic Law, and it is a map for the law-based reconciliation of humans to God and to each other.

The reconciliation, or atonement, sought by the Mosaic Law depends on human obedience and thus on human actions or deeds. It thus cannot be achieved just by human reflection or emotion. The kind of love commanded is volitional, depending on exercise of the human will in agreement with God's will represented by the Mosaic Law. Even so, as suggested, the obedience commanded is to involve the whole person in full commitment to God, with all of one's heart and soul. This is a tall order, but Moses points people to divine help and power in the quest for obedience. In this respect, Moses differs from Gautama and Confucius. An important question is whether such help is needed by humans. Another important question is whether the theistic option from Moses for life's meaning is preferable to its competitors, such as those noted in Chapter 2. We have no quick and easy answer, given variability in evidence possessed by humans, but Chapter 8 will relate such questions to a person's relevant evidence from experience.

Paul on Religious Practice for Christ-Based Atonement

Many commentators portray the apostle Paul as mainly an advocate of faith in God, with at best a subsidiary interest in obedient action toward God. This portrayal is misleading, because Paul thinks of faith in God as a special kind of obedience to God (Rom. 1:5, 10:16). The misplaced fear of many commentators is that if faith is a kind of obedience, it becomes a "work" of the kind Paul contrasts with divine grace and human faith in God (Rom. 4:2–5). This fear is misplaced, because, as Chapter 2 noted, obedient action should not be confused with a "work" in Paul's technical sense of behavior that aims to earn or merit God's approval of a person (Rom. 4:4). Acting, in short, is not automatically (attempted) earning, and therefore a divine requirement of obedient human action poses no threat to faith in God as Paul understands it.

Chapter 2 noted a neglected remark by Paul that reveals something centrally important to him: obeying the commandments of God. According to Paul: "Circumcision is nothing, and uncircumcision is nothing; but obeying the commandments of God is everything" (1 Cor. 7:19). In keeping with this high view of acting in obedience to God, Paul states: "You are slaves of the one whom you obey, either of sin, which leads to death, or of obedience, which leads to righteousness" (Rom. 6:16). Paul's idea of obedience to God *leading to righteousness* or approval from God is foreign to many commentators on Paul, but it is central to Paul's religious perspective. (A similar central role can be found in the teaching of Jesus as represented by Matthew's Gospel; see Matt. 7:21–23.) Intentional human action and obedience have an indispensable role in what Paul takes to be a meaningful human life acceptable to God.

Paul acknowledges various religious practices as important to a human life pleasing to God. For instance, he mentions baptism and the Lord's Supper (or the Eucharist communion meal) as practices in Christian churches, including the church he started at Corinth. Paul writes to the Corinthian church:

I thank God that I baptized none of you except Crispus and Gaius, so that no one can say that you were baptized in my name. (I did baptize also the household of Stephanas; beyond that, I do not know whether I baptized anyone else.) For Christ did not send me to baptize but to proclaim the gospel, and not with eloquent wisdom, so that the cross of Christ might not be emptied of its power. (1 Cor. 1:14–17)

We may infer that Paul did not regard baptism to be as important religiously as the proclamation of the gospel, or the good news, of what God has done in Christ for human redemption. He apparently thought of the proclaimed gospel as a better place than baptism to meet the God in search of divine–human reconciliation. Even so, he understood baptism, properly conceived, to be representative of dying and rising with Christ (Rom. 6:3–5), a process crucial to reconciliation with God.

Paul has a straightforward reason for his position:

I am not ashamed of the gospel; it is the power of God for salvation to everyone who has faith, to the Jew first and also to

the Greek. For in it the righteousness of God is revealed
through faith for faith; as it is written, "The one who is righteous will live by faith." (Rom. 1:16–17)

Paul regards human faith in God as a cooperative, obedient
response to God, and thus as a key part of human
reconciliation, or atonement, with God. Religious rituals,
in Paul's perspective, gain their religious value from their
contribution to human reconciliation to God. Their value is
thus instrumental, and not intrinsic.

Paul expresses his position on the Lord's Supper after
learning of a problem with the ceremony in the church at
Corinth. His summary of the original Lord's Supper is:

I received from the Lord what I also handed on to you, that
the Lord Jesus on the night when he was betrayed took a
loaf of bread, and when he had given thanks, he broke it
and said, "This is my body that is for you. Do this in remembrance of me." In the same way he took the cup also,
after supper, saying, "This cup is the new covenant in
my blood. Do this, as often as you drink it, in remembrance
of me." For as often as you eat this bread and drink the
cup, you proclaim the Lord's death until he comes.
(1 Cor. 11:23–26)

This is not just a historical matter for Paul; it bears on
subsequent human attitudes in response to the church's
communion meal. We might say it concerns how one relates
to God in the religious meal.

Paul explains his position:

Whoever eats the bread or drinks the cup of the Lord in an
unworthy manner will be answerable for the body and blood
of the Lord. Examine yourselves, and only then eat of the
bread and drink of the cup. For all who eat and drink without
discerning the body, eat and drink judgment against themselves. (1 Cor. 11:27–29)

This is no matter of a mere ritual or external behavior for Paul. Instead, it is an opportunity for one's forming an attitude toward God and God's crucified mediator for reconciliation, Jesus Christ. Paul seems to regard the Lord's Supper as a proclamation of God's message of reconciliation through the death of Christ. It is thus an opportunity for divine–human reconciliation and therefore something to be treated seriously.

Paul's focus on divine–human reconciliation includes a crucial role for God's Messiah, or Christ, rather than the Mosaic Law. Chapter 2 identified a central theme from Paul: "In Christ God was reconciling the world to himself, not counting their trespasses against them, and entrusting the message of reconciliation to us. So, we are ambassadors for Christ, since God is making his appeal through us; we entreat you on behalf of Christ, be reconciled to God" (2 Cor. 5:19–20). Paul here places Christ, and not the Mosaic Law, at the center of God's program of reconciling humans to God. This focus makes the redemptive program thoroughly interpersonal, with a personal mediator, Christ, between personal humans and the personal God. It also identifies interpersonal love (agapē), of the kind demonstrated by God in Christ, as the fulfillment of the Mosaic Law (Gal. 5:14; Rom. 13:10).

Paul assesses religious rituals by their contribution to one's reconciliation to God in Christ. This approach implicates the attitudes of people who participate in such rituals. If one's attitude toward a ritual is receptive to divine–human reconciliation, it is fitting for the ritual. Otherwise, it is not. So, merely external behavior in performing a ritual will not deliver what is needed, according to Paul's perspective.

Paul advocates human imitation of Christ as the way to reconciliation with God (1 Cor. 11:1), and this calls for heartfelt obedience to God, after the model of Christ himself (Phil. 2:5–11; cf. Mark 14:36). Is such obedience a live option for ordinary humans? Do they have the moral strength to realize it in their lives? These questions prompt the issue of whether Paul's God is too demanding for humans in general. They also lead us to ask how divine grace fits with the perfect but strenuous model for human obedience in Christ. (Chapter 8 returns to this topic.)

Muhammad on Religious Practice for Absolute Submission to God

Chapter 2 identified the experience of *being commanded* by Allah as central to Muhammad's religious experience. We saw confirmation of this idea in the *Qur'an*: "The guidance of Allah is the guidance, and we are commanded to surrender [or submit] to the Lord of the Universe" (*Qur'an* 6:71). Life's overarching meaning, in Muhammad's perspective, focuses on submitting completely to Allah by obeying the divine law based in the *Qur'an*. Submitting to Allah is thus law-based, and it is a law dependent on Allah's unique revelation to Muhammad. The *Qur'an*, we have seen, endorses "earning," "reward," and "wages" from God on the basis of human submission to its law.

The *Qur'an* characterizes God as being concerned with more than external human behavior. It portrays God as "the First and the Last, and the Outer and the Inner" (*Qur'an* 57:3). It also calls for an inward human state of awareness of God, beyond outer behavior: "Turning towards Him – and be conscious of Him, and perform the prayer, and do not be of the idolaters" (*Qur'an* 30:31). The practice of prayer, then, is not for just a public show or an empty ritual. It is to be coupled with being "conscious" of God, and the *Qur'an* closely aligns this state of being conscious with a state of being aware of being commanded by God (Muhammad's central religious experience).

The *Qur'an* associates the proper performance of religious rituals with love:

O you who believe! Whoever of you goes back on his religion – God will bring a people whom He loves and who love Him, kind towards the believers, stern with the disbelievers. They strive in the way of God, and do not fear the blame of the critic. That is the grace of God; He bestows it upon whomever He wills. God is Embracing and Knowing. Your allies are God, and His Messenger, and those who believe – those who pray regularly, and give charity, while bowing down. (*Qur'an* 5:54–55)

God's people are thus "a people whom He loves and who love him." The role of such love, divine and human, goes beyond external behavior to what motivates a divine–human relationship. It thus goes to inward psychological and volitional factors in action, including any religious action of humans.

We find a lesson about suitable motivation for two prominent religious practices in Islam: pilgrimage (*hajj*; to Mecca) and prayer (*salat*; five times each day). God announces to Muhammad:

We showed Abraham the location of the House: Do not associate anything with Me; and purify My House for those who circle around, and those who stand to pray, and those who kneel and prostrate. And announce the pilgrimage to humanity. They will come to you on foot, and on every transport. They will come from every distant point. That they may witness the benefits for themselves, and celebrate the name of God during the appointed days. (*Qur'an* 22:26–28)

The practices of pilgrimage and prayer thus depend on purity and celebration in motivation toward God. They are, then, to be properly motivated inwardly, and are not to be merely external practices.

Sacrificial offerings to God are to conform to the motives of pilgrimage and prayer:

Those whose hearts tremble when God is mentioned, and those who endure what has befallen them, and those who perform the prayer and spend from what We have provided for them. We have made the animal offerings emblems of God for you. In them is goodness for you. So, pronounce God's name upon them as they line up. Then, when they have fallen on their sides, eat of them and feed the contented and the beggar. Thus We have subjected them to you, that you may be thankful. Neither their flesh, nor their blood, ever reaches God. What reaches Him is the righteousness from you. Thus He subdued them to you, that you may glorify God for guiding you. And give good news to the charitable. (*Qur'an* 22:35–37)

The sacrificial offerings to God are to be occasions for gratitude to God as a result of the goodness God supplies in them. They are not centrally about the flesh and blood of animals; instead, they are mainly about the righteousness expressed by humans in making sacrificial offerings out of gratitude to God. This righteousness glorifies, or brings honor to, God for divine guidance given to humans.

The *Qur'an* portrays righteousness in terms of belief in God coupled with sincere actions pleasing to God:

Righteousness does not consist of turning your faces towards the East and the West. But righteous is he who believes in God, and the Last Day, and the angels, and the Scripture, and the prophets. Who gives money, though dear, to near relatives, and orphans, and the needy, and the homeless, and the beggars, and for the freeing of slaves; those who perform the prayers, and pay the obligatory charity, and fulfill their promise when they promise, and patiently persevere in the face of persecution, hardship, and in the time of conflict. These are the sincere; these are the pious. (*Qur'an* 2:177)

So, righteousness is faith in God joined with sincere conduct commanded by God. This is the center of the holy life commanded by God through Muhammad, and it is the way to absolute submission to God. It is the goal of a meaningful human life in Muhammad's statement of Islam.

We asked whether the apostle Paul's understanding of life's meaning was too demanding for ordinary humans, and we can ask the same of Muhammad's understanding. The main question is whether humans have the moral strength to achieve absolute submission to God, given God's morally perfect character and commands. Humans tend to have moral weakness, at least at times, and this weakness can yield conflicts between them and God's morally perfect character and commands. It thus seems to be an obstacle to absolute submission to God. God can be merciful, but divine mercy will not supply the human power needed to have absolute submission to God. At least, we would need some explanation of how such submission is to be achieved by humans.

One might respond by making humans mere pawns of God's sovereign will, but that would undermine *human* submission to God. It would end up as God's will and power submitting to God's dominating will. In that case, genuine human responsibility would be at risk, and genuine human agency would be too. Perhaps, then, Muhammad would allow for humanly acceptable submission to God without perfect or absolute submission. Maybe divine mercy would allow for such an option, given moral weakness in humans. (Chapter 8 returns to this topic.)

3 PERIL IN RELIGIOUS PRACTICE

Having identified some important features of religious life's meaning, we can see that such meaning is meaning for persons *as intentional agents*, for personal subjects and not for mere objects – rocks, trees, clouds, and so on. Such persons are not themselves practices or actions, even though at times they undertake practices or actions for various purposes. Some persons undertake religious practices at times, but they are not identical to those practices. They are the purposive agents who bring about those practices, for better or for worse. They are thus causally and morally responsible for those practices, even if it is difficult

at times to assess their full moral resp
particular case.

Some religious perspectives assume that hι
are to be treated as "ends in themselves," anc
means to some ends. The value of persons, in th
tives, is intrinsic, and not merely instrumental.
say that this is just the way persons are, with regι..u to their
value, or one might say that God made persons this way.
One also could offer a different basis for the value of persons, but the distinction between intrinsic value and merely
instrumental value amounts to an important difference,
bearing on how persons are to be treated.

The history of religion supplies some troubling cases of
treating religious practices as ends in themselves and persons as just means to those ends. In this reversal of value,
one might say that persons exist for (the benefit of) religious
practices rather than that religious practices exist for
(the benefit of) persons. Even religious practices of worship
can be treated in such a reversal. Human persons may exist
"for God" in some sense, but this would not entail that
persons owe their value to, or exist for the benefit of, practices of worship. Similarly, God may intend to have human
persons obey a religious law, but this would not entail that
such persons owe their value to, or exist for the benefit of,
such a law. Human persons still could have their value
just in virtue of who they are (i.e., their constitutional
makeup) rather than in virtue of the practices they undertake, such as in worship or in obeying a religious law.

Love-commands given to humans can block the reversal
of value in question, because they can give a primary status
of value to persons over religious practices. We find such
commands in various religious traditions, if with differing
emphases and ranges. The Mosaic Law includes the
following love-commands:

Hear, O Israel: The Lord is our God, the Lord alone. You shall
love the Lord your God with all your heart, and with all your

ul, and with all your might. Keep these words that I am commanding you today in your heart. (Deut. 6:4–6)

You shall not take vengeance or bear a grudge against any of your people, but you shall love your neighbor as yourself: I am the Lord. (Lev. 19:18)

We have noted that the Mosaic Law requires care and aid toward not just "neighbors" in a local or ethnic sense but also aliens and strangers in Israel. In doing so, the Law can protect the persons in question from being devalued for the sake of religious practices. It thus can maintain the value of those persons.

Jesus offers a clear restatement of the love-commands in the Jewish Bible:

One of the scribes asked [Jesus], "Which commandment is the first of all?" Jesus answered, "The first is, 'Hear, O Israel: the Lord our God, the Lord is one; you shall love the Lord your God with all your heart, and with all your soul, and with all your mind, and with all your strength.' The second is this, 'You shall love your neighbor as yourself.' There is no other commandment greater than these." (Mark 12:28–31)

Jesus draws from the Mosaic love-commands of Deuteronomy and Leviticus, and he gives them top priority: There is no commandment greater than the combination of these. As a result, he supplies a safeguard against putting (what benefits) religious practices above what is good for persons. If his love-commands have top priority, they will block a reversal of the value of persons relative to religious practices.

Jesus faced a reversal of the value of persons in some of the religious leaders of his time. A particularly controversial topic was the matter of keeping the Sabbath in relation to caring for persons. A case involving healing is the following:

[Jesus] entered the synagogue, and a man was there who had a withered hand. They watched him to see whether he would cure him on the sabbath, so that they might accuse him. And he said to the man who had the withered hand, "Come forward." Then he said to them, "Is it lawful to do good or to do harm on the sabbath, to save life or to kill?" But they were silent. He looked around at them with anger; he was grieved at their hardness of heart and said to the man, "Stretch out your hand." He stretched it out, and his hand was restored. The Pharisees went out and immediately conspired with the Herodians against him, how to destroy him. (Mark 3:1–6)

Given the priority of the love-commands for Jesus, he refuses to treat the Sabbath as an obstacle to caring for others in need. Indeed, he finds "hardness of heart" behind a refusal to care for others as a result of keeping the Sabbath. Such "hardness" includes a deficit in loving others, and it is thus at odds with the love-commands issued by Jesus. We see, then, that his love-commands can challenge a reversal of the value of persons relative to religious practices.

We find Jesus explicitly rejecting the reversal of value in question:

One sabbath [Jesus] was going through the grainfields; and as they made their way his disciples began to pluck heads of grain. The Pharisees said to him, "Look, why are they doing what is not lawful on the sabbath?" And he said to them, "Have you never read what David did when he and his companions were hungry and in need of food? He entered the house of God, when Abiathar was high priest, and ate the bread of the Presence, which it is not lawful for any but the priests to eat, and he gave some to his companions." Then he said to them, "The sabbath was made for humankind, and not humankind for the sabbath; so, the Son of Man is lord even of the sabbath." (Mark 2:23–28)

The pertinent assumption of Jesus is: "The sabbath was made for humankind, and not humankind for the sabbath." This is his basis for rejecting the value reversal that makes religious practices more valuable than persons. It also fits with his announced priority of the love-commands. He thus would say: Religious practices are made for people, and not people for religious practices.

A decisive, and divisive, issue concerns the scope of the love-commands. Do they extend just to one's neighbors as agreeable acquaintances, or do they have a broader scope, bearing even on persons who are real threats to one's well-being? We noted that the Mosaic Law extends the scope to aliens and strangers in Israel, but this does not go far enough for Jesus. He extends the scope even to one's enemies, to people who threaten one's well-being:

You have heard that it was said, "You shall love your neighbor and hate your enemy." But I say to you, Love your enemies and pray for those who persecute you, so that you may be children of your Father in heaven; for he makes his sun rise on the evil and on the good, and sends rain on the righteous and on the unrighteous. For if you love those who love you, what reward do you have? Do not even the tax collectors do the same? And if you greet only your brothers and sisters, what more are you doing than others? Do not even the Gentiles do the same? Be perfect, therefore, as your heavenly Father is perfect. (Matt. 5:43–48; cf. Luke 6:27–35)

Some parts of the Jewish Bible teach that God hates people who do evil (see, e.g., Psalms 5:11, 11:11), but Jesus corrects that view here. He assumes that God loves even God's evil enemies and therefore humans should follow suit, in loving their enemies. God's perfect love for all others, in other words, is to be shared by God's people for the sake of all other people. Jesus thus holds that divine love for humans is universal and love is to be the same *from* humans. He is at odds here with not only parts of the Jewish Bible but also what later would be parts of the *Qur'an* (2:190, 276; 3:140; 7:55; 42:40; 60:1).

The apostle Paul, citing the book of Proverbs, shares the view of Jesus regarding love of one's enemies, at least to the following extent:

If it is possible, so far as it depends on you, live peaceably with all. Beloved, never avenge yourselves, but leave room for the wrath of God; for it is written, "Vengeance is mine, I will repay, says the Lord." No, "if your enemies are hungry, feed them; if they are thirsty, give them something to drink; for by doing this you will heap burning coals on their heads" [Prov. 25:21–22]. Do not be overcome by evil, but overcome evil with good. (Rom. 12:18–21)

If we are to treat other people in a way that is morally good, rather than harmful, for them, we should not exploit or demean them for the sake of religious practice. Their value, in this perspective, exceeds that of a religious practice.

In agreement with Jesus, Paul bases his moral standard for how to treat other people on God's love for God's enemies.

God proves his love for us in that while we still were sinners Christ died for us. Much more surely then, now that we have been justified by his blood, will we be saved through him from the wrath of God. For if while we were enemies, we were reconciled to God through the death of his Son, much more surely, having been reconciled, will we be saved by his life. But more than that, we even boast in God through our Lord Jesus Christ, through whom we have now received reconciliation. (Rom. 5:8–11)

Out of divine love, in Paul's perspective, God did something good for God's enemies: God sent his Son and Messiah to prove and to enact divine love by dying for them in self-giving love. The divine goal is the reconciliation of humans, including God's enemies, to God. This reconciliation includes divine forgiveness, which is to be reflected in human action: "Bear with one another and, if anyone has a complaint against another, forgive each other; just as the Lord has forgiven you, so you also must forgive" (Col. 3:13; see Rom. 15:7).

The command to love strangers and one's enemies strikes many people as not only unreasonable but also likely harmful, if not deadly, to the person who obeys. Extending care to one's enemies for their benefit can, and sometimes does, leave one abused or dead. After all, one's enemies typically do not look after one's interests and often seeks one's harm. So, a love-command can seem to come at an excessive price as a counter to subjecting the value of persons to the value of religious practices. The peril of the love-command can seem to be more serious than the peril of exalting religious practices over persons.

One might retreat to a love-command that seems safe to the one who obeys. Such a command might be: Love other people but *only if* they are evidently no real threat to your well-being. This would be self-protecting love, and it would stand in sharp contrast to the kind of universal love commanded and practiced by Jesus. It is doubtful that Jesus would have risked losing his life for the sake of others if self-protecting love had guided him. Even so, many people will demand a good reason to accept a command to love or to forgive others who evidently pose a threat to them. Their default position is to withhold love and forgiveness from people who apparently put their well-being at risk.

The kind of love promoted by Jesus and Paul, we have seen, has its basis in the moral character of God (as they understood this character). In the absence of God and such a divine character, we will have a hard time finding a basis to empower or to command love or forgiveness of others that entails likely harm or death to the one who obeys. (For relevant discussion, see Moule 2011.) At least many people will demand such a basis but find it not to be available to them. They may find their available evidence for God's reality or at least for God's character of enemy-love to be inadequate. In addition, without God we seem to lack a source adequate to redeem any harm done to people who love their enemies. It is doubtful, then, people in general will be convinced of the universal love-commands promoted by Jesus and Paul. This is not, however, an unusual result for a religious position. Failure to convince people in general of a religious position does not typically discredit that position for everyone. In addition, such a failure does not entail the falsity of a religious position.

One might reject an appeal to love-commands on the ground that the love of others must be spontaneous in a way that cannot coherently be commanded. This, however, would be a mistake. If loving other people is a matter of agreeably *willing* what is good for them, love-commands can be coherent. We can and often do command what people should will, or intend, to do, and they can respond to such a command by exercising their will in one way rather than another. In particular, people can decide to exercise their will agreeably in favor of what is good for others. So, love-commands are a coherent option for people, and they can serve to counter an attempt to subject the value of persons to the value of religious practices.

4 LESSONS FOR RELIGIOUS PRACTICE

Chapters 1 and 2 raised a question about a responsible decision, all things considered, regarding the acceptance or practice of any of the religious positions offered. Such a decision, if epistemically responsible, would conform to one's available evidence concerning reality. If we neglect such evidence, we open the door to accepting and practicing religious proposals that lack any indication of capturing reality even in part. That would be to condone a kind of evidential arbitrariness in religious positions, thereby discrediting the evidential status of such positions. Many inquirers, seeking to capture reality at least in part, will avoid any position marked by such arbitrariness. Their response is understandable, especially when we consider the difficulty one faces in responsibly favoring one such arbitrary position over its many alternatives.

Inquirers about religion need a normative assessment of religious practices, in order to separate the (morally) good from the (morally) bad. For instance, the evil religious practices of ISIS should not get a pass from inquirers; instead, they should be condemned. The same holds for various other religious practices that bring real harm to people. Which normative standard, however, should serve the need, if we are to be responsible, all things considered? This question is among the most difficult questions facing inquirers about religion, but we cannot responsibly ignore it.

One issue is whether a person's normative standard will be self-made and have no bearing beyond that self-made status. Many inquirers, in any case, will want a normative standard that approaches a kind of normative objectivity beyond a merely subjective standpoint. To be socially binding, or intersubjective in scope, a normative standard for assessing religious practices cannot be merely subjective. It will need to have broader scope in its bearing on people, and it would be helpful to identify a basis for this scope. This may be a tall order, but it must be met if one aims to give a responsible endorsement of a religious position for a wide range of people.

Some inquirers will counter with a single normative standard that "naturalizes" religion, including religious experience, and removes any distinctive non-natural status. They aim to domesticate religion by portraying it as thoroughly natural in how it is explained. We need to attend to such a naturalist project if we seek a responsible position on the evidential status of religion and religious experience.

4

～

Religious Experience Naturalized

Chapter 3 asked whether it would be responsible, all things considered, to accept and practice any of the six religious perspectives offered. It did not defend an answer, given the need for further clarification of the question. One prominent philosophical approach, however, entails a negative answer: It would not be responsible as long as a religious perspective is at odds with something called "naturalism" about the world. This chapter explores the bearing of naturalism on religion and religious experience, in preparation for a broader assessment in Chapters 7 and 8.

1 A NATURAL WORLD

Whatever else we humans do, we face a changing physical world around and within us, whether we like it or not. Whatever else it does, this world does not bow and scrape before us humans. On the contrary, it bruises and bends us at times, regardless of our desires and hopes. Its hospitality toward us is thus questionable at best, and it certainly could be much more accommodating overall, if only coincidentally, for our well-being.

It would be misleading to call the nonintentional physical world our enemy, or our friend for that matter, because it does not have purposes, hostile or friendly, toward us. The nonintentional physical world is not a purposive agent, and therefore it lacks goals or aims. It does not function with anything like "in order to" in mind, because it does not have anything "in mind." Its causal functioning does not rise to that purposive level found among such intentional agents as humans, great apes, dogs, and cats. It is a matter of mere happenings, if law-based, in contrast with purposive actions. Our best sciences cohere with this characterization.

Physicalism and the Sciences

When is a world uniformly "natural," and when not? This question does not have an easy answer, but we can make progress toward a response. Our question is not just this: When is a world uniformly "physical," and when not? Naturalism about the world does not entail that the world is uniformly physical or material. It can acknowledge features that emerge, somehow, from a physical base without their being physical themselves. Many naturalists offer examples from psychological features of humans, for example, their believing, desiring, intending, fearing, or hoping something. Such psychological features of humans are not themselves physical, according to many naturalists, but their existence has a base of some kind in physical features of the world. Naturalists do not agree on how to specify the exact dependence relation to that base, even though talk of "supervenience" or "emergence" in various technical senses is common. (On some of the senses, see Moser and Trout 1995.)

We can make some good sense of talk of "physical" features of the world via an adequate notion of a thing's being *extended in space-time*. A chair, desk, or keyboard, for instance, is extended in space-time and therefore is physical, but the same is arguably not the case for a belief, desire, or intention, however such psychological features depend on brain states. If those psychological features are not physical, human persons are not uniformly physical; they then have irreducibly nonphysical features in their psychological makeup. Even so, human persons still could be uniformly natural, if their psychological features fall under a suitable category of what is "natural."

What, if anything, have the sciences to do with physicalism and naturalism? The question is fitting, because proponents of naturalism and physicalism often claim the sciences as backing their positions. The nature of the sciences is, however, more complicated than many people assume. The sciences, of course, have a lot to say in describing and explaining the physical world, but it does not follow that they back physicalism, or materialism, about the world at large. Cosmic physicalism is universal materialism, the view that all of reality is physical, consisting of things extended in space-time. In its typical status, this is a logically contingent, rather than a logically necessary, claim about reality. It logically could be false, and thus it does not qualify as necessarily true, if it is true at all.

The sciences, in their academic form in standard science textbooks (taken as a group), do not affirm cosmic physicalism. They do not claim that all of reality is physical; nor do they assume or otherwise depend on such a universal claim about reality. This is an empirical matter, and one can check the science textbooks for the fact of the matter. The key factor is that the sciences do not have a *scientific* means to confirm the universal truth of physicalism. This limitation may explain why the academic sciences properly restrict their claims to their own domains of scientific evidence: domains of physics, astronomy, chemistry, biochemistry, biology, geology, and so on. Given this restriction, the sciences stop short of the sweeping claims about overall reality found in some positions of philosophy and theology.

Some *scientists*, not to be confused with the sciences, do portray the academic sciences as linked to physicalism of a universal sort. After school hours, at least, these theorists step outside the boundaries of the academic sciences by offering universal claims about reality, such as the claims of universal physicalism. This move does not entail that they are doing science just because they are scientists. In fact, they are then moonlighting in a different discipline, perhaps in philosophy or theology.

Jerry Fodor has portrayed "the true scientific vision" as being committed to physicalism of a universal sort. He has claimed with regard to the biological sciences: "All that happens is this: microscopic variations cause macroscopic effects, as an indirect consequence of which sometimes the variants proliferate and sometimes they don't. That's all there is; there's a lot of 'because' out there, but there isn't any 'for'" (1998, p. 168). So, the physicalism of "the true scientific vision" is robustly causal but devoid of purpose or intention. It gives us a reality free of any purposive "for" or "in order to." Reality is thus "nonteleological," as many theorists would say.

Richard Dawkins has offered his physicalist portrait of reality: "In a universe of blind physical forces and genetic replication, some people are going to get hurt, other people are going to get lucky, and you won't find any rhyme or reason in it, nor any justice. The universe we observe has precisely the properties we should expect if there is, at bottom, no design, no purpose, no evil and no good, nothing but blind, pitiless indifference" (1996, p. 133). This is a straightforward physicalist vision of the universe, and it is held by many inquirers. It is doubtful, however, that this is a scientific vision, as least if the academic sciences and its textbooks are the standard.

Bertrand Russell, before Fodor and Dawkins, portrayed the sciences as leaving us with a world empty of anything like ultimate purpose:

Even more purposeless, more void of meaning, is the world which Science presents for our belief. Amid such a world, if anywhere, our ideals henceforward must find a home. That Man is the product of causes which had no provision of the end they were achieving; that his origin, his growth, his hopes and fears, his loves and his beliefs, are but the outcome of accidental collocations of atoms; that no fire, no heroism, no intensity of thought and feeling, can preserve an individual life beyond the grave; that all the labours of the ages, all the devotion, all the inspiration, all the noonday brightness of human genius, are destined to extinction in the vast death of the solar system, and that the whole temple of Man's achievement must inevitably be buried beneath the debris of a universe in ruins – all these things, if not quite beyond dispute, are yet so nearly certain that no philosophy which rejects them can hope to stand. Only within the scaffolding of these truths, only on the firm foundation of unyielding despair, can the soul's habitation henceforth be safely built. (1903, p. 46)

The sciences, in Russell's perspective, offer us a world that is "but the outcome of accidental collocations of atoms," even if laws of science govern. The laws of science themselves, according to Russell, do not result from purpose, and thus Russell acknowledges an ultimately "purposeless" world characterized by the sciences.

Russell is mistaken, as we see from an empirical view of the academic sciences. The sciences do not stick their neck out in the way Russell does in talking universally of "the purposeless ... world which Science presents for our belief." The problem is in the alleged universality of the sciences regarding "the world" as ultimately "purposeless" or "void of meaning." The academic textbooks of the sciences do not share Russell's universality regarding "the world" as a place ultimately "void of meaning." As we noted, the academic sciences limit themselves to their own domains of scientific evidence and thus avoid sweeping claims about "the purposeless ... world" as a whole.

Academic physics does not allege that the world of physics is reality *as a whole*. It is logically compatible with parts of reality being beyond the world of physics and even being meaningful or purposive in a way that physics is not.

For instance, academic physics does not rule out the disciplines of theology, ethics, or philosophy, or all of the purposes identified in those disciplines. A directly analogous lesson applies to the other academic sciences: astronomy, chemistry, biochemistry, biology, and so on. They, too, limit themselves to their own domains of scientific evidence. Russell's world of "science," then, is not that of the academic sciences. The sciences in their academic mode are more tolerant of a larger world, beyond the sciences themselves. The academic textbooks of the sciences confirm this lesson.

Daniel Dennett has proposed to restrict religion to the laws of science. He explains his naturalism about religion:

I might mean that religion is natural as opposed to *supernatural*, that it is a human phenomenon composed of events, organisms, objects, structures, patterns, and the like that all obey the laws of physics or biology, and hence do not involve miracles. And that *is* what I mean. Notice that it could be true that God exists, that God is indeed the intelligent, conscious, loving creator of us all, and yet *still* religion itself, as a complex set of phenomena, is a perfectly natural phenomenon. (2006, p. 25)

Dennett's naturalism thus applies to religion but not to God, if God exists. (Dennett does not believe that God exists.) His position excludes God from religion, if God exists, on the ground that religion is a "perfectly natural phenomenon" but God is not "perfectly natural," if God exists.

God's causal power is not limited by the laws of (natural) science, if God exists, but religion is thus limited, according to Dennett. So, if God chooses to act *within religion*, God will need to conform to the laws of science, in Dennett's perspective. This is an implausible restriction on God, if God exists. A more plausible view is that if God exists, *God* will choose whether to conform divine interventions in religion to the laws of science. God may or may not have good reasons to conform in that way; we cannot decide this matter one way or the other at the start. So, Dennett's restriction on God, if God exists, seems presumptuous at best. As responsible inquirers, we cannot simply assume that God would make religion a natural phenomenon, if God exists.

The academic sciences do not give the laws of science the hypothetical restriction on God entailed by Dennett's naturalism about religion. The explanation of this fact is straightforward: The sciences do not presume, support, or require naturalism about religion, because they do not presume, support, or require that religion conform to the laws of science. Much of religion, especially if God is involved, is arguably outside the domains of scientific evidence occupying the academic sciences. So, we do not find sweeping limitations of religion to naturalism offered in those sciences. Instead, we find empirical confirmation in scientific textbooks of the relative cognitive modesty of the sciences regarding matters outside the sciences.

If academic scientific textbooks represent the sciences, we may infer that the sciences are not committed to the truth or the reasonableness of unrestricted physicalism. The sciences, given their adopted focus, do not risk a claim on the universal truth of physicalism or its reasonableness. The topic of cosmic physicalism is properly outside their domain of evidence and assessment. If physicalism is naturalism in its ontological form, then the sciences are neutral on ontological naturalism in its universal guise. They may affirm, assume, or depend on *restricted* ontological naturalism, or physicalism, in one or more scientific domains, but that would stop short of a commitment to universal naturalism in its ontological form. Endorsing ontological naturalism for a limited range of domains does not entail endorsing such naturalism for all domains of reality. It allows for being neutral on some domains, such as the domains of philosophy, ethics, and theology.

Physicalists have offered different ways to approach some psychological features of humans, such as beliefs, desires, and hopes, which seem not to be physical. At the extreme, *eliminative* physicalists recommend that we simply eliminate talk of such psychological features while we wait for better replacement language from the sciences. This recommendation finds encouragement in the sciences having dropped talk of witches, demons, and ghosts for the sake of language more fitting to the sciences. (Dennett represents eliminative physicalism.) *Reductive* physicalists seek not just the elimination of psychological language remote from the sciences but its "reduction," by definition or law-governed correspondence, to language suited to the sciences. For instance, one might reduce talk of qualitative sensory states to talk of states correlated with brains.

Supervenience physicalists, having doubts about wholesale reduction and elimination, propose that the relevant psychological features can emerge from, or supervene on, physical states, in a law-governed manner, even if the reduction of corresponding language is not available. For instance, my pain from a throbbing toothache can emerge from my nervous system without our being able to reduce the language in question. Multiple nonreductive accounts of supervenience compete for acceptance, but the general option is sufficiently clear for now. (For details on these variations on physicalism, see Moser and Trout 1995.)

W. V. O. Quine confirms my comments on the relation of the sciences to universal physicalism:

Nowadays the overwhelming purposes of the science game are technology and understanding.... The science game is not committed to the physical, whatever that means.... Even telepathy and clairvoyance are scientific options, however moribund. It would take some extraordinary evidence to enliven them, but, if that were to happen, then empiricism itself – the crowning norm ... of naturalized epistemology – would go by the board. For remember that that norm, and naturalized epistemology itself, are integral to science, and science is fallible and corrigible. (1990, pp. 20–21)

Quine still can be a naturalist, conceived liberally, as long as he holds that all genuine "technology and understanding" focus on (some aspect of) "nature," broadly understood, rather than anything supernatural or non-natural. (We can leave the exact specification of "nature" to naturalists in such a case.) Even so, Quine holds that neither science nor naturalism based in science requires universal physicalism or even unrestricted empiricism. We shall see that neither theology nor religion is automatically excluded from responsible inquiry if the sciences and naturalism are suitably limited in explanatory scope.

Methodological Naturalism

Quine's overall position suggests naturalism as a method for belief and theory formation rather than as an exclusive, universal ontology regarding what exists. This is *methodological* naturalism, and many scientists use it as a portrait and guide for the sciences (but not automatically for all inquiry). It allows one to free the natural sciences from universal physicalism while maintaining naturalism in the methods of the sciences. What, however, is naturalism in the *methods* of the sciences? Proponents of methodological naturalism do not offer a singular answer, but we can clarify a bit.

At a minimum, naturalism in methods excludes supernaturalism or at least non-naturalism in methods, and it gives "nature" a central constraining role in acceptable belief or theory formation. It requires that the sources and processes of belief and theory formation be part of the causal nexus of nature. A supernatural source, such as God, and a non-natural source, such as a Platonic Form or a transcendent value, would be independent of that causal nexus.

Naturalism in the methods of scientific belief or theory formation is naturalism for the sciences, and not necessarily for inquiry outside the sciences. Again, we may use the academic sciences as the standard for sciences, while letting the corresponding academic textbooks represent those sciences. Those textbooks do not claim or assume that *all* methods of inquiry, outside and inside the sciences, must conform to the methods of the sciences or to naturalism in methods of inquiry. Instead, those textbooks focus on methods that serve the descriptive and explanatory aims of the sciences, without unrestricted generalization of those methods or aims as requirements for all inquiry. This kind of focus is responsible, and it shows proper modesty toward the scope of scientific methods and naturalism. It saves one from an unduly narrow monopoly on methods for belief and theory formation in general.

One might propose that the key to the methodological naturalism of the sciences is experimentation, in keeping with the prominent role of experiments in the sciences. This proposal, however, will not work. One problem is that some of the sciences are theoretical in a way that does not rely on experiments in any straightforward manner. This can result from the breadth of an area of scientific theory or from the nature of the objects about which a scientific theory offers explanations. For instance, scientific cosmology is typically not "experimental" in any direct way. Even so, it is explanatory, and it belongs to the academic sciences, as the relevant scientific textbooks indicate. In addition, we should allow for a use of experimentation outside the sciences, even in religion. (Chapter 7 returns to this topic.)

If a notion of experimentation fails to capture methodological naturalism in the sciences, some might look for a better alternative in empiricism: a view about the key role of perceptual experience in the sciences. Quine's aforementioned perspective on "science," however, recommends against this strategy. It does not limit science to empirical

science in any sense familiar to strictly empiricist philosophers. It permits that strict empiricism could "go by
the board" in science as the result of new extraordinary
evidence of parapsychological phenomena. Quine finds
such potential evidence to be compatible with science as a
fallible, error-capable pursuit of human understanding of
nature based on evidence.

Open to alternatives to strict empiricism, Quine's
naturalism endorses fallibilism about the sciences, given
their demonstrated capability of error. This is understandable in the light of the conflicting large shifts in the scientific
understanding of nature throughout its history. An a priori
commitment to the universal physicalist or strictly empiricist nature of science could yield a conflict with the best
contemporary science, and that conflict could hinder scientific understanding. So, Quine and like-minded naturalists
avoid such a commitment. The sciences, in their perspective, can accommodate, under extraordinary conditions,
even some *non*empirical methods to ground scientific
beliefs or theories. We should retain, however, enough
empiricism to maintain the empirical nature of our best
sciences; they are, after all, *empirical* sciences, even if they
do not demand a *strict* empiricism that excludes every
other method of inquiry. Perhaps Quine would agree.

The nonempirical methods of some religious inquiry,
including philosophical inquiry about God on the basis of
rational reflection, are logically compatible with a limited
naturalism for the sciences. Those nonempirical methods
need not focus on "nature" and thus need not be "scientific"
in that sense, but they can be fallible and yield human
understanding of reality (at least as conceived by its proponents). The sciences, in the view under consideration, are
the fallible pursuit of human understanding of nature, and
there is no requirement that such understanding be *fully*
guided by empiricism. In addition, although rarely noted
by extreme naturalists, the scientific pursuit of understanding of nature can find a logically compatible analogue

(not to be confused with an instance) in fallible theology and religion that advance human understanding of reality. Theology and religion, then, are not banned by a limited naturalism for the sciences or by the sciences themselves.

A proponent of methodological naturalism in the sciences might invoke the tendency of the sciences to explain phenomena by general *laws of nature*. The claim would be that we have not adequately explained something until we have subsumed it under a law of nature. This claim reflects a kind of knowledge called *scientia* in medieval philosophy and theology, and it offers a contrast with any alleged knowledge of individuals without general laws. It finds inspiration from a long-standing Aristotelian view that knowledge is "only of the universal," where such knowledge conforms to a general law (see De Burgh 1939).

It is controversial whether the sciences require that all explanation, even all scientific explanation, be explanation via general laws of nature. Even if some of the sciences (e.g., physics or chemistry) rely on such explanation, it is not clear that all of the sciences do. Parts of psychology, for example, explain human behavior by appeal to the intentions of an agent, but they do not (straightforwardly) rely on general laws of nature in doing so. Some historical explanation of human behavior has the same feature. So, there is no straightforward connection between scientific explanation, at least broadly conceived, and general laws of nature.

Some extreme naturalists endorse the following kind of comprehensive explanatory requirement from the sciences:

The sciences demand that all explanation of reality, at least in general and ultimately, be explanation in terms of nature alone; so, there is no ultimate exclusion of the sciences or naturalism from any domain of intended explanation of reality, including any theological or religious reality.

According to this view, the sciences aim to be comprehensive in their explanation of reality in terms of nature alone, at least in general and ultimately. If there is theological or religious explanation, the sciences aim to have explanatory coverage even there, in terms ultimately of nature alone.

An influential proponent of extreme naturalism for the sciences is Sigmund Freud. He claims that according to the sciences, "there is no other source of knowledge [or explanation] of the universe but the intellectual manipulation of carefully verified observations, in fact, what is called research, and that no knowledge [or explanation] can be obtained from revelation, intuition, or inspiration" (1933, p. 217). Excluding divine revelation as a source of knowledge, this position recommends a kind of *methodological monism* regarding a comprehensive naturalist source of knowledge and intended explanation of all domains of reality needing explanation. The sciences, in this view, serve as a singular, comprehensive methodological source of knowledge and such explanation. A proponent thus will hold: If the sciences do not aim to explain a phenomenon, at least in general and ultimately, in terms of nature alone, then it is not worthy of being explained, perhaps because it is not part of reality. (Chapter 5 challenges Freud's attempt to deflate religion as a reliable source of truth.)

Even if a naturalist explanatory monism for the sciences will simplify a theory of knowledge, it faces a serious problem. The academic sciences themselves do not endorse, presume, or support such monism for all explanation of reality. That is, such naturalist explanatory monism is no part of the sciences for all explanation of reality. The academic textbooks of the sciences do not endorse or assume it; nor do they depend on it in some other way. In particular, they do not require that all explanation of reality be explanation ultimately in terms of nature alone. For instance, the academic textbooks of the sciences do not require the explaining (even in general or ultimately) of theological, religious, or ethical reality in terms ultimately of nature alone. In addition, this fact does not result from an assumption of the sciences that there is no theological, religious, or ethical reality (needing explanation).

The sciences focus on describing and explaining their proper domains of *scientific* reality and evidence. This is an empirical truth confirmed by due attention to the academic textbooks of the sciences. An attempt or a demand of the sciences to explain all phenomena of *nature* in terms ultimately of nature alone does not entail an attempt or a demand to explain all phenomena of *reality* in terms ultimately of nature alone. The academic sciences accommodate this important truth, even though it is neglected by some extreme naturalists.

Dawkins acknowledges that religion can offer interpretations of facts, but he opposes any limitation on the intended explanatory scope of the sciences. He remarks: "A universe with a creative superintendent would be a very different kind of universe from one without. Why is that not a scientific matter?" (2006, p. 55). He adds: "God's existence or non-existence is a scientific fact about the universe, discoverable in principle if not in practice" (p. 50). So, a scientific fact need not be a physicalist or a naturalist fact, in Dawkins's language, if God's existence would be a scientific fact. What, then, makes a fact "scientific," in his perspective? The answer seems to lie in how a fact can be assessed.

Dawkins claims that the theses of theology and religion should be assessed as scientific hypotheses by what are "purely and entirely scientific methods." After raising a question about the divine resurrection of Jesus, Dawkins remarks: "The methods we should use to settle the matter, in the unlikely event that relevant evidence ever became available, would be purely and entirely scientific methods" (p. 59). He suggests that some attempts to make religion independent of scientific inquiry are popular only because we do not have any evidence in favor of (the truth of) the claim that God exists. Once evidence is available, according to Dawkins, we see that the sciences aim to cover the relevant claim with "entirely scientific methods."

Dawkins holds that the methods of the sciences demand evidence from probabilities. He remarks: "Even if God's existence is never proved or disproved with certainty one way or the other, available evidence and reasoning may yield an estimate of probability far from 50 per cent" (p. 50). In addition: "What matters is not whether God is disprovable (he isn't), but whether his existence is *probable*.... There is no reason to regard God as immune from consideration along the spectrum of probabilities" (p. 54). Many theists will agree with Dawkins here, but the big question is: What *kinds* of probabilities are required? Dawkins mentions statistical probabilities in some cases, but not all of science or probability is statistical.

Some philosophers acknowledge "epistemic" probabilities that bear on one's overall evidence but are not identical with statistical probabilities. Some of our evidence is experience-based and broadly probabilistic, and thus non-deductive, but not statistical. (See Kyburg 1970 and Moser 1989 for relevant discussion.) A key issue is whether religious experience can confer probability and thus epistemic justification on theological or religious commitments. If so, we would have an analogue to perceptual experience and perceptual justification, not all of which is statistical.

Dawkins dismisses personal religious experience as unreliable by appealing to "the formidable power of the brain's simulation software." He adds that "it is well capable of constructing 'visions' and 'visitations' of the utmost [seemingly] veridical power" (2006, p. 90). Note the use of the modal term "capable" here. The brain is indeed capable in the way indicated, but capability is not the same as *actual* performance. Being able to do something does not entail always doing it or even that it is probable that it is being done. My brain *can* construct an image of my cat, but it does not follow that my current experience of my cat is *nothing more* than a construction by my brain. More to the point, we lack the needed evidence, or probability base, to say that all personal religious experience emerges from *just* brain activity. Dawkins does not supply such evidence, and therefore his dismissal of personal religious experience is too quick, at best.

Dawkins does not offer an adequate explanation of the kinds of probability he demands, and therefore his position is obscure. It seems, however, that he requires the evidence base for the relevant probability to be socially readily shareable, if not actually socially shared, and not private. (By "socially readily shareable," I mean "shareable just by human means.") In Dawkins's requirement, the relevant evidence is "scientific" in qualifying as the kind of socially shareable evidence found in the sciences. We beg a key question, however, if we assume that all evidence from religious experience must be socially shareable in the way scientific evidence is. We cannot rule out that God would choose to give some humans evidence of divine reality that is not thus shareable. Dawkins does not rule this out with evidence, and he thus fails to undermine a role for religious experience in the conferring of probability and justification.

Dawkins rightly opposes the kind of fideism that disregards a role for evidence in the assessment of theology and religion. He makes the mistake, however, of assuming that there cannot be evidence from personal experience that confers probability in such domains. The academic sciences do not claim or depend on this view assumed by Dawkins. The academic textbooks of the sciences (taken as a group) bear this out, in their not demanding that the domains of theology, religion, and ethics be justified or explained just in terms of socially shared or readily shareable probabilities. We have no reason to suppose that they misrepresent the actual sciences in this regard. Dawkins, then, goes beyond the sciences he claims to represent in his assumption about relevant probabilities and religious experience.

Dawkins assumes that "the God question is not in principle and forever outside the remit of science" (2006, p. 71). We now see that the resilience of that assumption depends on the kind of evidence available in theology and religion. The evidence suited to the sciences is, in some sense, publicly readily available to inquirers and hence broadly intersubjective. It thus can be socially readily shared under circumstances where people are suitably positioned and perceptually capable relative to it. In contrast, we cannot say the same for all evidence offered in theology and religion, even if some of the evidence in those domains is intersubjective and publicly available to inquirers.

Some theology denies that all evidence for God's reality is publicly readily available. It proposes that God selectively reveals evidence of divine reality to people receptive to it and hides it, at least until an opportune time, from people who are not receptive, owing to their indifference or opposition to it. This strategy portrays God as being self-revealing in a way that is best for humans and thus sensitive to their receptivity. It would, in any case, be *God's* prerogative to reveal evidence of God in a way preferred by God. Dawkins (along with Dennett, as noted) misses this crucial point.

Suppose that God chose in divine self-manifestation to be sensitive to human receptivity and thus chose not to give publicly readily available evidence of divine reality to all inquirers. Would Dawkins be in a position to fault God in that case? It seems not, given God's superior status, cognitively and morally, relative to humans. So, we should not assume uncritically that all the evidence in theology and religion must correspond or does correspond to the publicly readily available nature of scientific evidence. Thus far we have no good reason to hold that the sciences undermine religious experience and evidence as a live option for human inquirers. (Chapters 7 and 8 return to the topic of suitable evidence for God's reality.)

2 AGENTS IN NATURE AND RELIGION

However we understand the natural world, the world we face seems to include personal agents (like us), who counter our will and other psychological features with their own will and other psychological features. What should we say of such agents, with regard to their fit with naturalism and the kinds of religious experience and meaning identified in Chapters 2 and 3? In addition, is naturalism a threat to the types of religious experience and meaning found in the six religious perspectives characterized previously? Our attention to those perspectives will save us from undue abstractness in relating religion to naturalism.

Gautama on Agents in Self-Practice for Awakening

Gautama has a central role for persons as intentional agents in his religious perspective. His recommended self-practice toward the religious experience of Awakening is for *self*-Awakening, that is, the Awakening of a self. It also is the practice of a *self* for the sake of such Awakening. As a result, Gautama offers an intentional, goal-directed path to Awakening, and its being intentional requires an intentional self, that is, an intentional agent, in contrast with a mere thing, event, happening, state, or process.

Gautama acknowledges that certain approaches to a self, such as what he calls a "doctrine-of-self-clinging," can block a holy life of Awakening. This view does not entail, however, that selfhood is itself altogether dispensable or inherently bad. The matter depends on what *kind* of self is involved, with regard to its fit with, including its flexibility toward, Awakening. Gautama, as Chapter 2 noted, highlights a crucial role for a *self in action* in following his recommended path to purity in self-Awakening: "Evil is left undone by oneself, by oneself is one cleansed. Purity and impurity are one's own doing. No one purifies another. No other purifies one" (*Dhammapada* 12:165). If "purity and impurity are *one's own doing*," neglect or omission of this role for a self will threaten the coherence or the practicality of following Gautama's path to a holy meaningful life, that is, a life of self-Awakening. There cannot be either mindfulness without a *mind* that is mindful or concentration without a self who is concentrating. Charity in interpretation requires that we understand Gautama accordingly.

Gautama gives a clear statement of a self who is engaged in the intentional, resolute activity of renunciation for the sake of self-concentration and self-Awakening:

As I remained thus heedful, ardent, and resolute, thinking imbued with renunciation arose in me. I discerned that thinking imbued with renunciation has arisen in me; and that leads neither to my own affliction, nor to the affliction of others, nor to the affliction of both. It fosters discernment, promotes lack of vexation, and leads to unbinding. If I were to think and ponder in line with that even for a night . . . even for a day . . . even for a day and night, I do not envision any danger that would come from it, except that thinking and pondering a long time would tire the body. When the body is tired, the mind is disturbed; and a disturbed mind is far from concentration. So, I steadied my mind right within, settled, unified, and concentrated it. Why is that? So that my mind would not be disturbed. (*Dvedhāvitakka Sutta, Majjhima Nikāya* 19)

The recommended goal is a mind, "my mind," not being disturbed or perturbed by the world's toxic changes, such as those found in suffering and frustration. The mind in question is a self, having the power of "resolute" concentration that can seek relief from (and avoid) being "disturbed" or perturbed. This self-concentration, as Chapter 2 noted, aims for self-insulation or relief from the world's psychologically corrosive effects from suffering and frustration.

Gautama identifies the experiential steps of a self's path to the purity of mindfulness. Such purity is at the center of self-Awakening, and it comes only with self-resolve. Note Gautama's repeated use of "I" as central to the path to Awakening:

Unflagging persistence was aroused in me, and unmuddled mindfulness established. My body was calm and unaroused, my mind concentrated and single. Quite secluded from sensuality, secluded from unskillful [harmful] qualities, I entered and remained in the first jhāna [meditative state of mind]: rapture and pleasure born of seclusion, accompanied by directed thought and evaluation. With the stilling of directed thoughts and evaluations, I entered and remained in the second jhāna: rapture and pleasure born of concentration, unification of awareness free from directed thought and evaluation – internal assurance. With the fading of rapture, I remained equanimous, mindful, and alert, and sensed pleasure with the body. I entered and remained in the third jhāna, of which the noble ones declare, "Equanimous and mindful, he has a pleasant abiding." With the abandoning of pleasure and pain – as with the earlier disappearance of elation and distress – I entered and remained in the fourth jhāna: purity of equanimity and mindfulness, neither pleasure nor pain. (*Dvedhāvitakka Sutta, Majjhima Nikāya* 19)

The culmination in the "purity of equanimity and mindfulness" assumes the presence of a mind that has reached this purity. Gautama's recurring use of "I" confirms that the process is intentional, or goal-directed, courtesy of a purposive self aiming at equanimity and mindfulness.

Gautama's advice for self-insulation or relief from troublesome obstacles to "imperturbability" assumes that a self has "past lives" different from that self's current life:

When the mind was thus concentrated, purified, bright, unblemished, rid of defilement, pliant, malleable, steady, and attained to imperturbability, I directed it to the *knowledge of recollecting my past lives*. I recollected my manifold past lives, i.e., one birth, two ... five, ten ... fifty, a hundred, a thousand, a hundred thousand, many eons of cosmic contraction, many eons of cosmic expansion, many eons of cosmic contraction and expansion: There I had such a name, belonged to such a clan, had such an appearance. Such was my food, such my experience of pleasure and pain, such the end of my life. Passing away from that state, I re-arose there.

There too I had such a name, belonged to such a clan, had such an appearance. Such was my food, such my experience of pleasure and pain, such the end of my life. Passing away from that state, I re-arose here. Thus I remembered my manifold past lives in their modes and details. (*Dvedhāvitakka Sutta, Majjhima Nikāya* 19)

Gautama thus acknowledges a self (an "I") that is robust rather than tenuous, a self that endures through many past lives. Many people have given no thought to such an approach to selves. Gautama would attribute this deficiency to a lack of self-Awakening. Our own evidence may or may not support his position here.

Gautama's overall view of a self aiming at self-Awakening in "imperturbability" does not fit with ontological naturalism, or physicalism. One consideration is that Gautama acknowledges "past lives" and rebirths, or reincarnations, of a self. The Jātaka in the Pāli canon is a collection of stories of Gautama's own previous lives, in various forms, throughout history. A self with past lives is not a self either consisting of or emerging just from physical states in a current life. In Gautama's perspective, one and the same self, as an individual self, survives across temporal eras in a way that a physicalist self would not. In a physicalist perspective, an individual, *token* self, in contrast with a *type* of self, would lose its token-identity with a change of physical basis across temporal eras. The latter change would result in a different token self. Selves in Gautama's account are token individuals, actual concrete selves, and not just types of selves. So, he is not endorsing physicalism about selves; instead, he is taking a different, nonphysicalist approach to selves.

Methodological naturalism, like ontological naturalism, is at odds with Gautama's perspective on selves. Gautama does not guide his view of selves by an appeal to "nature" or "natural methods," let alone to anything like the ancient sciences. (We may say the same about his personal theism, but, in keeping with his own practice, we have bracketed his theism from his practical religious advice.) Gautama's path to self-Awakening offers a practical method for human life, as Chapter 2 noted, but there is no reason to suppose that it follows or conforms to naturalism in ontology or methods. On the contrary, his method rests on normative considerations about what is good or at least right for a person, in the face of suffering and frustration, and those considerations do not manifest naturalism. His method does not require a physical base for all reality, evidence, explanation, or belief formation.

Gautama, we have seen, offers a threefold practical method. It can be summarized in terms of right conduct, right concentration, and right commitment aimed at psychological self-insulation or relief from life's destructive changes. As Chapter 2 indicated, he remarks: "And what is that ancient path, that ancient road, traveled by the Rightly Self-Awakened Ones of former times? Just this noble eight-fold path: right view, right resolve, right speech, right action, right livelihood, right effort, right mindfulness, right concentration. That is the ancient path traveled by the Rightly Self-Awakened Ones of former times" (*Samyutta Nikaya* 12:65). Gautama's method is thus inherently norma-tive regarding features independent of the sciences, and therefore it does not reduce to any method inapplicable to such features. His method focuses not on an ultimately nonnormative "natural world" but on the practical norma-tive means to stable conduct, concentration, and commit-ment. Gautama considered his method to be central to "the holy life" of self-Awakening, and this kind of life has no role in naturalism as typically conceived.

Ontological and methodological naturalists will balk at Gautama's religious perspective, especially its acknowledg-ment of "past lives" for human selves. Even so, we can ask why we, as responsible inquirers, should accept ontological or methodological naturalism as normative for Gautama's religious perspective, or any religious perspective, for that matter. Why suppose that we have a need of such natural-ism with regard to religion? This question becomes particu-larly relevant once we see that the sciences themselves do not require that theology and religion conform to the stand-ards of the sciences, let alone to the standards of universal ontological or methodological naturalism.

Gautama does not require that evidence for self-Awakening be publicly available in the way that scientific evidence is. This suggests that his religious approach is not guided by anything like the sciences as we know them. Gautama's main religious goal is to achieve the kind of self-Awakening or imperturbability resilient against human suffering and frustration. This goal lies outside the reach not only of the sciences but also of naturalism as typically conceived. It is doubtful that this is automatically a defect in Gautama's goal. So, naturalism is at most a questionable threat here.

Confucius on Agents in Self-Cultivation for Relational Virtue

Confucius, as Chapter 2 explained, assigns a central role to intentional selves in the religious quest for meaning in rela-tional virtue. He stresses, we saw, human self-control as the *self*-cultivation of virtuous reciprocity in interpersonal relationships:

The Master said, "Cultivate in yourself respectful attentive-ness." Zilu asked: "Is that all there is to it?" The Master replied: "Cultivate yourself to bring comfort to others." Zilu asked: "Is that all there is to it?" The Master replied: "Cultivate yourself to bring comfort to the people." (*Analects* 14.42)

The advice to "cultivate yourself to bring comfort to others" is benevolent *self-cultivation* for the good of others. It lies, we saw, at the center of what Confucius promotes as his reli-gious Way of human life.

Confucius offers a normative approach to a religious life, anchored in *ren* (goodness, including benevolence): "The Master said, 'Conquer yourself and return to *li* [proper, fitting conduct]: that is *ren*. If a person could conquer himself and return to *li* for a single day, the world would respond to him with *ren*. Being *ren* proceeds from oneself, how could it come from others?" (*Analects* 12.1). Confucius thus ascribes the *self*-cultivation of virtue to humans, leaving no place for God to cultivate virtue for them. Chapter 2 noted, accordingly, that God has no definite practical function in the religious Way of life recommended by Confucius, despite his personal commitment to theism.

Confucius identifies personal commitment to *ren* as the normative basis for knowledge and love:

4.1 The Master said, To settle in *ren* is the fairest course. If one chooses not to dwell amidst *ren*, whence will come knowledge?

4.2 The Master said, Those who are not *ren* cannot long dwell in straitened circumstances, and cannot long dwell in joy. The *ren* person is at peace with *ren*. The wise person makes use of *ren*.

4.3 The Master said, Only the *ren* person can love others and hate others.

4.4 The Master said, If one sets one's heart on *ren*, there will be none he hates.

Confucius evidently has in mind the kind of knowledge appropriate to "wisdom," given his reference to "the wise person." Such knowledge is directed toward goodness in human life, and thus it is not a matter of trivial facts. It is normatively significant knowledge, bearing on good conduct.

The advice from Confucius is to "settle" or to "choose to dwell" in the goodness that is *ren*. This happens when one "sets one's heart" on *ren*. His language of "settling," "choosing to dwell," and "setting one's heart" is inherently intentional, or goal-directed, and thus agent-centered. It is language of a personal agent who favors, in resolute action, the goodness of benevolence. This kind of agent is a conscious, self-determining doer, and not just a thing, event, happening, state, or process. The omission of such personal agents from the religion of Confucius would rob it of its main goal: the virtuous interpersonal relationship of such agents.

The self-determining agency acknowledged by Confucius includes human causal power to reach a valued goal. He remarks: "Is there any person who can direct his strength to *ren* for an entire day? I have never seen anyone whose strength is not sufficient – most likely there is such a one, but I have yet to see him" (*Analects* 4.6). This sufficient strength or power enables a person to move himself or herself, intentionally, toward the desired benevolence of loyal reciprocity with other persons. It also ensures personal responsibility in interpersonal morality and in various legal matters.

Note the talk by Confucius of "can direct his strength." Such self-directing of power toward a goal – what some call "final causation" – is distinctive of personal agents, and they contrast with mere things, happenings, events, states, or processes. The latter do not "direct" at all, even if they have so-called efficient causal influence. They lack the needed conscious focus and accompanying volitional resolve (toward a goal) to self-direct in the way suggested. As a result, lacking self-control, they are not morally or legally responsible. Confucius devotes his instructional attention to agents who are morally and legally responsible, rather than to mere things, happenings, events, states, or processes. It would be a category mistake to direct a program of instruction toward the latter items, because they are incapable of self-understanding and self-learning. They have no self to enable such understanding and learning. So, we do not consider them to be responsible students in school or participants in a court of law.

Confucius offers a portrait of responsible agents who should move toward responsible action *for others*, and not settle for private thoughts about virtue. He says of himself: "That I have not cultivated virtue, that I have learned but not explained, that I have heard what is right but failed to align with it, that what is not good in me I have been unable to change – these are my worries" (*Analects* 7.3). These are the worries of a self-reflective personal agent that stem from intentional self-examination. The world did not have to include agents of that sort, but it does, and this fact should attract our attention. Perhaps we cannot adequately explain this fact, but we still should acknowledge its reality. Our inability to explain it fully should not lead us to endorse an unduly restrictive bad theory, such as eliminativism about selves.

Mere things (e.g., rocks, clouds, and rivers) do not engage in self-examination, or in any examination, for that matter. As a result, they do not share the worries of Confucius, or any worries. Confucius worries that he has failed to change something in him that is not good. For instance, he worries that he has thought about virtue but not participated in virtue adequately. Talk and thought are cheap indeed in comparison with practicing actual virtue, and they do not add up to practicing virtue. A person can know what is virtuous but fail to be virtuous or to practice virtue. The cultivation of interpersonal virtue, according to Confucius, requires a person's acting in accordance with it, to actualize it in a life and a relationship. In this regard, wisdom for a meaningful life is practical and interpersonal, and not merely theoretical.

We have no reason to suppose that Confucius guided his religious perspective by ontological or methodological naturalism. He does not suggest that selves are either constituted by or emergent just from a physical base. In addition, he does not offer a method of inquiry about selves that is distinctively naturalistic in requiring an ultimate physical base for religious experience, evidence, explanation, or belief formation. Instead, he formulates his position with ethical insights about selves in relationships of interpersonal virtue. His own experience of interpersonal virtue serves as his basis for goal-directed action toward bringing more virtue to human relationships. In particular, his experience of "loyal reciprocity" is the basis for his intentional actions to bring about more loyal reciprocity among humans. This experience grounds his religious advice to pursue such reciprocity for a meaningful human life. That pursuit rests on a method that is participatory or practical, rather than simply reflective, toward goodness (as indicated by *Analects* 4.1–4, cited previously).

Confucius does not develop an epistemology or a general method of belief formation to support his religious perspective. We are, told, however: "The Master forbade four things: One must not act on guesses, one must not demand absolute certainty, one must not be stubborn, one must not insist on oneself" (*Analects* 9.4). We can read this remark as supporting fallibilism about belief, without fideism or dogmatism. The best way to avoid the extremes of fideism and dogmatism is to recommend conformity to one's available evidence. I suggest that we take Confucius to embrace such moderate evidentialism for the guidance of belief and action.

Neither ontological naturalism nor methodological naturalism is a serious threat to the religious perspective of Confucius. The relevant evidence does not require that he endorse either universal physicalism or universal methodological naturalism. If the sciences adopt methodological naturalism, by explaining their data from nature with purely "natural" terms and methods (however specified in detail), it does not follow that the view of selves and religion from Confucius must conform to those terms and methods.

We have noted that the academic sciences do not require that either all of reality or all domains of evidence be explained as having a physical base or as being accessed by ultimate physical processes. The scope of the academic sciences, as confirmed by science textbooks (taken as a group), is limited to their chosen domains of scientific evidence, and that evidence is publicly available to inquirers. The various ethical insights and underlying experiences invoked by Confucius are not all explainable in terms of publicly available evidence endorsed by the sciences. A lone moral reformer could have such insights and experiences, and use them for the improvement of moral understanding, eventually perhaps in a social context. In any case, the kind of ethical or normative evidence and advice found in the religion of Confucius lies outside the requirements of the sciences as identified by its textbooks. His religion, then, is not a chapter of the sciences.

Krishna on Agents in Constant-Adoration Theism

A practical role for God in religion enters, as Chapter 2 noted, with the perspective of Krishna on a meaningful life. We found this injunction to be central to Krishna's Constant-Adoration Theism: "Always think of me [Krishna], be devoted to me, worship me, and offer obeisance to me" (*Bhagavad-Gita* 18.65). He commands that singular devotion to him be constant, "always" in place as obedient worship. Such devotion is integral to suitable knowledge of God: "Only by loving devotion to me does one come to know who I am in truth. Then, having come to know me, my devotee enters into full consciousness of me" (*Bhagavad-Gita* 18.55).

The *Bhagavad-Gita* represents the divine Krishna as a personal agent, as one who intends to do things from conscious self-determination. For instance, Krishna self-manifests to his friend Arjuna, as Chapter 2 noted, and this includes Krishna's intention to draw Arjuna into a personal relationship of devotion to him. So, Krishna's role for personal agents in religion is not limited to human agents. Divine agency takes priority in his account, because God as the creator (see *Bhagavad-Gita* 13.17) is the personal agent who first invites receptive humans into a relationship of ongoing devotion to God. In addition, God bases this invitation not mainly on a human inference from evidence (as in much natural theology) but on divine presence in the experience of a human. God intervenes in human experience for a purpose, to attract human devotion to God. So, divine agency in goal-directedness toward humans is central to Krishna's message.

God's agency toward humans seeks to motivate, by way of response, human agency in devotion toward God. We noted this advice from Krishna:

With a serene, fearless, and unwavering mind, and staunch in the vow of celibacy, the vigilant yogi should meditate on me [Krishna], having me alone as the supreme goal. Thus, constantly keeping the mind absorbed in me, the yogi of disciplined mind attains *nirvāṇ* [awareness of true self in God], and abides in me in supreme peace.... The self-controlled yogi, thus uniting the self with God, becomes free from material contamination, and being in constant touch with the Supreme [God], achieves the highest state of perfect happiness. The true yogis, uniting their consciousness with God, see with equal eye, all living beings in God and God in all living beings. (*Bhagavad-Gita* 6.14–15, 28–29)

The primary religious goal, according to Krishna, is to be in constant adoration of God. All other goods for humans are to be instrumental to that goal. So, humans are to be purposive in all of their behavior, with goal-directedness toward the obedient worship of God. The meaning of human life, according to Krishna, centers on such worship of God.

Krishna does not seek to conform his positions on divine and human agency to any kind of naturalism. He has no compelling reason to do so, relative to his overall evidence of reality and a good, meaningful life. His view of God as spiritual and independent of the physical world does not fit with a physicalist view of agents. God does not either consist of or emerge just from a physical basis, in Krishna's perspective. God endures as a reality regardless of changes in the physical world. So, universal physicalism is not a live option in this perspective. Methodological naturalism also fails to constrain Krishna's religious position. He does not present his religious claims in conformity with guidelines about what nature includes or requires. Instead, he is guided by what he takes to be valued by God (with whom he claims self-identity).

We have no compelling way to challenge's Krishna's view of divine and human selves by an appeal to onto-logical or methodological naturalism. The universal physicalism of extreme ontological naturalism lacks the cogency to offer a serious challenge. We have noted that the academic sciences, as represented by its textbooks, do not require or recommend such physicalism. Their claims and assumptions are compatible with the existence of a God who is not physical, and thus they are more modest, onto-logically, than universal physicalism. If the sciences do not recommend universal physicalism, we will have difficulty in finding a cogent basis for it. In fact, we do have such difficulty, and it persists, especially in the face of theo-logical, religious, and ethical explanations of parts of human experience.

Methodological naturalism is not a serious threat to Krishna's approach to religion. We do not have a cogent version that falsifies or otherwise undermines the religious perspective of Krishna. The methods of the sciences will not bear such weight against religion, as we have noted, because those methods do not require uniformly naturalist explanations or processes for all areas of inquiry. We have invoked the textbooks of the academic sciences to confirm this lesson.

The sciences do not require exclusively naturalist explan-ations or processes for inquiry in theology and religion.

They thus do not demand, in this connection, a method of belief or theory formation that undermines inquiry in theology and religion. We have noted, in addition, that the publicly available evidence suited to the sciences does not find a uniform parallel in theology and religion. We do well, then, to acknowledge a kind of cognitive or evidential autonomy of theology and religion relative to the sciences. The "natural" phenomena of the sciences, in any case, do not clearly exhaust the phenomena of theology and religion needing explanation.

Moses on Agents in Law-Based Atonement Theism

Moses, according to Chapter 2, bases his religious perspective on a reported experience of God that contributes to divine–human atonement as reconciliation. Whatever else the God of Moses is, this God is an intentional, purposive agent in search of human redemption as reconciliation to God and humans. God uses the Mosaic Law as a means to such redemption, but the ultimate goal is the redemption of humans as interpersonal reconciliation from God.

The God of Moses displays goal-directedness in various self-manifestations and interventions in human experience. We have a clear statement of God's motive in choosing the nation of Israel as a focus for redemption:

You are a people holy to the Lord your God; the Lord your God has chosen you out of all the peoples on earth to be his people, his treasured possession. It was not because you were more numerous than any other people that the Lord set his heart on you and chose you – for you were the fewest of all peoples. It was because the Lord loved you and kept the oath that he swore to your ancestors, that the Lord has brought you out with a mighty hand, and redeemed you from the house of slavery, from the hand of Pharaoh king of Egypt. Know therefore that the Lord your God is God, the faithful God who maintains covenant loyalty with those who love him and keep his commandments, to a thousand generations, and who repays in their own person those who reject him. He does not delay but repays in their own person those who reject him. Therefore, observe diligently the commandment – the statutes and the ordinances – that I am commanding you today. (Deut. 7:6–11)

God seeks to fulfill divine commitments made in previous covenants, for instance, to Abraham, and Israel is the intended recipient of that covenant loyalty. God thus aims to fulfill divine promises in human history, working for and with actual people and groups of people in history. So, the religion of Moses becomes interpersonal in a divine–human context, involving a personal God interacting with human persons for definite redemptive purposes. Such intentional interacting is central to "the meaning (or purpose)" of the Mosaic Law (see Deut. 6:20–25).

God's intentional activity, according to the religion of Moses, creates duties and responsibilities for human agents. For instance:

Hear, O Israel: The Lord is our God, the Lord alone. You shall love the Lord your God with all your heart, and with all your soul, and with all your might. Keep these words that I am commanding you today in your heart. Recite them to your children and talk about them when you are at home and when you are away, when you lie down and when you rise. Bind them as a sign on your hand, fix them as an emblem on your forehead, and write them on the doorposts of your house and on your gates. (Deut. 6:4–9)

God expects intentional human obedience stemming from human love of God, in response to what God has done for humans. Such obedience, according to God's promise, will have benefits for humans. Thus: "If you heed these ordinances, by diligently observing them, the Lord your God will maintain with you the covenant loyalty that he swore to your ancestors; he will love you, bless you, and multiply you; he will bless the fruit of your womb and the fruit of your ground, your grain and your wine and your oil, the increase of your cattle and the issue of your flock, in the land that he swore to your ancestors to give you" (Deut. 7:12–13). God's intentional covenant loyalty seeks corresponding covenant loyalty from humans. This God is an intentional agent seeking reconciliation for humans, and humans are to follow suit in their response to divine loyalty.

Moses does not tailor his religion to either ontological naturalism or methodological naturalism. His view of God leaves no place for the universal physicalism of ontological naturalism. God is a spiritual agent who does not consist of or emerge just from a physical basis. Instead, the God of Moses is the creator of the physical world and, as such, precedes the physical order in existence. God thus does not depend for divine reality on the physical world. Instead, the dependence relation goes in the opposite direction, according to Mosaic religion (see the opening chapters of the book of Genesis). So, ontological naturalism as universal physicalism does not apply.

Methodological naturalism, as suggested, limits acceptable belief or theory formation to what is "natural" rather than "supernatural" or "non-natural." In particular, the relevant sources and processes are required to be based uniformly in the causal nexus of nature, or the natural world (understood in terms ultimately of what is physical). Moses does not treat such naturalism as a normative constraint on his religion. According to the book of Exodus: "The Lord used to speak to Moses face to face, as one speaks to a friend" (Exod. 33:11). Moses thus accepts direct revelation from God, who is supernatural rather than natural, and this revelation, rather than a natural process, forms his religion at its base.

God's being supernatural includes God's reality and action not being dependent on the causal structure of nature, which includes physical reality and what depends on it. Nature does not causally determine God's existence or activities, but God causally influences nature, in the account of Moses. By means of self-manifestations and other interventions in human experience, God also influences, in this account, what some people believe. The relevant experiential evidence from such divine activity grounds various theological and religious beliefs, according to the religion of Moses. It thus excludes fideism and dogmatism for people having such evidence. In addition, it saves the Mosaic religion from quick dismissal by methodological naturalism. It offers an experiential basis for religious commitment while avoiding an attempt to dispense with religious experience of God on naturalist grounds. Such religious experience is important evidence for some people, and it cannot be dismissed with any plausibility on the ground that nature itself opposes it or calls for an opposing kind of naturalism.

Paul on Agents in Christ-Based Atonement Theism

Paul shares the general position of Moses on the reality of a divine intentional agent and human intentional agents. There are genuine selves, in his perspective, and they differ from mere things, events, states, and processes. More to the point, they differ from the stuff of "nature," as typically understood in terms of what is ultimately physical.

Paul's God is the God of Moses but with a big twist: Paul's God has sent his divine son, Jesus Christ, to manifest God's moral character in action (of life and death) to enable and invite the reconciliation of humans to God. What the Mosaic Law did not do in this regard, God's Messiah has done, and Paul puts this divine redemptive activity front and center in his religious perspective. He thinks of this activity as powerful "good news" (a gospel) of God's redemptive grace and love, and he sees in it God's aim for humans to live for God rather than for the Mosaic Law. As he says: "Through the law I died to the law, so that I might live to God" (Gal. 2:19). He means "directly to God" in a way that allows God to advance new ways of seeking human redemption (such as through a crucified and resurrected Messiah), always in agreement with God's morally perfect character.

Paul is no physicalist about God or human persons. His God is the creator who existed prior to the physical world and does not depend for existence or action on the physical world. Echoing the Genesis creation story, Paul states: "It is the God who said, 'Let light shine out of darkness,' who has shone in our hearts to give the light of the knowledge of the glory of God in the face of Jesus Christ" (2 Cor. 4:6). So, Paul's view of God as a spiritual, goal-directed agent contradicts universal physicalism.

Paul's view of human selves does not fit with a physicalist view of persons. He anticipates the existence of human selves without physical, earthly bodies:

We know that if the earthly tent we live in is destroyed, we have a building from God, a house not made with hands, eternal in the heavens. For in this tent we groan, longing to be clothed with our heavenly dwelling – if indeed, when we have taken it off we will not be found naked. For while we are still in this tent, we groan under our burden, because we wish not to be unclothed but to be further clothed, so that what is mortal may be swallowed up by life. (2 Cor. 5:1–4)

The destruction of our physical bodies, in Paul's perspective, does not entail the destruction of us as persons or selves. Instead, it is an occasion for "being clothed with our heavenly dwelling." Paul regards a physical human body as a temporary "tent," and thus as something optional for the existence of a human. This contradicts physicalism about human persons. (We need not digress to the complexities of how Paul's perspective relates to Plato's mind–body dualism.)

Paul acknowledges an "inner person" who can endure and be renewed while his or her physical body is decaying or even destroyed (2 Cor. 4:16). In this respect, Paul is a mind–body dualist of a special sort. He distinguishes between "natural" (or "earthly") bodies and "spiritual" (or "heavenly") bodies for humans:

There are both heavenly bodies and earthly bodies, but the glory of the heavenly is one thing, and that of the earthly is another. There is one glory of the sun, and another glory of the moon, and another glory of the stars; indeed, star differs from star in glory. So it is with the resurrection of the dead. What is sown is perishable, what is raised is imperishable. It is sown in dishonor, it is raised in glory. It is sown in weakness, it is raised in power. It is sown a physical body, it is raised a spiritual body. If there is a physical body, there is also a spiritual body. (1 Cor. 15:40–44)

Physical bodies are perishable and therefore do not endure in God's everlasting kingdom. As Paul says: "Flesh and blood cannot inherit the kingdom of God, nor does the perishable inherit the imperishable" (1 Cor. 15:50). Humans, however, can inherit the kingdom of God, and therefore they are not identical to, or dependent for their existence on, "flesh and blood," that is, their physical bodies. So, Paul is no mind–body physicalist.

Methodological naturalism does not guide Paul's religious perspective. He acknowledges some belief formation on the basis of a non-natural process: communication directly from God. For instance, he states:

All who are led by the Spirit of God are children of God. For you did not receive a spirit of slavery to fall back into fear, but you have received a spirit of adoption. When we cry, "Abba! Father!," it is that very Spirit bearing witness with our spirit that we are children of God. (Rom. 8:14–16)

In Paul's perspective, God communicates directly with some people on occasion, without relying on what many call "natural processes" of belief formation. Paul attributes such communication to "the Spirit of God," who is a spiritual agent and not a natural process. This Spirit intervenes directly in human experience to invite, sustain, or deepen human reconciliation to God. The relevant kind of divine communication from this Spirit conflicts with methodological naturalism as typically understood.

Our previous doubts about universal ontological and methodological naturalism bear on Paul's religious perspective. This question arises: Why recommend that Paul's religious message conform to either kind of naturalism? Paul would balk at such a recommendation on the ground that his experiential evidence regarding God and other human agents counts against it. In particular, he would resist ignoring or dismissing his evidence from his religious experience concerning God's intervening for the sake of divine–human reconciliation. We noted his appeal to an experience of God's "bearing witness with our spirit that we are children of God." Paul would need a good reason to discredit this experience, and it is doubtful that naturalists could give him one. At least, naturalists would have a big explanatory task on this front.

The sciences, we have observed, will not underwrite an appeal to universal naturalism in opposition to Paul's religion. They do not require naturalism for all of reality. Instead, as noted, they limit their explanatory focus to phenomena of nature, thus allowing for phenomena of reality beyond their scope. We have seen that the academic textbooks of the sciences confirm this limit for good reason: The sciences maintain their credibility by not overextending themselves to domains outside their evidential reach, such as theology and religion. It is doubtful, then, that Paul's religious perspective on intentional agents, divine and human, faces a serious threat from the sciences or naturalism.

Muhammad on Agents in Absolute-Submission Theism

Muhammad shares the view of Moses and Paul about the reality of a divine intentional agent. This personal agent is the creator and the redeemer for the world. Chapter 2 noted the following contents of a religious experience of God by Muhammad:

1. Read [or: Proclaim]: In the Name of your Lord who created.
2. Created man from a clot.
3. Read [or: Proclaim]: And your Lord is the Most Generous.
4. He who taught by the pen.
5. Taught man what he never knew.

(*Qur'an* 96:1–5)

The *Qur'an* portrays God as the creator and the ultimate revealer of truths unknown to humans. God is thus an intentional agent with definite purposes toward humans.

A key purpose of God emerges from what Chapter 2 identified as Muhammad's formative religious experience: the experience of being commanded (by Allah). We found confirmation for the latter interpretation: "The guidance of Allah is the guidance, and we are commanded to surrender [or submit] to the Lord of the universe" (*Qur'an* 6:71). So, God's purpose is to command humans to submit to God as Lord of the universe. The redemption of humans by God comes in such submitting to God instead of following one's own desires: "God intends to redeem you, but those who follow their desires want you to turn away utterly" (*Qur'an* 4:27). Proper submission to God includes the submission of one's desires (along with the rest of one's life) to God's desires.

God seeks to guide human desires and other commitments via commands. For instance: "Say, 'We believe in God, and in what was revealed to us; and in what was revealed to Abraham, and Ishmael, and Isaac, and Jacob, and the Patriarchs; and in what was given to Moses, and Jesus, and the prophets from their Lord. We make no distinction between any of them, and to Him we submit'" (*Qur'an* 3:84). The commanded submission to God includes a command to announce belief in God and in what God has revealed to people, including Abraham, Moses, and Jesus.

Part of God's purpose for humans is to have them tested for discernment and commitment toward God:

We revealed to you the Book, with truth, confirming the Scripture that preceded it, and superseding it. So, judge between them according to what God revealed, and do not follow their desires if they differ from the truth that has come to you. For each of you We have assigned a law and a method. Had God willed, He could have made you a single nation, but He tests you through what He has given you. So, compete in righteousness. (Qur'an 5:48)

Part of God's purpose, then, is that humans have a resolute purpose toward discerning and complying with God's righteousness. Divine testing seeks to encourage humans to have such a purpose toward God.

The Qur'an portrays humans as needing to struggle to seek God and to resist turning away, given that they often have their own purposes relative to God's command to submit. It includes this prayer:

Our Lord, do not make us a target for those who disbelieve, and forgive us, our Lord. You are indeed the Mighty and Wise. There is an excellent example in them for you – for anyone who seeks God and the Last Day. But whoever turns away – God is the Self-Sufficient, the Most Praised. (Qur'an 60:5–6)

Divine redemption, then, occurs in a context of human conflict, and this context can instruct people about God. God's purposes, according to the Qur'an, will prevail in the conflict, and humans will stand or fall relative to their response to those purposes.

Muhammad's religious perspective shows no scruples to conform to universal ontological or methodological naturalism. Unrestricted physicalism is not a live option for Muhammad, because his God is a spiritual being who does not depend for existence on a physical world. This God neither consists in nor emerges just from a physical base. As creator, this God existed prior to the beginning of the physical world. Similarly, Muhammad does not understand human agents in terms of unrestricted physicalism. He holds that human souls can be removed from their physical bodies and endure in an afterlife (*Qur'an* 4:97, 7:37). A human person, then, is not adequately characterized by universal physicalism, in Muhammad's perspective.

Muhammad does not conform to methodological naturalism in his formation of religious beliefs. As we have noted, he acknowledges direct revelation from God, and this revelation does not require God to use uniformly "natural" processes for influencing the formation of human beliefs. In particular, Muhammad's formative religious experience of being commanded by God is not limited to natural processes for such an experience (see *Qur'an* 6:71, 7:54, previously quoted). God can intervene directly in human experience for the sake of commanding humans to obey the divine will. This consideration figures in the basis of Muhammad's being a prophet of God, one who receives God's direct revelation for the benefit of a wider audience of humans.

Universal ontological naturalism and methodological naturalism are not compelling threats to Muhammad's religion, at least given Muhammad's evidence from his religious experience. His experience of God's intervention in his life does not fit with universal naturalism, and it underlies a recommendation against it. In particular, his religious experience of being convicted by God's command serves as relevant evidence for him, at least, and it counts against a universal scope for naturalism, in its ontological or methodological forms. We have noted that the academic sciences will not challenge this consideration, because they do not require naturalism in an unrestricted form. The textbooks of the academic sciences restrict their explanatory domains to publicly available scientific evidence, and thus do not claim an explanatory monopoly over theology or religion. So, Muhammad's religious perspective, at least at its core, can survive the explanatory efforts of the sciences.

3 THE BEARING OF NATURALISM

Interest in naturalism is no mere modern trend. It dates back to some pre-Socratic philosophers, including Thales of Miletus (ca. 600 BCE) and Democritus of Thrace (ca. 450 BCE), although Thales seems to leave room for gods in nature. In any case, ancient Greek naturalism, or natural philosophy, attempts to explain the physical universe in terms of a single kind of natural thing, such as water, air, fire, or physical atoms. Its inspiration comes from a quest for unity, if not simplicity, in one's theoretical explainers, and some proponents would say that it tends toward empiricism, rather than just rational speculation, in inquiry. In any case, a desire for a naturalist explanation of the universe goes back at least to ancient Greece.

Modern naturalism shares the ancient naturalist quest for explanatory unity in (natural) explainers, but it adds considerable sophistication to the story, courtesy of distinctions gained in the later history of inquiry. Daniel Dennett, we noted, recommends that we think of religion as purely natural rather than supernatural. He offers a challenge to dissenters:

If it [religion] isn't entirely natural, if there really are miracles involved, the best way – indeed, the only way – to show that to doubters would be to demonstrate it scientifically. Refusing to play by these rules only creates the suspicion that one doesn't really believe that religion is supernatural after all. (2006, p. 26)

This challenge rests on a dubious assumption, one we found earlier in this chapter to occur also in Richard Dawkins (2006, p. 59). The questionable assumption is that all religious evidence of God's reality that supports religion as supernatural would be subject to the kind of available public assessment found in the sciences. We have no reason to assume this, despite the question-begging assumption of Dennett and Dawkins.

Here is a fair question for Dennett and Dawkins: Why should we assume that the sciences require that all evidence for *God's reality* be publicly readily shareable? So far as the textbooks of the academic sciences go, we should not assume this. They do not state or assume any such requirement for theology or religion, and this is empirically confirmable by attention to what those textbooks state. We have noted that the sciences do not commit one to either universal ontological naturalism or universal methodological naturalism. In reply to Dennett and Dawkins, the key point is that the sciences do not require that all evidence of reality be "scientific" evidence that is publicly readily shareable. In their eager support of naturalism about reality, Dennett and Dawkins assign an excessive requirement to the sciences for all evidence of reality. They thus fail to honor the proper cognitive modesty of the academic sciences. In short, they misrepresent our actual sciences.

Evidence that is not publicly readily shareable is not "purely subjective" in the way a belief can be purely subjective. For instance, if I have evidence from a pain experience resulting from a broken tooth, I cannot assume that you share this experience or evidence. In addition, I cannot give you this experience or direct evidence of mine, and I cannot "demonstrate it scientifically" to you. Even so, I actually have this experience and evidence, and I did not make them up, as if they are just a matter of my imagination. I do have the pain experience, and it is part of my relevant evidence.

Analogous points hold for my interactive experience of communication with another person. I can have that experience, and it can be evidence for me, even though I cannot assume that you too have this experience. More to the point,

I cannot give you this experience or direct evidence of it; nor can I "demonstrate it scientifically" to you. These limitations do not detract from the reality of this experience or evidence; nor do they undermine the reality of a similar experience of God and the related evidence. The methodological naturalism of Dennett and Dawkins, however, neglects this kind of evidence. It thus fails to challenge the reality of a significant kind of religious experience and evidence.

The desired explanatory unity from methodological naturalism can conflict with the actual evidence one has from experience. The kind of evidence just noted serves as a relevant example. Methodological naturalism will become implausibly a priori and dogmatic if it blocks the suggested kind of evidence from experience. Such evidence is a live option for a person, even so far as the sciences go, and it figures in the basis of much religious commitment. The academic sciences themselves properly allow for this option. Neither the academic sciences nor naturalism, then, undermines religious experience or commitment as a live option for evidence-guided humans. Our next question is whether our best psychology also leaves religious experience and commitment as live options for such humans. Some influential theorists have offered a negative answer, but we shall identify good reasons to question their answer.

5

∾

Religious Experience Psychologized

Chapter 4 considered whether universal naturalism about real objects and belief-forming processes discredits the reality or the reliability of religious experience and religious commitment based on such experience. It also explored whether the academic sciences require a commitment to universal naturalism and thus raise a devastating challenge to religious experience and religious commitment. We saw that neither naturalism nor the sciences discredit the reality or the reliability of all religious experience or commitment.

Many people think that the academic discipline of psychology offers, even without relying on a commitment to naturalism, a serious challenge to the reality or the reliability of religious experience and commitment. They think that certain psychological motives for religious commitments undermine the reality or the reliability of those commitments, even though the acknowledgment of these motives does not commit one to naturalism. Sigmund Freud is the most influential advocate of this anti-religious perspective, having devoted three influential books to the topic (1927, 1930, 1939). (His first book on the topic, *Totem and Taboo* (1913), is summarized in his 1933 essay.) He endorsed naturalism, as we shall see, but his psychological case against religion does not rest just on naturalism. We need to attend to Freud's overall case, and to identify its bearing on the six religious figures characterized in Chapters 2–4.

1 FREUD'S PSYCHOLOGICAL WORLD

Chapter 4 highlighted the role of intentional agents, in contrast with mere objects, in the religious perspectives of our six influential figures. Intentional agents do things, such as making commitments to views and to other agents. In addition, they are morally responsible for many of the actions they perform, and they can be responsible in other ways, too. For instance, they can be cognitively responsible as inquirers for the way they handle their available evidence. If they ignore, distort, or suppress relevant evidence, they may be negligent rather than responsible as inquirers. For instance, I could have a favorite theology handed down to me by my ancestors, but I vigilantly ignore evidence indicating that it is contradictory. This approach to my evidence could hinder my acquiring the truth about my favorite theology. It would leave me negligent rather than responsible from an evidential or cognitive point of view. We need to ask whether psychology indicates evidential or cognitive negligence in all religious people or at least in all proponents of a religious perspective.

Freud alleges a kind of negligence in all religious people, and he links this negligence to their psychological motives for religious commitment. We shall see that Freud's allegation of negligence suffers from inadequate support from our actual evidence. Specifically, his allegation fails to give adequate attention to religious experience of a morally relevant sort.

The Future of an Illusion

We have various motives for believing things about the world. Some of these motives are harmless from the standpoint of truth-seeking (and error-avoiding), such as when we are motivated by gaining true belief (and avoiding error) on the basis of our overall evidence. Other motives are more dangerous from that standpoint, such as when we want to protect at any expense a traditional belief handed down to us by our ancestors. The latter motive can lead us to neglect relevant evidence, and when we do that, all bets are off regarding our gaining true belief (and avoiding error).

Freud worries that "religious ideas, in spite of their incontrovertible lack of authentication, have exercised the strongest possible influence on mankind" (1927 [1961], p. 29). For instance, some people are willing to die for their commitments or at least to build their lives around them, thus making them a priority. Freud wonders what accounts for this priority of religious commitments in many human lives, and he considers his inquiry in this area an important psychological topic. He finds his preferred explanation in the psychological motives for religious commitments.

Freud claims, regarding religious commitments:

[They] are not precipitates of experience or end results of thinking: they are illusions, fulfilments of the oldest, strongest and most urgent wishes of mankind. The secret of their strength lies in the strength of those wishes. As we already know, the terrifying impression of helplessness in childhood aroused the need for protection – for protection through love which was provided by the father; and the recognition that this helplessness lasts throughout life made it necessary to cling to the existence of a father, but this time a more powerful one. Thus, the benevolent rule of a divine Providence allays our fear of the dangers of life; the establishment of a moral world-order ensures the fulfilment of the demands of justice, which have so often remained unfulfilled in human civilization; and the prolongation of earthly existence in a future life provides the local and temporal framework in which these wish-fulfilments shall take place. (p. 30)

Freud alleges that religious commitments "are not precipitates of experience," but he does not provide the needed supporting evidence. If we can trust the testimony of many people in this area, we can take seriously that their religious commitments do result from religious experiences, regardless of the reliability of those experiences. We began this book with such testimony from Tolstoy, and then identified similar testimony from Gautama, Confucius, Krishna, Moses, Paul, and Muhammad. Freud seems not to have the evidence needed to dismiss this kind of testimony across the board as unreliable, even if some religious commitments lack a basis in religious experience.

Freud claims, in the previous quotation, that religious commitments "are illusions, fulfilments of the oldest, strongest and most urgent wishes of mankind." They get their motivational strength, in his view, from the strength of underlying wishes. Humans, according to his story, wish to remove or at least to curb their fear of life's dangers and frustrations, and many humans consider God to be able and willing to satisfy this wish. They thus attribute importance to a religious commitment to God. The assumed God figures centrally in their wish fulfillment by removing or curbing fears and frustrations that have persisted since childhood.

Freud speaks of "illusions" that contribute to wish fulfillment for religious people. He explains:

An illusion is not the same thing as an error; nor is it necessarily an error.... What is characteristic of illusions is that they are derived from human wishes. In this respect they come near to psychiatric delusions. But they differ from them, too, apart from the more complicated structure of delusions. In the case of delusions, we emphasize as essential their being in contradiction with reality. Illusions need not necessarily be false – that is to say, unrealizable or in contradiction to reality. For instance, a middle-class girl may have the illusion that a prince will come and marry her. This is possible; and a few such cases have occurred.... Thus, we call a belief an illusion when a wish-fulfilment is a prominent factor in its motivation, and in doing so we disregard its relations to reality, just as the illusion itself sets no store by verification. (pp. 30–31)

Freud holds that because religious commitments have wish fulfillment as a prominent factor in their reality, we "disregard [their] relations to reality." Even if many people disregard their relations to reality, however, we must ask whether these people *should* do so as responsible inquirers. After all, a belief could be motivated by a wish fulfillment for a person while having, *at the same time*, a firm basis in that person's available evidence regarding reality. There is no incompatibility here, even on Freud's understanding of wish fulfillment and illusion.

Freud holds that only science can decide the reliability of religious commitments if they concern a reality independent of us:

Of the reality value of most of them [religious commitments] we cannot judge; just as they cannot be proved, so they cannot be refuted. We still know too little to make a critical approach to them. The riddles of the universe reveal themselves only slowly to our investigation; there are many questions to which science today can give no answer. But scientific work is the only road which can lead us to a knowledge of reality outside ourselves. It is once again merely an illusion to expect anything from intuition and introspection; they can give us nothing but particulars about our own mental life. (pp. 31–32)

Freud contrasts science and religion on the ground that science "has given us evidence by its numerous and important successes that it is no illusion" (p. 55). In his view, then, religious commitments that entail a mind-independent reality must meet the evidential standard of science. (Chapter 4 noted, and challenged, the similar view of Richard Dawkins.)

Freud, as quoted previously, holds that religious commitments "need not necessarily be false – that is to say, unrealizable or in contradiction to reality," even though they rely on wishful illusions. He states nonetheless:

On the one hand, religion brings with it obsessional restrictions, exactly as an individual obsessional neurosis does; on the other hand, it comprises a system of wishful illusions together with a disavowal of reality, such as we find in an isolated form nowhere else but in amentia, in a state of blissful hallucinatory confusion. (p. 43)

This is a sweeping judgment regarding religion in general, and it calls for supporting evidence that Freud has not provided. The main point, however, is that Freud is clarifying his earlier claim that a religious commitment "need" have no "contradiction to reality." Even if it "need" have no such contradiction, he now claims that religion (at least typically) *does* include a denial or "disavowal of reality," and he contrasts this with science.

Freud offers an analogy with a baby-delivering stork to illustrate his view of how religion denies or disavows reality:

The truths contained in religious doctrines are after all so distorted and systematically disguised that the mass of humanity cannot recognize them as truth. The case is similar to what happens when we tell a child that new-born babies are brought by the stork. Here, too, we are telling the truth in symbolic clothing, for we know what the large bird signifies. But the child does not know it. He hears only the distorted part of what we say, and feels that he has been deceived; and we know how often his distrust of the grown-ups and his refractoriness actually take their start from this impression. We have become convinced that it is better to avoid such symbolic disguisings of the truth in what we tell children and not to withhold from them a knowledge of the true state of state of affairs commensurate with their intellectual level. (pp. 44–45)

When we tell a child that a stork has delivered a baby to a family, we are telling the child something false, for whatever reason. Freuds holds that religion typically denies or disavows reality in a similar manner, in stating something false. He has in mind at least the familiar religious claim that God has acted somehow in a human life, in analogy with the stork's delivering a baby to a family. He thus thinks that the wishful illusion in religion is false, at least regarding a familiar religious view about God doing something in a human life. His example of the stork makes this clear, even if he hedges a bit elsewhere.

Freud offers nothing near adequate evidence for his claim that religion typically includes a denial or disavowal of reality. An appeal to science will not deliver the needed evidence for him. As noted in Chapter 4, the sciences do not require that all responsible inquiry conform to its standards for socially readily shareable evidence (i.e., shareable just by human means). In particular, the textbooks of the academic sciences do not demand that all religious evidence be socially shared or even socially readily shareable. That is, they do not require that all such evidence be scientific evidence. Freud, then, subjects religion to a requirement of conformity to scientific evidence even though the sciences themselves do not do so. In addition, he does not make the needed case that the sciences set this requirement, and our actual evidence regarding the sciences, including from its textbooks, does not support his position.

Freud seems to think that if socially shareable evidence from science is not required of religion, the result will be a misleading use of introspection and intuition instead. In that use, he claims, we end up with "nothing but particulars about our own mental life." This claim, however, is not obviously true. Sometimes introspection puts one in touch with experiences that represent nonsubjective occurrences. For instance, by introspection I can come to a moral conviction of my having mistreated someone. This conviction, via introspection, can put me in touch with a nonsubjective reality that goes beyond my "own mental life." It is a live option, so far as Freud's evidence goes, that a religious experience can function in this way. In this regard, Freud is misleading about the nature of religious evidence and its relation to scientific evidence.

A critical shortcoming of Freud's *The Future of an Illusion* is its neglect of religious experience and its role in religious commitment. In particular, it neglects how religious experience, beyond any wish, can motivate a religious commitment. It also neglects how religious experience can motivate a religious commitment even when a wish is present (and the commitment is overdetermined). As a result, Freud does not offer a cogent case in *The Future of an Illusion* to dismiss or discredit religious commitment as unreliable. A neglect of religious experience typically leads to this kind of failure.

Civilization and Its Discontents

In his second treatment of religion, in *Civilization and Its Discontents*, Freud attends to religious experience of a particular kind in his case against religion. He describes the position of a critic of *The Future of an Illusion*:

He was sorry I had not properly appreciated the true source of religious sentiments. This, he says, consists in a peculiar feeling, which he himself is never without, which he finds confirmed by many others, and which he may suppose is present in millions of people. It is a feeling which he would like to call a sensation of "eternity," a feeling as of something limitless, unbounded – as it were, "oceanic." This feeling, he adds, is a purely subjective fact, not an article of faith; it brings with it no assurance of personal immortality, but it is the source of the religious energy which is seized upon by the various Churches and religious systems, directed by them into particular channels, and doubtless also exhausted by them. One may, he thinks, rightly call oneself religious on the ground of this oceanic feeling alone, even if one rejects every belief and every illusion. (1930 [1961], p. 24)

The critic's main point is that Freud has neglected the key role of religious experience in religious commitment. This is, as suggested, true of Freud's discussion in *The Future of an Illusion*. The critic, however, offers an approach to religious experience that leads to serious problems. It is an understanding of religious experience as an "oceanic feeling of something limitless, unbounded," and it invites criticisms from Freud.

Freud reports not being able to find the relevant "oceanic feeling" in himself, and he objects to its not being easily assessed by science. He offers a genetic (or "psychoanalytic") approach to the matter, on the following ground: "The idea of men's receiving an intimation of their connection with the world around them through an immediate feeling which is from the outset directed to that purpose sounds so strange and fits in so badly with the fabric of our psychology that one is justified in attempting to discover a psychoanalytic – that is, a genetic, explanation of such a feeling" (1930, pp. 25–26). In other words, Freud recommends that we find a psychological motive for the feeling in question, and he aims to do so.

Freud's explanation of the "oceanic feeling" is straightforward:

Originally the ego includes everything, later it separates off an external world from itself. Our present ego-feeling is, therefore, only a shrunken residue of a much more inclusive – indeed, an all-embracing – feeling which corresponded to a more intimate bond between the ego and the world about it.... The ideational contents appropriate to it [the original, primary ego-feeling] would be precisely those of limitlessness and of a bond with the universe – the same ideas with which my friend elucidated the "oceanic" feeling. (1930, p. 29)

Freud thus acknowledges that the oceanic feeling occurs in many people as a result of their original "ego-feeling."

He asks, however, whether this feeling, rather than something else, is the actual source of religious needs.

Freud denies that the oceanic feeling is a primary source
of religious needs, on the ground that it cannot compete
with widespread human feelings of helplessness and fear.
He explains:

The derivation of religious needs from the infant's helplessness
and the longing for the father aroused by it seems to me
incontrovertible, especially since the feeling is not simply pro-
longed from childhood days, but is permanently sustained by
fear of the superior power of Fate. I cannot think of any need in
childhood as strong as the need for a father's protection. Thus,
the part played by the oceanic feeling, which might seek
something like the restoration of limitless narcissism, is ousted
from a place in the foreground. The origin of the religious
attitude can be traced back in clear outlines as far as the feeling
of infantile helplessness. (1930, pp. 35–36).

Freud thus allows for the role of feelings in motivating a
person's religious commitments. He denies, however, that
these feelings, involving felt helplessness and fear, save
these commitments from illusion or even delusion. In fact,
he claims that these commitments are delusions, as we shall
see momentarily.

A serious problem with Freud's case against the reliability of religious commitments is its implausibly narrow
approach to the relevant religious experiences. The
oceanic feeling is not representative of the religious
experiences to which many religious people testify. So,
Freud's negative diagnosis of the oceanic feeling does not
apply automatically to religious experiences in general.
In addition, as we have seen in Chapters 2–4, not all
religious experiences involve a father figure who saves
one from the vicissitudes of fate. (Chapters 7 and 8 attend
to some religious experiences that do not fall under
Freud's diagnosis.)

In Freud's diagnosis, religious commitment qualifies as delusion, and not just illusion, on the following ground:

One can try to re-create the world, to build up in its stead another world in which its most unbearable features are eliminated and replaced by others that are in conformity with one's own wishes. But whoever, in desperate defiance, sets out upon this path to happiness will as a rule attain nothing. Reality is too strong for him. He becomes a madman, who for the most part finds no one to help him in carrying through his delusion.... A special importance attaches to the case in which this attempt to procure a certainty of happiness and a protection against suffering through a delusional remoulding of reality is made by a considerable number of people in common. The religions of mankind must be classed among the mass-delusions of this kind. No one, needless to say, who shares a delusion ever recognizes it as such. (1930, p. 51)

He adds: "Religion ... imposes equally on everyone its own path to the acquisition of happiness and protection from suffering. Its technique consists in depressing the value of life and distorting the picture of the real world in a delu-sional manner – which presupposes an intimidation of the intelligence" (1930, p. 56). This is not just a claim that religion results from wish fulfillment and therefore is an illusion. It is the stronger claim that religion distorts reality and thus is a "delusion," a denial of reality.

Freud assigns to religion "a delusional remoulding of reality in conformity with one's own wishes." He alleges that religion undertakes this distortion in its "attempt to procure a certainty of happiness and a protection against suffering." Religion can support this attempt in various ways, but Freud claims that its attempt stems from infantile helplessness and corresponding fear. Religion, he assumes, settles for wishful delusion in its response, whatever the details of the response.

Once again Freud settles for a sweeping claim that fails to apply to religion in general. *Some* versions of religion do distort reality in the way suggested, by stipulating a source of happiness lacking in supporting evidence. For instance, we seem not to have durable evidence for any god who brings happiness just to one ethnic or racial group, to the neglect of others. It does not follow, however, that religions in general distort reality in the way suggested. Freud himself has not supplied the evidence needed to generalize to all religions. So, religion in general is not threatened by Freud's anti-religious diagnosis in *Civilization and Its Discontents*.

Moses and Monotheism

Freud extends his criticism of religion in his final book, *Moses and Monotheism*, but he does not retract his previous objections. He offers a psychological account of the role of human conscience in religious and ethical commitment:

In the course of individual development, a part of the inhibiting forces in the outer world becomes internalized; a standard is created in the Ego which opposes the other faculties by observation, criticism, and prohibition. We call this new standard the super-ego. From now on the Ego, before undertaking to satisfy the instincts, has to consider not only the dangers of the outer world, but also the objections of the super-ego, and has therefore more occasion for refraining from satisfying the instinct. (1939, pp. 183–84)

The internal conviction of morality and religion, in Freud's view, is nothing deeper than the internalizing of outer influences on a person. As a result, Freud sees no need in this context for anything as mysterious as God or distinctively religious values.

Freud holds that human conscience has a straightforward social explanation involving a key role for a person's parents and other influential people:

The super-ego is the successor and representative of the parents (and educators), who superintended the actions of the individual in his first years of life; it perpetuates their functions almost without a change. It keeps the Ego in lasting dependence and exercises a steady pressure. The Ego is concerned, just as it was in childhood, to retain the love of its master, and it feels his appreciation as a relief and satisfaction, his reproaches as pricks of conscience. (1939, p. 184)

Parents and educators thus replace the role of God in influencing a human conscience from early life. They form in a child, according to Freud, the attitudes characteristic of religion and ethics. So, God is dispensable in this domain, by Freud's lights.

Freud extends his account of conscience with a social approach to "instinctual renunciation":

Instinctual renunciation appears to play a prominent part in religion, although it had not been present in it from the beginning.... Here it is the parents' authority – essentially that of the all-powerful father who wields the power of punishment that demands instinctual renunciation on the part of the child and determines what is allowed and what is forbidden. What the child calls "good" or "naughty" becomes later, when society and super-ego take the place of the parents, "good" (in the sense of moral) or evil, virtuous or vicious. But it is still the same thing: instinctual renunciation through the presence of the authority which replaced and continued that of the father. (1939, pp. 188–89)

A human ego will renounce a response from instinct, according to Freud, because an authority figure, after the model of an authoritative father, prohibits an instinctive response, calling for its renunciation. Religious prohibitions can and do follow this pattern, in Freud's view.

One might think of religious prohibitions as "sacred" prohibitions, on the ground, noted by Freud, that "everything connected with religion is sacred" (1939, p. 190). Freud identifies such prohibitions with a supposed will of a severe father figure:

I should confidently anticipate that an investigation of ... cases of sacred prohibitions would lead to the same result as that of the horror of incest, namely that what is sacred was originally nothing but the perpetuated will of the primeval father. This would also elucidate the ambivalence of the word – hitherto inexplicable – which expresses the conception of sacredness. It is the ambivalence which governs the relationship to the father. "Sacer" does not only mean "sacred," "blessed," but also something that we can only translate by "accursed," "worthy of disgust" ("auri sacra fames"). The will of the father, however, was not only something which one must not touch, which one had to hold in high honour, but also something which made one shudder because it necessitated a painful instinctual renunciation. (1939, p. 192)

Freud holds that religious faith in a divine being as a father figure takes on "enormous power that enables it to overwhelm Reason and Science" (1939, p. 194). In addition, he thinks that we can account for this by genetic psychological considerations. So, psychology can explain and thereby deflate or domesticate the source of religious commitment.

Freud explains:

We understand that primitive man needs a God as creator of the world, as head of his tribe, and as one who takes care of him. This God takes his place behind the dead fathers of whom tradition still has something to relate. Man in later times – of our time, for instance, behaves similarly. He also remains infantile and needs protection, even when he is fully grown; he feels he cannot relinquish the support of his God. So much is indisputable. (1939, p. 202)

An infantile need and a corresponding wish for protection, in Freud's view, lead to the tendency of religious commitment to "overwhelm reason and science." In particular, they result in neglect of the need for due supporting evidence for such a commitment.

Freud holds that firm human wishes often yield unduly easy commitment to what will satisfy those wishes, thus diminishing the value of needed evidence to support a commitment. He remarks: "It is the general experience that the human intellect errs very easily without our suspecting it at all, and that nothing is more readily believed than what – regardless of the truth – meets our wishes and illusions half-way" (1939, p. 203). Freud thinks that this tendency underlies commitment to monotheism as belief in one supreme God.

Freud explains:

I do not believe that one supreme great God "exists" today, but I believe that in primeval times there was one person who must needs appear gigantic and who, raised to the status of a deity, returned to the memory of men.... One result of this is the emergence of the conception of one great God. It must be recognized as a memory, a distorted one, it is true, but nevertheless a memory. It has an obsessive quality; it simply must be believed. As far as its distortion goes, it may be called a delusion; in so far as it brings to light something from the past it must be called truth. The psychiatric delusion also contains a particle of truth; the patient's conviction issues from this and extends to the whole delusional fabrication surrounding it. (1939, pp. 204–5)

This diagnosis presents monotheistic religion as a distortion of reality, a "delusion" and a "fabrication" regarding ultimate reality. It portrays such religion as "raising to the status of deity" someone (typically, a human father figure) who does not have that status. This is where the alleged "delusion" and "fabrication" enter. The result, according to

Freud, is a religion that distorts reality for the sake of a human quest for protection.

Our main question for Freud is whether he has the needed evidence to generalize his charge of fabrication to all cases of religious commitment to monotheism. This is a demanding charge, as it requires that ultimate reality not include a supreme divine being who is a morally good agent. Freud has not supplied the needed evidence for that claim about ultimate reality. Even if some people with religious commitments fabricate in the way suggested by Freud, it is a separate issue whether all do so. Only evidence with general scope would make Freud's case, but we do not have it, at least from him. We turn to his attempt to explain his case against religion in more detail.

A Philosophy of Life

Chapter 4 noted Freud's understanding of science as having "a categorical rejection of certain elements which are alien to it": "It asserts that there is no other source of knowledge of the universe, but the intellectual manipulation of carefully verified observations, in fact, what is called research, and that no knowledge can be obtained from revelation, intuition, or inspiration" (1933, p. 217). So, in his view, science denies that religious knowledge can be obtained from revelation. His claim is not simply that *scientific* knowledge cannot or does not come from revelation (from God). It is, instead, that no knowledge can come from such revelation, according to science.

Freud makes the following claim about "intuition and inspiration," and he would say the same about alleged revelation from God:

They can safely be counted as illusions, as fulfilments of wishes. Science takes account of the fact that the mind of man creates such demands [of wish fulfillment] and is ready to trace their source, but it has not the slightest ground for thinking them justified. On the contrary, it does well to distinguish carefully between illusion (the results of emotional demands of that kind) and knowledge. (1933, p. 218)

Science does distinguish between *scientific* knowledge and illusion, but this falls short of an unqualified distinction between knowledge and illusion *in general*. At least, Freud does not show from the sciences that they exclude *all* knowledge from divine revelation, even if they acknowledge or assume a difference between scientific knowledge and knowledge from revelation. Chapter 4 suggested that the relevant difference involves the kind of publicly readily shareable evidence in the sciences that need not be present in religious evidence. Freud does not consider this important distinction, and therefore his general criticism of religion misses the mark.

Freud supports his view of the scope of science as follows:

The bare fact is that truth cannot be tolerant and cannot admit compromise or limitations, that scientific research looks on the whole field of human activity as its own, and must adopt an uncompromisingly critical attitude towards any other power that seeks to usurp any part of its province. (1933, p. 219)

Is this true of the academic sciences found in universities? It seems not. Do their academic textbooks teach that no knowledge is to be found in philosophy, ethics, or theology, for instance? It seems not. We can examine those textbooks and find that they do not exclude, implicitly or explicitly, philosophy, ethics, or theology as potential sources of knowledge. It looks as if Freud is twisting the nature of science to his anti-religious sentiment, but, in any case, he has not given us evidence from science itself for his sweeping characterization of science. Instead, he has assigned to science a general stricture not to be found there. He thus misrepresents our actual science.

Freud clearly states his hypothesis of wish fulfillment in religion, as follows:

Even the grown man ... rightly feels that fundamentally he is just as helpless and unprotected as he was in childhood and that in relation to the external world he is still a child. Even now, therefore, he cannot give up the protection which he has enjoyed as a child. But he has long ago realized that his father is a being with strictly limited powers and by no means endowed with every desirable attribute. He therefore looks back to the memory-image of the overrated father of his childhood, exalts it into a Deity, and brings it into the present and into reality. The emotional strength of this memory-image and the lasting nature of his need for protection are the two supports of his belief in God. (1933, p. 223)

"The two supports" for belief in God, according to Freud, are not a matter of evidence or religious experience but something less relevant to knowledge. They are a psychological need for protection and a memory of an overrated father. Neither of these factors yields evidence that supports the truth of a religious belief. It is, of course, an empirical issue whether these two factors are *the* only two supports for belief in God. If we look carefully at actual religious lives among humans, we must be doubtful of such a simplistic diagnosis. We then find that religious experience figures crucially in the support of much religion. Chapters 1–3 have documented this truth, thereby offering crucial evidence in religion neglected by Freud.

Freud tries to deflate the view that religion can give protection and happiness to humans:

The assertions made by religion that it could give protection and happiness to men, if they would only fulfil certain ethical obligations, were unworthy of belief. It seems not to be true that there is a power in the universe, which watches over the well-being of every individual with parental care and brings all his concerns to a happy ending. On the contrary, the destinies of man are incompatible with a universal principle of benevolence or with ... a universal principle of justice. Earthquakes, floods and fires do not differentiate between the good and devout man, and the sinner and unbeliever. (1933, p. 228)

It would be special pleading, at best, to claim that one's religious commitment is joined by a kind of parental care that brings all of one's concerns "to a happy ending" in this earthly life. I doubt that any careful religious writer has ventured such a bold, far-fetched claim. So, it is puzzling that Freud tries to hang this claim on religion. In doing so, he misses his intended target. Some religions are eschatological, suggesting a reconciliation of all things in an afterlife, but that position does not entail "a happy ending" in this earthly life. The fullness of time is not the present time, as various religions propose. So, Freud sets up a straw man in his attempt to undermine religious commitment. He thus misses the mark.

Freud tries to temper his criticism of religion while maintaining its force. He writes:

This [diagnosis regarding wish fulfillment] does not precisely imply a refutation of religion, but it is a necessary rounding off of our knowledge about it, and, at least on one point, it actually contradicts it, for religion lays claim to a divine origin.... While the different religions wrangle with one another as to which of them is in possession of the truth, in our view the truth of religion may be altogether disregarded. Religion is an attempt to get control over the sensory world, in which we are placed, by means of the wish-world, which we have developed inside us as a result of biological and psychological necessities. But it cannot achieve its end. (1933, p. 229)

From the standpoint of our actual evidence, it is premature to conclude that "the truth of religion may be altogether disregarded." Even if human wishes figure somehow in many religious commitments, it does not follow that those commitments lack truth or evidence. They still could be grounded in religious experiences that serve as evidence for their truth. At least, Freud has not undermined this live option, and Chapters 2–4 above have presented evidence for it. We turn now to consider how the six religious figures of those chapters fare in the light of Freud's case against religion.

2 RELIGION AFTER FREUD

We have seen that Freud has two main objections to religious commitment, regarding its origin in wish fulfillment and its conflict with science. We shall ask whether such objections bear on the six religious figures we have discussed in previous chapters.

Gautama after Freud

As Chapter 2 explained, the nontheistic practical religion of Gautama seeks relief in self-Awakening from debilitating human suffering and frustration. The relevant self-Awakening is experiential, and not just reflective or intellectual, as it includes an awareness of relief from various kinds of destructive "becoming" (or change) in human life. The experiential awareness of relief can occur via a practice of concentration on the cessation of various destructive changes in one's consciousness. This process does not result in the absence of change in a human life; instead, it leaves one "imperturbable" in the presence of corrosive changes. That is, it insulates a person from the toxic changes that impede self-Awakening.

Gautama's experience of self-Awakening, including an experience of relief from certain destructive changes, is not the same as a wish to be protected from such changes, nor is it a memory of a wish. Instead, it is a qualitative awareness of something valuable in a human life, including an awareness of relief from certain destructive changes. Freud's diagnosis of religion thus does not find an easy foothold here. It would allege that Gautama suffers from an infantile wish for protection from life's harms, and that this wish motivates a quest for self-Awakening as a source of the desired protection. It also would allege that Gautama offers a religious perspective in conflict with the kind of supporting evidence (i.e., "scientific" evidence) needed by any perspective worthy of being considered true.

In defense of Gautama's religious perspective, we should acknowledge that Freud's ascribing an infantile wish for protection to Gautama would miss the mark. It would neglect the kind of religious experience of self-Awakening that grounds Gautama's perspective. The latter experience is a matter of qualitative awareness (of a specific relief) in a way that a mere wish is not. We also should acknowledge that a demand for socially shareable "scientific" evidence would beg a key question against Gautama. It is an open question whether Gautama's experience of self-Awakening must be socially shareable in the way scientific evidence typically is. Responsible inquiry does not allow us simply to assume that Gautama's religious experience must conform to typical scientific evidence. In addition, as noted, the sciences themselves do not underwrite the latter requirement, contrary to Freud's suggestion. So, Gautama's religious perspective is not undermined by Freud's case against religion.

Confucius after Freud

Confucius, according to Chapter 2, offers a religious perspective based on religious experience of loyal reciprocity in a human relationship. We have noted that Confucius, like Gautama, does not invoke God to develop his practical religious perspective. Instead, he relies on various features of moral experience and finds overarching meaning and religious significance in them. In his perspective, virtuous human relationships figure centrally in a meaningful human life, and they share an experience of loyalty and reciprocity. A religious life depends on a person's self-cultivation of virtue in interpersonal relationships.

The religious perspective of Confucius does not appeal to, or rely on, a wish to be protected from life's dangers; nor does it exalt a father figure to satisfy such a wish. Instead, it maintains a focus on virtuous human relationships and their central role for loyal reciprocity. Freud thus will find no basis in Confucius for his hypothesis of infantile wish fulfillment. Likewise, he will find no ground for his allegation of a memory of an exalted father figure who offers human protection. So, Freud's psychoanalytic genetic diagnosis will miss the mark in relation to Confucius.

Freud's postulated standard of "science" might seem to challenge the virtue-oriented religious perspective of Confucius. We do not seem to have publicly shareable evidence from the sciences that can confirm the position of Confucius regarding the primary value of loyal reciprocity for life's meaning. It is doubtful, in any case, that Confucius thought of his position as confirmable by publicly shareable evidence from scientific inquiry. He seems, instead, to allow for evidence from personal moral experience that may or may not be public in virtue of being socially readily shareable. For instance, one can have an experience of moral conviction of wrongdoing that does not depend on its being socially readily shareable. Such conviction could serve as a kind of moral evidence pertinent to one's moral perspective on life. At least, it is an open question whether such moral conviction must await confirmation from socially shareable evidence from the sciences. So, Freud's demand for scientific evidence from a religious perspective is questionable at best. I have suggested that it misrepresents the character of significant religious evidence in human experience, including moral experience. I also have suggested that it misrepresents the scope of scientific evidence.

Krishna after Freud

Chapter 2 noted that Krishna offers a theistic interpretation of religion in practice, and he thus contrasts with Gautama and Confucius. He proposes that the meaning of a human life, from a religious perspective, centers on constant adoration of God. God plays a key role in practical religion, because God empowers people, via religious experience, to undertake obedient worship of God. In undertaking such worship, according to Krishna, one experiences devotional union with God and even bliss in doing so. This union, in Krishna's perspective, relays divine power to worshippers and thereby empowers them to flourish in a meaningful human life.

The religious experience in worship, as portrayed by Krishna, involves a qualitative awareness that differs from a mere wish or wish fulfillment. This is understood as an awareness of a self-manifestation of God's character, including its unique bliss, to a human. Such an awareness can have qualitative content that figures in evidence for a religious commitment to God. In such a case, one's religious commitment would not have its basis only in a wish for protection or in a memory of a father figure exalted to divine status. So, Freud's anti-religious diagnosis would not apply. It would fail from neglect of the role of religious experience in the evidence for religious commitment. A critic may doubt the reliability of the religious experience in question, but the experience still merits attention for its actual role in religious commitment.

Freud would question the "scientific" basis for the religious perspective offered by Krishna. In particular, he would ask whether Krishna's perspective finds support from the kind of socially shareable evidence common to the sciences. Krishna would be unmoved, denying that divine self-manifestation to a human must yield socially shareable evidence of the kind found in the sciences. God's self-manifestation in a situation could intervene in the experience of one person, such as Krishna's friend Arjuna, but not extend to the experience of another person. This could be the result of God's choice, based on divine knowledge of the situation and the relevant persons. So, Freud's appeal to what he mistakenly regards as scientific evidence misses the mark. We have offered a good reason to question Freud's assumption that the sciences demand that theology and ethics conform to scientific evidence.

Moses after Freud

Chapter 2 characterized the theistic religious interpretation of Moses in terms of law-based atonement or reconciliation. We saw that the religious perspective of Moses was based on a religious experience of divine self-manifestation to Moses. This experience included announcements and commands to Moses, and it resulted in the Mosaic Law as the foundation of Jewish religion. Initially, Moses responded with fear and hiding, thus giving behavioral evidence that his religious experience was no matter of casual intellectual reflection. Instead, his religious experience was a challenge to his own desires and expectations for his life. He thus tried to sidestep the divine claim on his life, by asking God to call on someone else: "O my Lord, I have never been eloquent, neither in the past nor even now that you have spoken to your servant; but I am slow of speech and slow of tongue.... O my Lord, please send someone else" (Exod. 4:10, 13). In the end, Moses conformed to the call in his religious experience, and this response led to the liberation of the Jewish people from ancient Egypt.

Freud would latch onto the fear Moses has in his religious commitment. He would suggest that Moses is engaged in wish fulfillment for the sake of curbing his fear of a destructive future. Moses, in Freud's story, postulates God in order to have a willing and powerful savior from fear and destruction. This postulation, according to Freud, is delusional fabrication, entailing a denial of reality. It is no better, from the standpoint of genuine knowing, than infantile wish fulfillment, and thus it should be disregarded as a candidate for knowledge or even reasonable belief.

Freud's simple diagnosis neglects the complexity of the situation. Moses does not get the kind of God he naturally would wish for, that is, a God who readily fulfills his desires. Instead, he faces a God who frustrates many of his settled desires and wishes, and who ultimately leaves him out of the promised land of Canaan. God announces to Moses: "You broke faith with me among the Israelites ... by failing to maintain my holiness among the Israelites. Although you may view the [promised] land from a distance, you shall not enter it – the land that I am giving to the Israelites" (Deut. 32:51–52). Clearly, if Moses was going to postulate a God to satisfy his wishes, he picked the wrong God. Something more than infantile wish fulfillment is going on with Moses, and the key to understanding his life and religious perspective is in his religious experience. In neglecting that experience, Freud misunderstands the life and the religion of Moses. As a result, his criticism misses the mark.

Freud would subject the religious perspective of Moses, along with all other religious perspectives, to his understanding of the "dictatorship" of scientific evidence. Here, however, he would go wrong, as in the case of Krishna noted previously. Freud would demand that Moses produce socially readily shareable evidence for his religious experience and thus meet a "scientific" standard for evidence. We have noted that God may or may not choose to meet a standard of socially readily shareable evidence in a particular case. There thus would be no universal requirement binding God to conform to *Freud's* preferred standard for evidence. In addition, the sciences themselves do not underwrite the universality of Freud's preferred standard. The academic textbooks for the sciences, we have noted, do not impose a standard of socially readily shareable evidence on all domains of inquiry, including theology and ethics.

They focus their concern on scientific inquiry and its corresponding evidence. Freud's anti-religious challenge, then,
does not undermine the religious perspective of Moses, at
least at its core.

Paul after Freud

As Chapter 2 explained, the apostle Paul had his life as a
Pharisee interrupted by a religious experience of the risen
Jesus. He came to think of God as primarily not a law-giver
but the Father of the crucified Messiah, Jesus Christ, who
gave his life in order to reconcile humans to God. Paul
thinks of God as offering forgiveness to humans through
Jesus as Messiah, and thereby as inviting humans to be
reconciled to God in interpersonal fellowship conformed
to God's morally perfect will. God is not an abstract
principle, in this perspective, but is a personal agent who
intervenes in human experience via self-manifestation of a
perfect moral character. This character manifests divine
love to humans at the opportune time, in order to promote
the reconciliation of humans to God (Rom. 5:3–5; 2 Cor.
5:19–21). On this experiential basis, anchored in conscience
(Rom. 9:1), humans can be led by God to conform to God's
perfect will and purpose for a human life (Rom. 8:14–16).

Paul's perspective on God as the Father of the crucified
Messiah did not fit with his earlier image of God as the
giver of the Mosaic Law. It called for a significant revision
in his wishes and hopes for the God of Israel, and this
revision changed his perspective on the role of non-Jews
in God's plan of redemption, especially in relation to the
Mosaic Law. The revision in question is not just a matter of
wish fulfillment, as if Paul had a deep-seated wish that God
would use a crucified Messiah to extend salvation to non-
Jews. In addition, we have no evidence indicating that Paul
had a memory of a father figure that explains his perspective of salvation via a crucified Messiah. Freud's diagnosis
falls short here, because it neglects the role of religious

experience in Paul's perspective. Paul, we might say, was led by religious experience to embrace and to develop his distinctive religious perspective. If we omit such experience, we lack the resources to make sense of Paul's religious trajectory from being a Pharisee to being a Christian. Freud's diagnosis suffers from this deficiency.

Freud will insist on socially shareable evidence of a scientific kind to confirm Paul's religious perspective, and any other religious perspective, for that matter. Paul would balk at such a requirement, for good reason. Nothing in reality or in our evidence binds God to give only socially shareable evidence in divine self-manifestation. As a result, Freud's requirement lacks needed support in what Freud claims to value, that is, actual evidence. In addition, as noted, the sciences do not support Freud's requirement for all domains of inquiry. They do not require that inquiry in theology and ethics, for instance, proceed only by socially shareable evidence of the kind found in the sciences. Freud, then, fails to make a compelling case against Paul's religious perspective.

Muhammad after Freud

Chapter 2 portrayed the religious perspective of Muhammad as focusing on absolute submission to God, in keeping with the *Qur'an* 6:71, 7:54. Muhammad's theistic perspective relies on a particular kind of religious experience, that is, an experience of being commanded by God. This experience anchors Muhammad's conveying of revelation in the *Qur'an*, and thus separates it from mere talk. It gives it resilience in evidence for those people who have the relevant experience. Such people report having an experience of being commanded or called to submit in worship and obedience toward God. They are thus motivated to undertake a religious commitment that leads to a religious life of Islam.

Muhammad does not base his case for a religious life of Islam on the fulfillment of human wishes to avoid childhood fears, even if God can counter various human fears. Instead, he bases his case on God's authoritative command to humans to submit to God's will. This command comes to humans in their experience, in an experience of being commanded by God. When one has the latter experience, and bases a religious commitment to God on it, one is not engaged in mere wish fulfillment. Instead, one then is being led to a religious commitment by a religious experience, the experience being one's ground for one's commitment. In that case, one is not holding the commitment just on the basis of a memory of a father figure exalted to the status of a deity. The matter is then more complicated, because one is responding to a qualitative experience and not just an infantile wish or a general memory. So, Freud's diagnosis finds no easy foothold in Muhammad's presentation of an Islamic religious perspective. It neglects the key role of religious experience in that perspective.

Muhammad does not conform his case for a religious life to Freud's demand for publicly shareable evidence suitable to the sciences. Instead, Muhammad's basic evidence is more akin to that found in one's moral conviction, say, in the experience of conscience, from a moral command. Such conviction can be experienced by an individual without being publicly readily shareable. In that respect, it can differ from typical scientific evidence that is thus shareable. Freud has given us no reason to disregard such religious evidence, and it is not easy to see how one could exclude all such evidence in a responsible manner. We have seen that the sciences themselves do not exclude such evidence in general, because they do not exclude evidence-based inquiry in theology and ethics. The fact that the sciences proceed on the basis of publicly shareable evidence does not entail that they demand such evidence in all areas of inquiry. Freud fails to attend to this important lesson. As a result, his case against religion fails to convince, owing to its neglect of relevant evidence.

3 RELIGIOUS EXPERIENCE IN PSYCHOLOGY

Psychology attentive to actual relevant evidence is no universal threat to religious experience or to religious commitment. It becomes a threat only when one introduces, in one's preferred conception of psychology, standards for evidence that the sciences themselves do not support. We have identified Freud's mistake on this front, along with a similar mistake by Dawkins. Of course, one can try to dismiss religious commitment by attributing a dubious origin to it, such as an origin in infantile wishes. This attempt, however, neglects the actual source of much religious commitment, a source in religious experience. We have identified Freud's mistake on this front, too, and Chapters 2–4 have offered the needed evidence for a key role for religious experience in significant religious commitment.

If Freud had attended to actual religious experience, and thus had gone beyond his own simple genetic story, he would have seen the actual basis of much religious commitment. In that case, he would have stopped short of his sweeping, ungrounded claims about religion as a delusion, a denial of reality, and something worthy to be disregarded. He then would have been true to his frequent talk of the importance of (evidential) support appropriate to knowledge. He still would need to correct his mistaken view about the sciences as requiring that all evidence be socially shareable scientific evidence, but that is an empirical matter settled by the textbooks of the academic sciences. Academic psychology, in any case, is no enemy of religious experience or religious commitment in general. In fact, it can benefit religious commitment by attending to the actual sources and evidence for such commitment. (For details, see Hood et al. 2009.) In that case, it will be a friend of religion based in suitable evidence. We turn now to the role of ethics in religious commitment.

6

∾

Religious Experience Moralized

Chapter 5 explained that a religious perspective need not fall prey to Freud's anti-religious diagnosis from psychoanalytic motives. It thus denied that we responsibly can dismiss the reality or the reliability of all religious commitments on the ground that they stem just from dubious psychological factors, such as infantile wishes. Another attempt to dismiss the reality or the reliability of religious commitments proposes that they are best understood as *just* value commitments of a kind familiar in morality. The aim of such an attempt is to dispense with religion as a distinctive source of truth on the ground that it is covered adequately by morality alone. Such a replacement of religion by morality, according to this story, removes the needless mystery created by religion. It enables us to make do with morality instead, thereby domesticating religion as something much more familiar. We shall see that this story of the attempted replacement or domestication of religion by morality faces some big problems.

1 RELIGION MORALIZED REDUCTIVELY

Religion is moralized *reductively*, let us say, when it is reduced to or replaced by morality. (Alternatively, we might say that the *claims* of religion are reduced to or replaced by the claims of morality.) In that case, morality would be shown to supply everything important offered by religion. If religion happens to claim something not covered by morality, we can omit it without significant loss, in this reductionist perspective. Given that we already have morality, we would not have to take on an extra burden with religion, if this approach succeeds. Many people will be sympathetic to this approach, if they aim to minimize our explanatory or theoretical burdens.

Compatible Magisteria

Matthew Arnold famously suggested that religion is just "morality touched with emotion" (1883, p. 17), and others have shared this sentiment. In recent years, Stephen Jay Gould has contrasted religion with science in a way that suggests, if only initially, that religion is centrally a matter of morality, without anything that threatens the sciences in their cognitive pursuits. We shall see that a reductionist story about religion may offer a simple approach, but it does not do justice to actual religions of the kinds introduced in Chapters 2–4. We will do well to keep such religions in mind, in order to avoid fabrications about religion and religious experience. They will serve as a benchmark for measuring the correctness of a strategy to moralize religion reductively. We also shall see that Gould's approach to religion includes, in the end, a tolerable perspective that avoids trying to reduce religion to morality.

Gould introduces his approach to religion with a conciliatory tone. He offers the following statement that suggests a "merely value-meaning" approach to religion, along with a "merely factual" approach to science:

I do not understand why the two enterprises [of science and religion] should experience any conflict. Science tries to document the factual character of the natural world, and to develop theories that coordinate and explain these facts. Religion, on the other hand, operates in the equally important, but utterly different, realm of human purposes, meanings, and values – subjects that the factual domain of science might illuminate, but can never resolve. Similarly, while scientists must operate with ethical principles, some specific to their practice, the validity of these principles can never be inferred from the factual discoveries of science. (1999, pp. 4–5)

Science gets the domain of facts, in Gould's proposal, and religion gets the domain of human values, which are not "facts" in his sense. Gould includes human "purposes" and "meanings" with human "values," but none of these three phenomena includes, in his perspective, facts of the object-ive sort pursued by science. In addition, the relevant pur-poses, meanings, and values are normatively significant for humans (as a result of human commitments), and they can be considered part of "morality" in a broad sense. At least Gould often talks that way.

Gould presents science and religion as two "non-overlap-ping magisteria" (NOMA, for short) characterized by mutual "respectful noninterference" (1999, p. 5). He explains: "NOMA is a simple, humane, rational, and altogether con-ventional argument for mutual respect, based on non-overlapping subject matter, between two components of wisdom in a full human life: our drive to understand the factual character of nature (the magisterium of science), and our need to define meaning in our lives and a moral basis for our actions (the magisterium of religion)" (p. 175). NOMA thus denies that the sciences have comprehensive explana-tory value, on the ground that they do not seek to cover or include at least the value-meaning domain of religion.

Science and religion are "non-overlapping magisteria," in Gould's language, because they are different domains of inquiry and subject matter that do not compete. He explains:

The net, or magisterium, of science covers the empirical realm: what is the universe made of (fact) and why does it work this way (theory). The magisterium of religion extends over questions of ultimate meaning and moral value. These two magisteria do not overlap, nor do they encompass all inquiry (consider, for example, the magisterium of art and the meaning of beauty). To cite the old clichés, science gets the age of rocks, and religion the rock of ages; science studies how the heavens go, religion how to go to heaven. (p. 6)

Gould correctly states that neither science nor religion encompasses "all inquiry." The academic sciences, including the psychology of religion, allows for inquiry in religion that is not part of scientific explanation in terms ultimately of nature alone. The academic science textbooks confirm as much. In addition, religion typically allows for inquiry in the sciences that is not part of religion, as various religious perspectives illustrate. Religion, however, will be "respectful" of science in Gould's sense only if it avoids claims to causal and factual significance that contradict scientific claims. We shall return to the latter point soon.

Gould thinks of morality that bears on a special human ideal as particularly important to religion. He remarks: "I will accept ... the etymology of the word ['religion'] itself – and construe as fundamentally religious (literally, binding us together) all moral discourse on principles that might activate the ideal of universal fellowship among people" (p. 62). He adds a restriction on science that leaves room for religion in such morality: "The magisterium of science cannot proceed beyond the anthropology of morals – the documentation of what people believe, including such important information as the relative frequency of particular moral values among distinct cultures, the correlation of those values with ecological and economic conditions, and even (potentially) the adaptive value of certain beliefs in specified Darwinian situations" (pp. 65–66). Such empirical "anthropology of morals" leaves untouched actual moral deliberation and advice among humans, including the justification of moral decisions and principles.

We end up with a symmetry of tolerance between religion and science. Gould remarks: "If religion can no longer dictate the nature of factual conclusions residing properly within the magisterium of science, then scientists cannot claim higher insight into moral truth from any superior knowledge of the world's empirical constitution" (pp. 9–10). He offers the following questions as illustrations of "moral issues about the value and meaning of life": "Are we worth more than bugs or bacteria because we have evolved a much more complex neurology? Under what conditions (if ever) do we have a right to drive other species to extinction by elimination of their habitats? Do we violate any moral codes when we use genetic technology to place a gene from one creature into the genome of another species?" He finds that such questions "engage different concerns that simply cannot be answered, or even much illuminated, by factual data of any kind" (pp. 54–55). If this is right, the sciences will not be able to displace either ethical inquiry or religious inquiry that includes ethical inquiry.

Religious inquiry, in Gould's perspective, includes ethical inquiry, but it must abide by "the first commandment" for NOMA: "Thou shalt not mix the magisteria by claiming that God directly ordains important events in the history of nature by special interference knowable only through revelation and not accessible to science" (pp. 84–85). In short, religion is not allowed to use divine miracles to merge the two magisteria by settling matters about "nature" in a way inaccessible to science. In Gould's language, "NOMA does impose this 'limitation' on concepts of God" (p. 85). He protects the separation of the magisteria on this ground: "So long as religious beliefs do not dictate specific answers to empirical questions or foreclose the acceptance of documented [empirical] facts, the most theologically devout scientists should have no trouble pursuing their day jobs with equal zeal" (p. 84). Religion, then, must not claim authority over science regarding "empirical questions" or "documented [empirical] facts." (He does mean *empirical* facts, as we shall see.) Science alone, according to NOMA, has authority over such matters.

God and Science

Is much of religion suppressed by NOMA? Religion, in Gould's perspective, functions in the realm of "human purposes, meanings, and value," but not in a realm of *divine* purposes, meanings, and values identifiable in nature but inaccessible to the sciences. If the purposes in question were thus identifiable but inaccessible, religion would tap in to something causal and factual in an empirical way that violates the spirit of NOMA. Even so, Gould allows for religion's endorsing a kind of deism in theology. He grants, without disapproval, that some scientists "still hold a conception of God (as an imperial clock winder at time's beginning in this version of NOMA) that leaves science entirely free in its own proper magisterium" (p. 22). The key demand is that religion not affirm anything that contradicts a scientific finding.

Gould asks about a "violation of NOMA commonly encountered among people whose concept of God demands a loving deity, personally concerned with the lives of all his creatures – and not just an invisible and imperious clock winder." He explains:

Such people often take a further step by insisting that their God mark his existence (and his care) by particular factual imprints upon nature that may run contrary to the findings of science. Now, science has no quarrel whatever with anyone's need or belief in such a personalized concept of divine power, but NOMA does preclude the additional claim that such a God must arrange the facts of nature in a certain set and predetermined way. For example, if you believe that an adequately loving God must show his hand by peppering nature with palpable miracles, or that such a God could only allow evolution to work in a manner contrary to facts of the fossil record (as a story of slow and steady linear progress toward *Homo sapiens*, for example), then a particular, partisan (and minority) view of religion has transgressed into the magisterium of science by dictating conclusions that must remain open to empirical test and potential rejection. (pp. 93–94)

According to Gould, "science has no quarrel whatever with anyone's ... belief in such a personalized concept of divine power," but he demands that religion not affirm anything that contradicts a scientific thesis. In particular, NOMA rules out any claim of religion that "God must arrange the facts of nature in a certain set and predetermined way," that is, a way indifferent to the evidence of the sciences. The central requirement here is that religion avoid "dictating conclusions that must remain open to empirical test and potential rejection." *Empirical* claims, in short, demand *empirical* evidence, even if they emerge from religion.

Advocates of religion can accept Gould's central requirement for religion if they are careful about which claims "must remain open to empirical test" and about what the relevant "empirical test" involves. If Gould were to demand that all empirical evidence be socially readily shareable (i.e., just by human means), as is common in the sciences, many advocates of religion would balk, and rightly so. It is not an a priori truth, and arguably not a truth at all, that God would have to make experience and evidence of divine reality socially shareable in the way the evidence of the sciences is. So, an advocate of religion could accept Gould's central requirement and deny that the relevant empirical test is always based on socially readily shareable empirical evidence. Gould does not affirm this option, but he does not exclude it, either.

Gould endorses this controversial position: "Science simply cannot (by its legitimate methods) adjudicate the issue of God's possible superintendence of nature.

We neither affirm nor deny it; we simply can't comment on it as scientists" (1992, p. 119). I suspect he means "God's actual superintendence of nature," because the "possible superintendence" is just a matter of logical coherence and can be settled by coherent imagination. He evidently holds that God could superintend nature without distorting or undermining the evidence in the sciences or self-manifesting in it. This seems right, because God could be suitably elusive and subtle in divine superintendence, by hiding all identifiable divine fingerprints. God could super-intend nature in various ways without corrupting the scientific evidence available to humans or self-manifesting in it. We have no good reason to deny this; so, Gould is on the right track here.

Richard Dawkins, as Chapter 4 noted, contradicts the position offered by Gould. We identified this claim and rhetorical question by Dawkins: "A universe with a creative superintendent would be a very different kind of universe from one without. Why is that not a scientific matter?" (2006, p. 55). We also noted his following claim: "God's existence or non-existence is a scientific fact about the universe, discoverable in principle if not in practice" (p. 50). The disagreement between Dawkins and Gould depends on what is expected of divine superintendence and on the scope of scientific evidence.

Chapter 4 acknowledged that, according to Dawkins, the sciences demand of all reasonable inquiry probabilities on the basis of socially readily shareable evidence. Gould, in contrast, portrays the sciences as less monopolistic toward reasonable inquiry, as allowing for reasonable inquiry outside the sciences that does not contradict scientific evidence. In particular, Gould leaves room for the latter kind of inquiry having a basis in evidence that is not socially readily shareable. We have no firm basis to exclude such inquiry, and the sciences, as Chapter 4 explained, do not exclude it.

We should doubt Dawkins's suggestion, in opposition to Gould, that a divine superintendent for nature would show up (as being divine) in our scientific evidence. We have no good reason to agree with Dawkins here. As suggested, God as superintendent could be elusive and subtle in relation to our available scientific evidence, leaving no identifiable fingerprints of divine activity. We shall return to a potential reason for such divine elusiveness in Chapters 7 and 8, but the point now is that Dawkins has not made an adequate case to reject divine superintendence on the basis of our scientific evidence. Gould's position is not only more resilient than that of Dawkins but also more in agreement with the academic sciences. The academic sciences do not claim a monopoly on all reasonable inquiry. In this respect, Gould offers a more accurate portrait of the sciences than Dawkins does.

It is significant that God could superintend nature without corrupting scientific evidence or self-manifesting in it. If such superintendence is not excluded by the sciences, then neither is the option of God's self-manifesting to a person without providing socially shareable evidence of the kind familiar in the sciences. As a result, we have no basis in the sciences for excluding a God who is involved, if with due subtlety, in nature or in a person's experience. This is true even if we deny that God's interests are solely ethical relative to humans and their experience. We should expect the sciences, however, to exclude any scientific claim coming from a religion lacking scientific evidence. We thus should not expect the sciences to allow for any kind of fideism (denying a need for evidence) that infects scientific facts and claims. *Scientific* evidence rightly bears on all scientific claims, even if they stem from a religion. We should not assume, however, that all evidence is scientific evidence.

Religion without Reduction

We have no firm basis for a reduction of religion in general to ethics, and Gould's NOMA perspective fits with this truth. One hindrance to such a reduction is the role of theology, beyond ethics, in much religion. Another hindrance is the central role of religious experience in religion; such experience is not reducible to ethical experience, at least in typical cases. We cannot reduce religion to moral principles or even to principles of meaning, because that would omit the motivation for religious commitment in religious experience, which is neither a moral principle nor a principle of meaning. We find this truth confirmed in the religious figures characterized in Chapters 2–4.

The nontheistic religious perspectives of Gautama and Confucius might seem reducible to ethics in some way, but this is only apparent. The obstacle comes from a religious experience of overarching supreme value and meaning that goes beyond ethics. Gautama identifies an experience of such value and meaning with an experience of self-Awakening. It includes an experience of relief from the perturbing effects of life's corrosive frustrations. This experience does not reduce to ethics or to an experience of ethical rightness or goodness. It is an experience of value for a person, but that value is broader and more practical than ethical value as typically understood. It bears on life as a whole, and not just its ethical aspects, and it is inherently practical toward an overarching goal for life.

Confucius may seem to offer a religious perspective that reduces to ethics, but we need to look more carefully. Chapter 2 noted that he affirms the primary value of his Way (*dao*) for human life focused on virtuous reciprocity: "The Master said, 'Set your heart on the *dao*, base yourself in virtue, rely on *ren*'" (*Analects* 7.6). We thus found that he locates overarching, primary meaning for human life in a certain kind of loyal reciprocity in virtuous human relationships. We proposed that his experience of such reciprocity was central to his core religious experience. In its breadth for life's meaning, his religious perspective goes beyond an ethics as typically understood. It commands that one focus one's whole life on loyal reciprocity in relationships. His religious perspective includes an ethics based on a religious experience generalized to all of life. It thus is an experience-based perspective for a whole meaningful life, with no restriction to a set of ethical injunctions or commitments. It includes an ethics, but it is not reducible to an ethics. It is a comprehensive life-perspective with an experience-grounded demand to base oneself in the virtue of loyal reciprocity. It is thus inherently practical toward an over-arching goal for a life.

The theistic religious perspectives outlined in Chapters 2–4 clearly do not reduce to an ethical perspective. They involve theology in a way that exceeds any morality. The theistic religion of Krishna, as Chapter 2 noted, has God (as Krishna) become one's singular focus for a good, meaningful life. God takes on this focus via human devotion to God, in worship and obedience, and it ideally is constant devotion. We have noted the following remark of Krishna in *Bhagavad-Gita* 18.65: "Always think of me, be devoted to me, worship me, and offer obeisance to me." Such devotion is to be constant, "always" functioning as ongoing obedient worship. This is no matter of simply conforming to ethical standards. Instead, it is centrally a matter of relating to *God*, always, in a manner pleasing to God. It thus is a divine–human interpersonal relationship that exceeds ethics as typically understood.

The theistic religious perspective of Moses is steeped in ethics but does not reduce to ethics. It has a basis in religious experience of God, including Moses's experiences of God's self-manifestations for the sake of redeeming people. Chapter 2 noted that the exodus story of Israel offers a promise-and-conflict model of relationship between God and Israel. A central lesson, we saw, is that humans need atonement as reconciliation with God, because human moral failures conflict with God's character and commands. Humans themselves do not have the power needed for such atonement, and this results in God's undertaking a redemptive plan for them, for the sake of their having a good, meaningful life. The plan includes God's giving Israel a law, the Mosaic Law, to guide their reconciliation to God. The Mosaic Law is replete with moral content, but the special, covenant relation between God and Israel is not just moral. It is an ongoing relationship of deepening reconciliation between Israel and God. It thus exceeds any moral perspective, while including a moral perspective.

The religious position of the apostle Paul is inextricably ethical, but it is much more than ethics. Chapter 2 characterized Paul's religious perspective in terms of one's entering into interpersonal reconciliation to God, ever more deeply, with trust in God and fellowship with God. In this perspective, the resurrected Christ, rather than the Mosaic Law, provides the personal guidance and power for this redemptive process. Chapter 2 noted that Paul's religious experiences extend beyond his experience of the risen Jesus on the road to Damascus, and that he expects some of these experiences to be shared by other people. He refers to God's self-manifestation to some humans (Rom. 10:20), and this includes God's manifesting his unique personal character to certain humans, for the sake of their being reconciled to God. He thinks of this character, as noted, in terms of God's love (*agapē*) being poured into human hearts, that is, their volitional, psychological centers (Rom. 5:3–5). This kind of divine intervention can be personal evidence of God's reality and goodness for a recipient, but it is not reducible to ethics. As a result, Paul's religious perspective does not reduce to an ethical perspective.

The theistic religion of Muhammad is based on divine moral commands, but it exceeds ethics. It stems from a distinctive religious experience. As Chapter 2 noted, the experience of *being commanded by God* is at the center of Muhammad's religious experience: "The guidance of Allah is the guidance, and we are commanded to surrender [or submit] to the Lord of the Universe" (*Qur'an* 6:71). Muhammad regards God's status as the one who commands human obedience to be as important as God's status as the one who creates humans. Many people report their having an experience of God's commanding them to submit in obedience and worship, and this experience motivates their commitment to a religious, including an Islamic, way of life. This experience of being commanded was central to Muhammad's life, and it motivated his taking the message of the *Qur'an* to a sizable group of people. It also distinguished Muhammad's religious perspective from a mere ethical perspective. As a result, the religion of Muhammad does not reduce to ethics, despite its having a central role for ethics.

The religious perspectives outlined in Chapters 2–4 do not reduce to an ethical position. They include something distinctively religious that goes beyond ethics. For instance, they include religious experience that is not just a matter of ethics. Even though ethics cannot be eliminated from those religious perspectives, ethics cannot fully explain them. So, those perspectives resist any reduction to ethics.

2 RELIGION MORALIZED NONREDUCTIVELY

Religion can be "moralized" in a way that gives it moral significance without reducing it to ethics. Many philosophers and theologians have proposed ways of doing so, but we have no consensus of how to do so. (For a broad survey of relevant positions, see Baillie 1929, chaps. 5 and 6.) We shall consider some positions that identify important lessons about the relation between morality and religion.

Immanuel Kant

In modern western thought, Immanuel Kant has had unmatched influence on positions relating religion to morality. Contrary to some popular interpretations, Kant did not aim to reduce religion to morality. Instead, he sought to give morality a central role in religion, including in the justification of religion. He explains:

The service of God consists simply and solely in following his will and observing his holy laws and commands. Thus, morality and religion stand in the closest connection with one another. They are distinguished from one another only by the fact that in the former moral duties are carried out from the principle belonging to every rational being, which is to act as a member of a universal system of ends; whereas in the latter these duties are regarded as commandments of a supremely holy will, because fundamentally the laws of morality are the only ones which agree with the idea of a highest perfection. (1783 [1978], p. 143)

Kant thinks of "the idea of a highest perfection" as the idea of God, the supreme being with a morally perfect character. So, his talk of a "supremely holy will" is talk of *God's* perfect moral will. He thinks of morality as a "universal system of ends," because he thinks of morality as bearing on all rational agents with regard to their ultimate ends. Morality, in his view, cannot be just a means to some independent ends.

Kant has in mind theistic religion, and he does not relate his perspective to nontheistic religious perspectives, such as those offered in the practical religions of Gautama and Confucius. Even so, he acknowledges that morality can and does function in perspectives that do not acknowledge God. One can follow God's will, in his view, without acknowledging God's existence.

Kant represents God as seeking to make people *worthy* of having happiness from God, who uses morality to that end. He explains:

God is the only ruler of the world. He governs as a monarch, but not as a despot; for he wills to have his commands observed out of love, and not out of servile fear. Like a father, he orders what is good for us, and does not command out of mere arbitrariness, like a tyrant. God even demands of us that we reflect on the reason for his commandments, and he insists on our observing them because he wants first to make us worthy of happiness and then make us participate in it. God's will is benevolence, and his purpose is what is best. If God commands something for which we cannot see the reason, then this is because of the limitations of our knowledge, and not because of the nature of the commandment itself.... He may often use wholly incomprehensible means to carry out his benevolent aims. (p. 156)

God thus has a purpose in giving moral commands to humans, even if they lack a full understanding of this purpose. The purpose includes our reflecting on moral commands and obeying them. God, in Kant's view, uses morality to bring about what is best for humans. He remarks: "[God's] governing presupposes purposes, and God's government presupposes the wisest and best" (pp. 156–57). At least "the best" would be in God's intention, even if it is frustrated in reality by humans who exercise their free will in imperfect ways.

Kant contends that morality needs God for its completeness. God "completes" morality, in this perspective, by working for its "conviction, import, and emphasis" in human lives. In doing so, God aims to improve people morally in a way that makes them worthy of their happiness from God. This happiness conforms to God's moral commands, thus amounting to *morally righteous* happiness. Kant explains:

God's governance of the world in accordance with moral principles is an assumption without which all morality would have to break down. For if morality cannot provide me with the prospect of satisfying my needs, then it cannot command anything of me either.... How can I know by reason and speculation what God's will is, and what it consists in? Without morality to help me here, I would be on a slippery path, surrounded by mountains which afford me no prospect.... The knowledge of God, therefore, must complete morality....

In order to provide my heart with conviction, import, and emphasis, I have need of a God who will make me participate in happiness in accordance with these eternal and unchangeable laws, if I am worthy of it. (p. 159)

God thus would round out morality, in practice, by giving it motivating power in human lives. Morality would gain practical conviction from God in receptive humans, courtesy of God's role as the empowering benefactor for those committed to a moral life. The practical benefit from God, leading to righteous happiness from God, comes only with human conformity to God's moral commands.

Kant makes morality integral to religion, owing to the central role of God's morally perfect character and will in properly motivated theistic religion. It would be unconvincing, however, to suppose that we have a cogent theoretical argument for God's existence on the basis of morality. God's existence is not transparent in morality itself in a way required by such an argument. Instead, God's existence figures in the motivating component of morality when one properly seeks righteous happiness suited to God's character and will. A person, however, need not seek such happiness, and thus one could be without a practical reason to acknowledge God as motivating benefactor.

Can a *rational* human be without a practical, morally relevant reason to acknowledge God? The answer will depend on what we build into rationality. If it does not require morality leading to lasting righteous happiness, we may not have a basis to include all rational humans. In that case, morality (leading to lasting righteous happiness) and rationality could diverge in a person, and a rational person could be without a practical reason to acknowledge God. If, in addition, one's morality can exist without one's seeking lasting righteous happiness, one's morality will not require acknowledgment of God's existence. In that case, one's morality will not demand theistic religion.

Clearly, not every morality will require religion, let alone theistic religion. In addition, not every religion will yield a sound morality. Some religions, such as that of ISIS (or Daesh), are morally evil and thus call for moral revision. So, there is no simple positive relation between religion and a sound morality. Perhaps all religions yield some morality or other in virtue of giving standards for conducting a proper meaningful life. Even so, the latter standards can fail to capture what is actually morally good or valuable. In that case, a religion will leave us with an inadequate morality at best.

John Baillie

Under Kant's influence, John Baillie has tried to moralize religion in a nonreductive manner. He identifies three relevant views of religion in relation to morality: (1) "Religion is a projection of our moral values into the real order of things"; (2) "Religion is an apprehension of reality through, and in terms of, our moral values"; and (3) "Religion is a moral trust in reality" (Baillie 1929, p. 318). Baillie offers position 3 as encompassing the best interpretations of positions 1 and 2. Position 1 is suggested by Freud (see Chapter 5), but it does not entail that the relevant projection is distorting or deceiving regarding reality. The projection may match the real order of things. The third position echoes Kant's idea of human trust in the promise of the moral law.

Baillie explains how theistic religion takes one beyond just an ethical position:

What religion does is to deliver me from loneliness by giving my ideals a mooring, and as it were an enfranchisement, in the "scheme of things entire." It gives me the assurance that in following the gleam of righteousness and love and honour, I am entering no unsubstantial region of my own fancying, but am rather identifying myself with the inmost nature of things, and bringing my finite will into line with the Infinite Will that made and moves the stars. And thereby is opened out to me a wholly new outlook upon life. I am now at home in the universe. I am no longer a slave but a son. I am not fighting alone, against impossible odds, for a fantastically hopeless cause, and with the paralysing suspicion in my heart that it cannot really matter whether I win or lose, because in the end it can make no difference to anything. Nay, rather it is Reality's own battle that I am fighting, and the stars in their courses are fighting with me and the very Force that moves them is on my side. (p. 326)

Baillie worries that ethics apart from theistic religion could be a "hopeless cause" that "in the end can make no difference to anything." He thus thinks that ethics needs a "mooring" in a divine will whose purpose is to shore up human wills committed to an ethical life.

The divine purpose to aid human wills, in Baillie's perspective, contributes enduring meaning for ethical human lives. He adds:

The citizenship of the *civitas Dei*, like lesser citizenships, gives us more than mere security, precious as that is; it gives to our lives a new depth of meaning by enabling us to envisage them in a wider system of relations; and, at its best, it gives us a new Companionship and a new and purely blessed sense of being at home in a Father's house. We must thus beware of stating the benefits of religion too narrowly; but we must also beware of stating them too negatively. (p. 330)

The God of theistic religion, in Baillie's judgment, gives a hospitable, satisfying home to moral agents devoted to following the divine will. This home includes lasting meaning for people committed to a morally good life. This meaning comes from the will or purpose of a lasting personal agent who is a Father and Companion for receptive humans.

Baillie contends that without theistic religion, moral effort is ultimately "effort wasted" (p. 333). He asks:

If, day by day, I were to carry about with me in my heart a purely naturalistic picture of the universe; if I kept reminding myself, as I tried to do my duty, that it made no difference to anybody or anything outside our little human society whether I did it or not, and that in the end it would make no difference even to that society, because that society can in the end have nothing before it but utter extinction and an eternal night in which nothing that it now cares for will leave any trace or echo at all; if I nourished in myself a steady belief in these negations, would my conscience still remain unimpaired in its "tenderness," and my zeal for that which is good be undiminished in its ardency? (p. 354)

Baillie doubts that a sincere answer to his question can be affirmative. He therefore follows Kant in holding that morality must be completed by a God who, by divine intent, makes moral effort meaningful in a lasting way. This is at best an argument from a *motivational need* in ethics, and we can imagine that this need is not satisfied in reality. So, we would need a better line of argument, if we seek an argument for God's reality.

The core of Baillie's Kantian argument from morality to God is:

If I am right in feeling that it is absolutely demanded of me that I be pure in heart, and just and honourable in all my dealings, then can this mean less than that reality demands these things of me? And if reality demands these things of me, then reality must be interested in moral value, it must have a stake in the moral issue; it must be on the side of the good and against the unworthy and the evil. But that is to say that it is a moral Being itself, not indifferent to moral distinctions but, on the contrary, supremely sensitive to them, and really and deeply caring whether good or evil prevails.

The ultimate reality must thus be One Who loves the Good. (p. 352)

This is too quick to convince. The premature leap goes from reality demanding something valuable to reality being a personal, purposive agent who cares about and loves what is good.

Some nontheistic naturalists have developed moral realism without a role for God. Nature, in their perspective, gives rise to objective values, and those values must be followed if humans are to flourish (see Railton 1986). This does not involve a superhuman personal agent making a demand; instead, it is a naturalistic feature of nature, conducive to human flourishing. A naturalistic value will last only as long as nature lasts, but this does not undermine naturalism about values. Naturalists do not expect values to satisfy lasting purposes or agents. The Kantian argument in question does not undermine such naturalism, and therefore it fails to convince.

Baillie came to acknowledge that Kant's original line of argument does not yield the kind of God needed by a robust religious ethics. He ultimately found Kant's argument too narrow and indirect:

[Kant] taught that [moral] guidance is originally revealed to us in the form of a self-evidencing law – a mere obligation detached, as it were, from Him who lays the obligation upon us; and that the knowledge of Him who thus obliges us is afterwards reached as an inference from the felt nature of the obligation. We, on the other hand, have argued that the Source of the obligation is Himself directly revealed to us and that it is in this vision of His glory and His holiness that our sense of obligation is born. It is His perfection that rebukes us; it is His love that constrains us.

Hence it is no mere law that is revealed to us, but a living Person, and what we call the moral law is but an abstraction

which our limited and limiting minds make from the concrete-
ness of the living Glory that is revealed. (1939, p. 162).

Baillie thus holds that the evidence for God in moral
experience is more direct than Kant held. God self-manifests
to us in our moral experience when "it is [God's] perfection
that rebukes us, [and] it is [God's] love that constrains us."
This self-manifesting of God in our moral experience differs
from an inference to God's reality on the basis of our experience. It has a directness of self-revelation by God that inference to God lacks. As Baillie notes: "It is not merely that
through our values we reach God or that from them we
infer Him, but that in them we find Him" (1929,
pp. 131–32).

Kant's emphasis on "practical reason" remains formative
in Baillie's position as follows:

Kant's great rediscovery was that of the Primacy of the Practical Reason, as he called it. It is not in the realm of sense, he
believed, that we are all really in touch with absolute objective
reality, and certainly not in the realm of the supersensible
objects of scientific and metaphysical speculation, but only in
the realm of the practical claim that is made upon our wills by
the Good. Ultimate reality meets us, not in the form of an
object that invites our speculation, but in the form of a demand
that is made upon our obedience. We are confronted not with
an absolute object of theoretical knowledge but with an absolute obligation. We reach the Unconditional only in an unconditional imperative that reaches us. There is here, as it seems to
me, most precious and deeply Christian insight. (1939, p. 157)

The key assumption is that God would seek the moral
improvement of humans, leading them to become worthy
of their happiness from God. So, God would not want to be
an object of mere speculation or reflection for humans. God
would be deeply interested in the direction of human wills,

because their moral direction (away from or toward a good life) resides there. God's morally perfect character thus would give importance to moral considerations in divine self-manifestation to humans.

The divine influence on human moral direction would not be coercive, but it would allow for human freedom and thus for genuine moral agency in humans. Kant and Baillie agree here. Baillie identifies how God self-reveals to humans in this regard:

A sense of converse with the Living God ([such] as Kant clearly saw to be excluded by his own system) lies at the root of all our spiritual life. That life finds its only beginning in the revelation to our finite minds of One whose transcendent perfection constitutes upon our lives a claim so sovereign that the least attempt to deny it awakens in us a sense of sin and shame; and thus is initiated the sequence, ever extending itself as the revelation of the divine nature becomes deeper and fuller, of confession, repentance, forgiveness, reconciliation, and the new life of fellowship.

There is no other spiritual sequence than this. (1939, p. 159)

This kind of divine self-revelation is morally relevant to humans, given the moral claim it makes on humans, and it leaves its mark in human moral experience. We still can ask why its mark should be taken to be that of a personal, intentional agent. In other words, we can ask why the relevant evidence in our moral experience should be regarded as indicating a personal, intentional God who has a meaningful goal for our lives. We turn now to this important matter.

Arthur Campbell Garnett

Baillie has suggested, as noted, that God self-reveals to us in moral experience when "it is [God's] perfection that rebukes us, [and] it is [God's] love that constrains us." Arthur

Campbell Garnett has explained what this self-revelation entails in moral experience. In doing so, he has identified a role for moral experience in theistic religion and a role for theistic religion in a certain kind of moral experience.

The object of religious commitment, according to Garnett, must have significant meaning, and this agrees with the portrait of religion we offered in Chapter 1. He remarks: "One cannot make an object of devotion of bare infinity, even if one spells it with a capital 'I.' To become an object supremely worthy of devotion the Infinite must be filled with meaning" (1955, p. 97; cf. Garnett 1952, p. 268). The meaning in question must be morally relevant, if a God worthy of devotion is involved; it cannot be simply mystical or rational. Garnett credits Kant with the latter insight, in calling "attention to the experience of the ethical imperative as both the actual basis of religious faith and the best starting point for its logical justification" (1955, p. 99). Here he agrees with the main thrust of Baillie's position outlined above.

Garnett thinks of moral constraints as applying a kind of morally relevant pressure on humans, and this consideration can bear on religion, including theistic religion. He explains:

When [a person] feels a moral constraint placed upon himself, he feels it as the pressure of something other than himself, and yet not in any way sensory or physical. In part he may feel it as pressure of the demands of other human beings, but in so far as it is genuinely felt as moral, it is more than mere social pressure. It is a pressure recognized as that of a rule of right that presses equally upon himself and other human beings. (1955, p. 101)

The relevant moral pressure can come in one's conscience, and it can lead one to go against the moral judgments of one's human social group, including one's parents and educators. One can be a moral rebel as a result of it. So, a simple explanation in terms of human social pressure will be inadequate. (Freud missed this important point.)

Garnett contends that God is involved in the process of human moral experience that leads to moral renewal. God, in his perspective, takes a certain initiative in the matter of humans finding God in moral experience. He remarks:

[A human] does not go readily and willingly seeking God, or creating pleasant images of Him. His first thought of being found by God is one of awe mingled with fear. For *the God he has found seeking him is the embodiment of the moral law.* (1955, p. 101)

The fault-finding power of the moral law in a human life is, in this perspective, the power of God, who seeks to be morally corrective toward wayward humans. So, it is no surprise that common human fear of the moral law is coupled with fear of God. God appears to be a threat to one's self-approved moral standing.

Garnett acknowledges a positive as well as a negative side to divine use of the moral law, and the positive side indicates the meaning of human life. He explains:

The power that condemned [in moral experience] has been found to be a friend. It had pressed upon the self as something alien but inescapable, opposing, and condemning, yet in sur-render to it has been found an unexpected peace, strength, and joy. Here is the deepest mystery of life to ponder. Can it be that in this experience life finds not only its deepest fulfillment, but also the secret of its ultimate meaning? ... [The power] is an other and higher Will than ours, that seeks in and through each of us the good of all. Herein is the meaning of life revealed. It is the meaning of the universe – that the life of [humans] is drawn from a larger Life, the life of One who makes His will felt in ours, a will that calls us to do justly, to love mercy, and to walk humbly with Him, our God. (1955, p. 103)

The proposed ultimate meaning of human life is to live cooperatively with the God who intervenes for human benefit in moral experience. This God seeks to undermine selfish human tendencies for the sake of the common good of humans. So, this God begins as a perceived enemy but, with human cooperation, emerges as a beneficial companion for humans. In that case, humans move from experiencing God's will as bad to experiencing it as good and meaningful.

The evidence of God's will in moral experience allows for human freedom to reject God's offer of companionship and even the claim that God exists. In addition, it aims to build trust in God rather than either speculative or sensory knowledge about God. Garnett adds:

The plodding reason, seeking from the evidence of the senses an answer to the question "Whence does [one] come, and why?" finds no response. The kind of reality revealed by the senses does not speak of ultimate origin or purpose. Nor can reason deduce an answer from this other reality faced in our moments of conscientious struggle and decision. Yet nothing in all experience is more real, more vital, more important, more fraught with meaning – though a meaning to be guessed at rather than read. With its feet planted firmly on the reality of the inward struggle and decision, faith takes its leap. (1955, p. 103)

Garnett fails to convince here, in grounding faith in "a meaning to be guessed at rather than read." A more durable approach would state that one can interpret, in terms of a best available explanation, one's moral experience to include the meaning involving an intervening divine will. Chapters 7 and 8 will make a case for this more resilient approach in contrast with guesswork. We shall see that Garnett has no need to resort to his misleading language of guesswork. His dubious language stems, we shall see, from a neglect of the key role of an inference to a best available explanation of one's experience.

Garnett's own theistic account portrays human commitment to God, including a faith commitment, to call for interpreting moral experience as indicating God's immediate causal presence. He explains:

The theistic vision ... takes the vivid, lived experience of conscience, a power with which [one] wrestles and from which [one] strives to escape, a reality that is personal and immanent, and it interprets this reality as not only immanent but, while still personal, also transcendent. Thus, it finds within the most intimate recesses of the self the impression of something greater beyond us. The idea of God is the interpretation of a lived impression, as the idea of the sun is the interpretation of the light in our eyes, and the idea of the rock is the interpretation of the pressure on our hands. Thus, God is seen not as an abstraction, a hypothetical entity invented as the indirect cause of immediate experience. He is a concrete object of immediate experience. He is also thoroughly objective. (1955, p. 104)

Garnett's description does not fit well with his earlier talk of our commitment to (meaning from) God as a *guess*. We do not typically think of our acknowledgment of the sun and rocks as guesses, but Garnett likens our interpretive acknowledgment of God to our acknowledgment of the sun and rocks. So, his earlier talk of a guess is dubious by his own account, even if we accept his concession that it is possible for a theistic interpretation to be mistaken. Such a possibility of mistake does not entail actuality of mistake; nor does it entail that we are dealing with a guess.

Garnett locates the key evidence of divine intrusion in human conscience of a distinctive sort. What we may call "traditional conscience" gives us moral input from human sources, perhaps social human sources, and not from God. In contrast, what Garnett calls "critical conscience" demands of humans "an impartial concern for the welfare of all [humans], that is the root of all conscience; and it is this, and this alone, that can reasonably be attributed to the influence within us of the divine moral power of the universe" (1955, p. 105). The impartial concern in question goes beyond much of the material of ordinary, traditional conscience. It is involved in the kind of altruistic love commanded in the New Testament.

Unselfish, altruistic love, according to Garnett, provides the basis of moral life in critical conscience from God. He states:

[In the New Testament] we see the single principle of the critical conscience, *agapē*, productive love, set forth as the basis of the moral life. We see the assertion of [the human] universal capacity for conscientious insight into that law as not merely a God-given concept but as the presence and working of the divine life in [humans]. And we are told that the essence of the divine life is love. When we turn from the New Testament to the records of religious, and particularly of Christian, life we find these conceptions borne out in experience. It is the duty of productive love to one's fellows that is endorsed by the critical conscience. It is in facing up *to* the implications of this duty that the best of [persons] find themselves falling short and faced with a demand that condemns them. It is this demand that, in a life of religious devotion, is recognized as the ideal. And it is in the vision of that ideal as embodied in the Source of all life, Whose will we feel constraining ours to be loyal to the ideal, that the religious personality finds its inspiration and strength. (1955, p. 113)

Garnett thus links the demand of altruistic love in critical conscience to a life of religious devotion and to a religious personality. We need to qualify his approach as that of a *theistic* religion of moral goodness, because religious devotion need not be avowedly theistic. Chapter 1 noted that not all religions are committed to genuine moral goodness, and Chapters 2–4 identified some nontheistic religious perspectives.

The heart of theistic religion, according to Garnett, can be found in the critical conscience of moral experience. It includes that one is loved by God, that one should love God with all one's heart, that one should love one's neighbor as oneself, and that in such love the human spirit is made whole (1955, p. 117). Garnett contends that ethics without such religion is deficient:

Without a God worthy to serve, [a person's] extrovert interests are apt to become one-sided, confused, conflicting, and weak. But still worse, [one] is apt to become more or less introverted.... The states of the self, the prestige and power and sensory gratification in which those satisfied feelings are found, become the ends predominantly sought. Pride and sensuality become the dominant motives, in place of wholesome constructive interests in the affairs of the world. And out of pride and sensuality grow hatred, harshness, unwarranted fears, lust, and greed. From these dangers [one] is saved if [one] has a high God to serve with true devotion; [one] must find something beyond [oneself] that [one] can recognize as more worthy than self, which [one] can learn to love more than [one] loves [oneself]. This is religion. Ethics alone is not enough. (1955, p. 190; see also Garnett 1945, chap. 1)

In this perspective, theistic religious commitment is grounded in the critical conscience of moral experience, but it exceeds the domain of morality or ethics. It does so, because its main object, the personal God, is irreducible to that domain. Indeed, God challenges that domain from moving toward harmful extroversion or introversion, and critical conscience is the venue for that divine existential challenge in human moral experience.

Garnett elaborates on the need of robust ethics for theistic religion:

[Ethics] teaches [a person] to love his neighbor *as* himself. But this can still leave him divided between the balanced interests of self and neighbor – with the strong tendency that self will win. Thus, the second of the two great commandments [in the teaching of Jesus, to love God and to love other humans] requires the support that comes alone from obedience to the first. [One] must love his God first, that thereby he may find it in him to love his neighbor consistently and well. And he must love his God, not as he loves himself, but with all his heart and all his strength and all his mind. Then he can rejoice in the conviction that God loves him; and he will find that spontaneously he loves his neighbor whom God also loves; and he can even safely (without introversion) love himself equally with his neighbor, loving himself not as an end, but as an instrument in the service of God. (1955, p. 191)

Garnett offers the altruistic God of theistic religion as the only source to meet the human need of supreme devotion. Of course, humans may have this need but lack a personal God in reality to satisfy it. So, one cannot argue from the need to the reality of God. Instead, one must find evidence of God in human moral experience, particularly in its critical conscience as God's self-manifestation reveals God's perfect moral character.

Garnett improves on Kant's perspective on religion and morality by identifying some features of human moral experience that arguably indicate divine intervention for human good. The role of critical conscience is central to this perspective, and it merits more attention. (Chapters 7 and 8 return to the role of conscience in theistic religious experience.) Garnett misses, however, an opportunity to identify how moral experience can serve as a ground for a theistic interpretation. His appeal to a "guess" is, as suggested, not compelling and even misleading. Guesswork will not convince anyone looking for evidence for a theistic interpretation of moral experience. The next chapter develops this lesson, in connection with an account of theistic evidence in human moral experience.

3 MORALIZING WITHOUT REPLACEMENT

In the case of theistic religion, involving a morally good God, we should expect religion to be inextricably related to moral goodness. If God is the supreme object of religion, as in theistic religion, then religion will be directed ultimately toward something morally good. The big question is whether our experience of moral goodness can recommend religion on the basis of credible grounds. The key issue is: Can religious commitment be evidentially or cognitively grounded on the basis of human moral experience? If so, can this approach be extended to nontheistic religions? We turn now to such questions.

7

Religious Experience Cognized

Foundations

Chapter 6 argued that religion does not reduce to ethics, even though ethics typically looms large in religions. It considered the broadly Kantian view that a distinctive moral experience is particularly relevant to religious commitment. This chapter will extend our attention to that view, with a special focus on theistic religion. It will ask whether a certain kind of moral experience can evidentially or cognitively ground theistic religious commitment, and, if so, how it can do so. Chapter 1 characterized religious commitment in terms of an overarching practical meaning for human life, and therefore we shall ask about the evidential or cognitive grounding for a commitment to such meaning.

My focus in this chapter and the next will be on experiential evidence characteristic of Jewish and Christian theism. Such evidence, however, is not exclusive to Jewish and Christian theism or even to theists. It can be found in a wide range of versions of theism, including Islamic, Hindu, and Buddhist theism of various sorts. It also can be found among some people who are not theists at all, including various nontheistic followers of Gautama and Confucius. If it is evidence of a perfectly good God, we should expect it to be found widely among humans, even if they do not always perceive it for what it actually is: evidence of a perfectly good God. Space limitations prevent me from documenting the broad and diverse reality of the evidence in question, but one could pursue this wider evidence without much difficulty. It is readily available to inquirers.

1   COGNIZED RELIGIOUS EXPERIENCE

Let us say that a religious experience is *cognized*, or made cognitively relevant regarding an objective fact, when it is undefeated evidence for a commitment regarding the human-independent world. In that case, the relevant experience *indicates*, if fallibly, something about what we may call "external (or objective) reality," and not just something subjective, illusory, or delusional. So, if an apparent experience of God is cognized, it is undefeated evidence for God's reality. Its being undefeated requires it not to be undermined or overridden by other experiences or evidence one has. We use the word "cognized," because undefeated support of this kind is fitting for genuine knowledge of external reality. A religious experience can *be* cognized regarding objectivity, however, without one's *showing* it to be so. An experience's being cognized (by being undefeated evidence for external reality) and one's showing it to be so are two different things. The former can, and often does, exist without the latter. *Having* good evidence is not *presenting* such evidence.

Two big questions face a theistic interpretation of religious experience: What would evidence of a personal God look like, and what would make it cognized, that is, undefeated evidence, for affirming the reality of a human-independent personal God? When discussions of God's existence neglect these questions, they fail to make needed progress. It will not do to opt out of a role for supporting evidence, as in the case of fideism about divine reality, because this would invite a kind of arbitrariness toward reality in theistic commitment. Even if our evidence misleads us at times, and it does, as responsible inquirers we must have our beliefs guided by it. In cases where our evidence does mislead, it is other evidence that indicates its being misleading, if anything does. So, evidence matters, even if it is fallible, because evidence is a truth indicator, and truth indicators matter. They matter in guiding responsible inquiry as doing the best we can in inquiry, given our overall experience.

2 INTERPERSONAL INQUIRY

Inquiry regarding the reality of a personal God is potentially *interpersonal* inquiry. In such a case, human inquiry goes beyond the natural sciences to include inquiry about irreducibly personal features in experience, such as the role of an intentional will in the experienced data needing explanation. Some of the social sciences, including segments of psychology and sociology, go beyond the natural sciences in that manner. Given their disciplinary scope, however, they stay clear of formulating theology, even when they attend to empirical psychological or sociological matters in religion. Inquiry about God, when responsible, also takes inquirers beyond the natural sciences, on the assumption that God inherently would be a personal, goal-directed agent with intentions and plans, that is, an agent who intends to do something. In such inquiry, one personal agent asks about the nature or reality of another (potential) personal agent, and, in that regard, we have interpersonal inquiry.

If God inherently would be an intentional agent and aim to guide humans as their Lord toward a goal, then direct evidence of God's nature or reality would include direct acquaintance with a *guiding will*. In that case, human agents would have the opportunity for a direct experience of a guiding agent irreducible to themselves. Such an experience would be irreducibly interpersonal, and it would fall into the category of a direct "I–Thou" relation, in the first and second person, between a human and God. (Such a relation has received attention from Kierkegaard (1846), Martin Buber (1923), and H. H. Farmer (1942), among others.)

If God is the "Lord" over humans, as many theists claim, we should expect God to seek to lead or guide cooperative humans toward the satisfaction of a divine purpose. Mere information would not serve the needed role of personal guidance for humans. God would not be the Lord, at least in practice, over humans without some effort to lead them toward a divine goal, and this effort would emerge somehow in human experience under certain circumstances. Divine lordship over humans would include this effort at its core, and it would offer an opportunity for a kind of divine experiential immanence at odds with typical deism. We need to characterize this experiential immanence, if we are to understand human knowledge of God, in contrast with knowledge in the natural sciences.

If we take the term "God" to be a supremely honorific title, rather than a name, we can make some progress in our inquiry. We then can use the term without assuming that God exists, or that there is an actual titleholder. In addition, we then can rely on the content of the title to guide our expectations regarding evidence of God's reality or non-reality. The theistic religious perspectives outlined in Chapters 2–4 agree in portraying the titleholder of "God" as being *worthy of worship* and thus worthy of unqualified commitment. As a result, they represent God as being morally perfect, free of any moral defect. They do not agree on what exactly moral perfection requires, but they do claim that God is free of moral wrongdoing. This takes talk of "God" out of a domain of debilitating abstractness, and it enables us to ask about relevant evidence of divine reality. For instance, we then can acknowledge that the relevant evidence of God's existence must be evidence of a God worthy of human trust. Even so, questions about God typically leave us with a further question: *Which* God? That is, what kind of God is at issue? We now have the start of an answer.

Someone might propose a morally inferior notion of God, but that would be to change the subject from traditional monotheism, and, more to the point, it would be premature now. One might consider that option if the morally superior notion ultimately finds no actual titleholder, but we have not reached that place of failure. The God in question, in any case, would not be limited in intervention or work to a particular (say, a Jewish or a Christian) context that completely excludes other versions of theism or religion. This God could work for redemption among all people and religions, even among polytheists, agnostics, and atheists. In addition, this God could be accurately represented, if only in part, in a range of religious perspectives.

Our adopted notion of God will bear directly on our epistemic assessment of whether God exists, owing to the parameters for relevant evidence suited to that notion. In addition, an approach to evidence can set standards for evidence or justification that conflict with, or otherwise challenge, an evidence-based commitment to God's reality. The lesson, in any case, is that one's notion of God matters for epistemic assessment of belief in God, and the same is true of one's notion of evidence for reasonable commitment. Cognitively responsible inquiry about God needs to attend carefully to both considerations

The job description for a God worthy of worship would be anything but easy to satisfy by a typical moral agent. A serious problem arises from the required moral perfection. Moral indifference toward humans would not be a live option for the kind of God in question, and the same is true for *any* moral option at odds with moral perfection. A morally perfect God would seek to engage humans as moral agents, not just as thinkers, toward needed redemption as reconciliation with God for their moral and spiritual good. Their needed redemption would consist in such ever-deepening reconciliation with God, in keeping with God's perfect moral character. It would counter their being wayward from cooperating with God and God's perfect character. So, God would seek to lead or guide cooperative humans toward what is best for them, all things considered, including what is morally and spiritually best for them.

A perfectly good God would not settle for revelation via abstract arguments, particularly those comprehensible only to a small group of intellectuals. Otherwise, God would not be perfectly caring toward all people. So, typical arguments of natural theology (such as ontological, cosmological, and teleological arguments) would not be the main avenue for divine self-revelation to humans, if they would be an avenue at all. (On such arguments, and their failure to indicate the reality of a God worthy of worship, see Moser 2020.) Whatever beliefs they yield, such arguments lack the kind of motivational power needed to reconcile a person to God, particularly in an agreement of wills as a basis for cooperative action. They thus do not nudge one to obey or to trust God, however favorable one's beliefs *about* God are.

It is doubtful that arguments (and intellectual contents, in general) by themselves are motivational for persons. Motivation, instead, needs a basis in one's motivational set, including one's desires and intentions. Mere beliefs will not do the motivational work on their own, because they do not have an inherent basis in one's motivational set. So, merely having a proof or a sound argument for God's existence will not move one to a significant practical difference in one's life. This is not just a point about agnostics or atheists; it bears on theists too. So, a perfectly caring God would have a different approach to self-revelation to humans. Such a God would have a kind of immanence in human experience, for the sake of *leading* people, without coercion, to what is morally and spiritually good for them, including reconciliation with God. Otherwise, God would be deficient in caring for them.

We now face a crucial but widely neglected question: What kind of immanence from God should we expect? More specifically, what kind of religious experience should we expect among humans from a God worthy of worship? Not every experience will indicate the reality of an intentional God worthy of worship. An experience of impersonal nature will fail here, as will an experience of any agent who is morally deficient. The evidence of the titleholder for "God" must be adequate to indicate God's unique moral character as perfectly loving and redemptive toward humans. The standard for evidence, then, is high, and it excludes many familiar candidates in history. Indeed, the list of excluded candidates is extensive. For instance, mere beauty, goodness, or truth will not suffice as an indicator of a personal God, contrary to many theists.

God, as redemptive, would *do* something to try to bring a human's moral character into agreement with God's moral character, for the sake of divine–human reconciliation. We must say "try to" here, because this would be a cooperative rather than a mechanical process. God would honor the purposive responsible agency of humans, and this would entail honoring their potential decision to resist or ignore conformity to God's moral character. Otherwise, there would be no genuine intentional *agents* to be reconciled to God, at least in the area of divine–human reconciliation. We then would have nondivine persons as mere extensions of God's all-encompassing will, but no nondivine persons with their own wills, at least in divine–human relations. This is not, however, the picture offered by the common human experience of agency in action; in that picture, we can resist God's moral challenges to us. In addition, it is not the picture offered by the theists characterized in Chapters 2–4, who assume responsible human agency in their frequent moral injunctions to people.

It would be a mistake to oppose the justification of religious commitment on the basis of religious experiences because such experiences are not "cognitive," that is, because they "alone would not constitute a basis for our gaining knowledge of some objective reality." Richard Gale takes the latter direction (1991, p. 287). He holds that a cognitive experience cannot be person-relative in the evidence it supplies, but instead that it must be evidence even for people who have not had this experience or an experience of its kind. This is arguably too strong. It seems, for instance, that the pain in my mouth is evidence for me regarding my having a toothache, but it need not be similar evidence for you, particularly if you have no experience of this kind. So, many epistemologists now accept the person-relativity of some evidence in experience. This is preferable to Gale's extreme requirement on experience as evidence.

Chapter 4 raised doubt about the suggestion of Richard Dawkins (2006, pp. 52, 59) that the evidence for God's existence is to be treated like evidence for a scientific hypothesis. It would be a mistake, as Chapter 4 contended, to demand that evidence of God's reality be socially readily shareable, in the way typical "scientific" evidence is. (We have characterized being "readily" shareable in terms of being shareable just by typical human means.) As a morally challenging personal agent, God would differ in significant ways from typical scientific objects, and this would yield a relevant difference between scientific evidence and the interpersonal evidence for God. We beg a key question if, with Dawkins, we simply assume otherwise. If God gives you evidence of God's reality, say, by divine self-manifestation, it does not follow that God gives the same to me or that you can give me your evidence. So, one's evidence of divine reality need not be socially readily shareable in the way scientific evidence is. Many critics of theistic evidence miss this important point.

God's giving evidence of divine reality to humans would occur in actual human experience, and it would arise in a purposive context chosen by God. We may characterize such a context as one of *redemptive testing* by God, because God's aim would be to elicit reconciliation as obedience and trust in God from humans. Humans would have the option of failing the test by resisting or ignoring the desired reconciliation. We need to clarify the context of redemptive testing. We will continue to talk of what God *would* do or be like (if God exists), in order to avoid begging any question about God's actual existence.

3 TESTED IN *AGAPĒ*

If God is worthy of worship, then God is perfectly good and thus perfectly loving and caring toward all persons. In that case, God would seek to have people freely cooperate in becoming loving toward others as God is loving toward others, in relationship with God and others. Part of this divine effort would include God's testing people to reveal, if only to themselves, who they really are, including what kind of people they are, as moral agents. A divine aim would be to reveal where they stand relative to the divine effort to form a flourishing community or society of people who love others as God does. The following Biblical passage acknowledges part of this effort: "The Lord your God is testing you, to know whether you indeed love the Lord your God with all your heart and soul" (Deut. 13:3). The test also includes an assessment of our love for our neighbors, regarding whether we love our neighbors as ourselves (see Lev. 19:18; cf. Mark 12:30–31).

An important Biblical theme is that one's loving God must be accompanied by loving one's neighbors. The writer of 1 John thus states: "Those who say, 'I love God,' and hate their brothers or sisters, are liars; for those who do not love a brother or sister whom they have seen, cannot love God whom they have not seen" (1 John 4:20). By this standard, the redemptive test from God would be ongoing and morally rigorous for humans. As a result, we may prefer to ignore it, to change the subject to something less rigorous. We may even prefer to change the standard for divine reality or evidence to something more convenient for us.

A perfectly loving God would calibrate divine testing to the abilities of the agents being tested. Even so, such a God would seek to cultivate love of others wherever it can be cultivated, and this would entail real, even painful struggles for most humans to learn to love others as God does. We can distinguish between divine testing and morally or spiritually harmful testing. A morally perfect God, being perfectly loving toward others, would do no moral or spiritual harm to others. God still could allow for physical harm, including death, for the sake of (testing for) moral or spiritual good among humans. (Death need not be the end of the redemptive story, given divine power over it.) God would be willing to cultivate love for others at the expense of lesser goods or pleasures, and this could be a painful experience for humans. The "testing" of Job serves as an example, and it casts doubt on our now having a full explanation of why God allows suffering among humans. (Chapter 8 returns to the latter topic.)

One might propose that every experience of human life is designed and caused by God for the purpose of testing humans. Some proponents of extreme divine sovereignty might endorse such a bold view, but it seems doubtful that a perfectly loving God could design and cause the evil events and experiences of, say, the Holocaust. That would be at odds with a morally perfect character. In a world of many free agents, some of whom are evil, it seems much more plausible to say that God could turn the evil designs and efforts of others into a test for advancing divine love. Jesus in Gethsemane and on Calvary may be a model for this kind of redemptive testing and suffering (see Heb. 8:5–9). This does not suggest that God punished Jesus on the cross; instead, it proposes that God turned the evil of others into a redemptive opportunity that became a test for all human agents involved.

Abuses in talk of divine "testing" are common, just as abuses occur with talk of "love" and even of "God." We should be attentive to a notion of *redemptive*, or restorative, testing in *agapē*, because it can illuminate an important part of human experience in relation to a redemptive God. Many of the Biblical writers seem attuned to such testing as a challenging intervention from God in human experience.

They assume that God would care enough about humans to assess and test them on where they stand in their relation to God's moral character and will. Redemptive testing could serve as a needed wake-up call to humans who have strayed from what they need morally and spiritually in relation to God.

Some inquirers about religion neglect that a perfectly good God would want humans to learn to love others, even their enemies, as God does, and this neglect can obscure their inquiry. It can cloud how God, as perfectly good, would be available to be known in moral experience by humans. We humans are in no position to set the terms for how God would be known by us, because God would be sui generis and unmatched by humans in moral perfection. So, as perfectly good, God would seek to be known by humans *on God's perfectly good terms*. Otherwise, God would fail to be perfectly good in the area of human knowledge of God, and hence would fail to be worthy of worship, thereby being disqualified to satisfy the perfectionist title "God."

God's terms for being known by humans would fit with God's perfect moral character, the character required for being worthy of worship. Those terms would require that humans, for their own good, conform to God's perfect moral character rather than that God conform to or condone defective human ways. God would be morally negligent in failing to uphold such a perfect-character standard in being known by humans. So, humans would face a challenge in coming to know God, a challenge from the unique, morally perfect character of God. The self-manifestation of that character would contrast sharply with a typical human moral character, and that contrast would be morally significant. The resulting challenge would include a moral demand to conform to God's character of perfect goodness. This would require that one put morally righteous *agapē* toward God and others at the top of one's priorities for life, and thus that one love others as God does. A big question concerns how this is to be done by humans, who seem to have selfish tendencies that interfere with their loving others as God does.

A problem arises for humans (including agnostics, atheists, and even many theists) who do not see or feel divine love in their lives. Like Jesus at Calvary (Mark 15:34), they feel abandoned by God, if God exists; or they feel the world at large to be abandoned by God, if God exists. It is hard to blame them for that feeling if their overall experience agrees with it. I doubt that we can blame them, in any case, for not being moved by speculative inferences about a fine-tuner, designer, or first cause in the service of a natural theology. A different kind of evidence is needed.

At first glance, we may experience the world as the kind of place abandoned by God if God exists. The basis for Jesus's cry of abandonment on Calvary thus seems to be writ large in our troubled world, at least on its surface. Theologians and apologists for theology would do well not to ignore or disparage this painful reality for many people. We shall ask whether a certain role for being convicted by *agapē* in theological discernment offers a helpful response.

W. R. Matthews has identified a common human problem, as follows:

There are, I suppose, many in these days who long for the assurance that God is a reality and not a fiction, and the lover of men, but who are looking for that spiritual assurance in the wrong place. They turn over the arguments for and against the Christian belief in God, "and find no end in wandering mazes lost"; or they seek for some overwhelming religious experience which will sweep doubt away, only to be haunted by the suspicion that this experience when it comes is nothing but a drama played on the stage of their own minds. (1936, p. 182)

Humans need an alternative to being lost or haunted in those familiar ways of seeking God. We shall see that such an alternative would be available to them under certain circumstances of being convicted by *agapē* in moral conscience.

Matthews elaborates by taking a lead from the author of 1 John:

The guidance which comes from the earliest days of our [Christian] religion would not indeed lead us to despise intellectual enquiry and mystical vision, but it would not lead us to begin with them. It would tell us to start loving our fellows, to cultivate the settled and resolute will for their good. So, by coming to know what "love" means we shall come to know what "God" means, and *by realizing [love's] power, its reality as a human force, we shall be in contact with a power which is more than human, with the creative energy of the world.* "Beloved, let us love one another, for love is of God and everyone that loveth is born of God and knoweth God. He that loveth not knoweth not God, for God is love." [1 John 4:7–8] (1936, p. 182, emphasis added)

A key claim here is: "by realizing [love's] power, its reality as a human force, we shall be in contact with a power which is more than human, with the creative energy of the world." One's acting with love toward other people, in this perspective, will enable one to experience love as a power that transcends human power. We need to clarify this claim and to consider its plausibility.

We find some clarification in a notion of divine self-authentication for the sake of leading humans in moral experience. David Forrest explains:

God verifies Himself not as an idea, but as a power "to kindle or restrain" in every impulse, resolve, and aspiration. We are sure of Him, because of what He is to us, because of the place He has in our life, ruling, rebuking, uplifting. It was this inward and indisputable knowledge which Christ Himself had and which He strove to realise in others. (1906, p. 107)

The key idea is that God would be self-authenticating and self-evidencing in divine intentional power toward humans, at least toward humans willing to consider such power without opposition or indifference. This fits with the recurring Biblical theme that God authenticates himself for humans: "When God made a promise to Abraham, because he had no one greater by whom to swear, he swore by himself" (Heb. 6:13; cf. Gen. 22:16, Isa. 45:23). The claim that God self-authenticates divine reality for humans does not entail that either a religious experience or a religious document or statement is self-authenticating regarding God's existence. God is not to be identified with a religious experience or a religious document or statement.

The main question becomes: What would the relevant divine power look like in human experience? God would have unmatched causal power, but what kind of power would serve for divine self-authentication in human experience? Such questions rarely emerge in theology and the philosophy of religion, but they are central to responsible inquiry about God. They demand straightforward answers from a theistic approach to religion and religious experience.

The divine power in question would be that of a morally perfect will, given that God inherently would be an intentional agent worthy of worship and thus morally without defect. Being morally perfect, God would seek the moral perfecting of humans, at least humans willing to cooperate, in a manner that depends on God's experienced moral power. Such perfecting would enhance human reconciliation with God and would serve the overall good of humans, including in their relationships with each other. The relevant kind of perfecting emerges in the New Testament, with various expressions. The writer of 1 John, for instance, comments on being "perfected" in divine love: "If we love one another, God lives in us, and his love is perfected in us" (1 John 4:12).

The kind of reconciliation pertinent to the perfecting of humans is found in Paul's summary of his Good News: "In Christ God was reconciling the world to himself, not counting their trespasses against them, and entrusting the message of reconciliation to us" (2 Cor. 5:19). In honoring human agency, such reconciliation would seek human cooperation with God's will, without divine coercion of a human will. (On the relevant kind of reconciliation, see Moser 2017, chap. 5; see also Taylor 1946, Martin 1981, and Marshall 2008. John 15:13–15 portrays it as a distinctive kind of *friendship*.) God could constrain human options, leading people to choose for or against God's will, but this would not be to coerce a particular choice. We should expect evidence of God's reality and character to be *volitionally sensitive* to individual persons and thus elusive, variable, and morally challenging toward human reconciliation with God. Such evidence would come through a moral challenge, from uncoercive pressure from God's intentional will on a human will, rather than through mere casual reflection on evidence.

We need to clarify how the uncoercive perfecting of divine love is to function in interpersonal divine–human interaction. Otherwise, we will not adequately understand the nature of direct evidence for God's reality and character. In that case, we will lack an adequate religious epistemology, including an adequate phenomenology of religious experience. Because the evidence for God's reality, as one worthy of worship, is inseparable from evidence for God's moral character, we should expect the relevant evidence to be associated with the self-manifestation of God's morally perfect goodness, including divine love for all other agents. God's perfect moral character would not be just another feature of God, as if it could be set aside in relating to God. The idea of inherent moral perfection is central to the meaning of the perfectionist title "God" as one worthy of worship.

The divine power that serves as direct evidence would be the power of God's morally perfect character as self-manifested in perfect love to agents for the sake of divine–human reconciliation. This power would represent God's inherent character without coercing humans in their response to God. Such power would not be easily copied by false gods, because they would lack the needed moral character. What is morally imperfect will fall short of the divine power of moral perfection. Only God would be able to self-manifest a morally perfect divine character, because only God would have control over the self-revealing of God's personal character. We can benefit from some clarification of such morally unique power in its relation to humans.

4 LED BY GOD

We should ask about the *recognition* of divine perfect love, but we should not assume uncritically that the needed recognition can be free of *cooperation* with such love. Otherwise, we could obstruct our understanding of how a morally perfect God would interact with humans. The writer of 1 John offers a comment that aids understanding: "Whoever says, 'I am in the light,' while hating a brother or sister is still in the darkness. Whoever loves a brother or sister lives in the light, and in such a person there is no cause for stumbling. But whoever hates [his or her brother or sister] is in the darkness, walks in the darkness, and does not know the way to go, because the darkness has brought on blindness" (1 John 2:9–11).

The writer of 1 John suggests that one's lack of (sharing in or cooperating with) *agapē* toward others leaves one in spiritual "darkness." Such darkness could include a case of spiritual "blindness" regarding knowing the way to go, including the way to (knowing) God. A key claim is: "Whoever does not love does not know God, for God is love" (1 John 4:8). The writer holds that love of others is a basis for knowing that one has entered "the life" from and with God: "We know that we have passed from death to the life because we love the brothers" (1 John 3:14, my translation). According to 1 John, we face an evidential or cognitive consequence from our practical failure to share in or cooperate with *agapē* toward others. One could say that God either causes the blindness in question (cf. John 12:40) or sets circumstances up so that they bring about the blindness. We need not digress to that matter. (For relevant discussion, see Meadors 2006.)

The writer of 1 John holds that the relevant love is not merely human but is "from God" (1 John 4:7). The writer remarks: "We love because he [God] first loved us" (1 John 4:19). A pressing question concerns how one knows, if one does, that the relevant love is from *God* rather than from humans alone. We can find some illumination from the apostle Paul, in his following remark that ultimately bears on divine love: "All who are led by the Spirit of God are children of God" (Rom. 8:14). This remark prompts a question: What is it to be "led by the Spirit" of God? In Galatians 5:18, Paul speaks of being "led by the Spirit" in connection with loving others, among other "fruit" of God's Spirit.

James D. G. Dunn comments as follows: "[Paul] was able to urge his converts to walk by the Spirit, be led by the Spirit, etc. (as in Rom. 8:4, 14; Gal. 5:16, 18, 25). In other words, so far as Paul was concerned, loving conduct was something much more spontaneous than can be tested by simple reference to the rule book and precedent – it was much more in the nature of obedience to an inward compulsion" (1998, p. 323). Perhaps, as Dunn suggests, being led by God's Spirit includes an experience akin to an inward compulsion, such as an inward compulsion to love others. Even so, we have to ask whether this compulsion is from *God* rather than from a natural source. We would gain nothing by simply assuming that it is from God. Supporting evidence is needed.

An important issue concerns the role of a human agent in the relevant experience of being led by God. Joseph Fitzmyer comments: "'Being led by the Spirit' ... is the Pauline way of expressing the active influence of the Spirit in Christian life, i.e., the reaction of Christians to the leading of the Spirit; Christians are under the vital guidance of God's Spirit, which leads them *when they allow it* and thereby mortify the deeds of the body" (1993, p. 499, emphasis added). In this perspective, being led by the Spirit does not entail the suppression of a human will; instead, it requires human cooperation in allowing the leading by the Spirit.

Helmut Thielicke concurs: "We are not happy owners [of the Spirit] who can identify ourselves with the Spirit and count upon it that he will automatically impel us toward what is posited in a new entelechy. It is a mistake to take the 'led by the Spirit' of Romans 8:14 (*agesthai*) to imply automatic impulsion" (1982, p. 26). This view fits with the position that humans must allow themselves to be led by the Spirit, and this includes a kind of human cooperation with God (see also Bultmann 1951, p. 336, rejecting the kind of coercive role suggested by Käsemann 1980, p. 226). The role of human cooperation is clear in Paul's understanding of advised human "sowing to the Spirit" (Gal. 6:8) and his injunction to "walk by the Spirit" (Gal. 5:16). Such talk would be irrelevant if being led by the Spirit disregarded a cooperative human will.

A serious problem would arise if God were to coerce people in leading them to become obedient children of God. A troublesome question is: Why, if the coercion of humans is a divine option beneficial to them, has not God coercively led all people by now to become obedient children of God, thus sparing them the considerable stresses and strains of life without a positive relationship with God? If a perfectly loving God could use coercion in that supposedly beneficial manner, it would seem pointless and perverse to allow people to undergo such stresses and strains. Divine coercion thus would complicate theism in this regard, given that many people have not received the supposed benefit of being coerced by God to obey.

If God seeks to preserve genuine human agency in submission to God, we can make some sense of the trials of ongoing human life without a positive relationship with God. At least some of those trials may serve to challenge human agents to reorient, without coercion, their priorities for life agreeable to God. No full theodicy for such trials is available to us now (as Chapter 8 indicates), but we can make some theological sense of some trials, typically in hindsight.

We can identify a distinctive role for *God* as an intentional power beyond humans in their being led by God, if we ask what, if anything, would be the goal of their being led. We find a suggestion in two prayers of the apostle Paul: "May the Lord make you increase and abound in love for one another and for all" (1 Thess. 3:12). "This is my prayer, that your love may overflow more and more with knowledge and full insight to help you to determine what is best" (Phil. 1:9–10). The writer of 1 John, as indicated previously, offers the same suggestion that being led by God entails being "perfected" in divine love: "If we love one another, God lives in us, and his love is perfected in us" (1 John 4:12). God's love could be perfected in a human *partially* or *incompletely* at a time. In that case, it would not make the relevant human perfect *overall* (cf. 1 John 1:8), but it would make perfect some feature of a person, such as an act or attitude of love at a time. So, humans need not be perfectly loving overall, or without exception, to be in a process of being perfected in divine love.

Relative to the *overall* status of a human, that human could be an incomplete work in progress toward overall perfect love. So, divine love could be in a process of *being perfected* in a person overall. The central role of a process over time figures in Paul's following remark: "Not that I have already ... reached the goal; but I press on to make it my own, because Christ Jesus has made me his own. Beloved, I do not consider that I have made it my own; but this one thing I do: forgetting what lies behind and straining forward to what lies ahead, I press on toward the goal for the prize of the heavenly call of God in Christ Jesus"

(Phil. 3:12–14). With a similar emphasis on maturation over time, Paul talks of a cooperative process of "making holiness perfect in the fear of God" (2 Cor. 7:1). The righteous love in *agapē* would include the kind of "holiness" Paul had in mind, and God could foster it through a developmental process in order to honor maturing human agency. It thus would be holy love in progress, for the sake of human maturation. (On the relevant kind of maturity, see Lehmann 1963.)

God may want humans now to be cooperative works in progress, needing a process over time, to perfect divine love in them. If God is perfectly loving, the central goal of the process would be the cooperative perfecting of all humans in divine love, in relationship with God and other humans, and this goal would be intrinsically valuable. Perfect love would aim to be uncoercive, universal, and relational in that way. Otherwise, it would face a moral defect that undermines moral perfection, and thus would be inappropriate to a God worthy of worship. We have no reason to hold, in any case, that God would have to perfect divine love in a person synchronically or instantaneously overall. The divine effort instead could be diachronic, and it thus could attend to the cooperative maturation of humans over time in relation with God's perfect moral character.

5 CONVICTED IN *AGAPĒ*

Our talk of "being led" by God toward divine love suggests a distinctive moral *experience* of being led in the perfecting of divine love in one's life. This experience ideally would figure in an ongoing interpersonal and dispositional relationship with God. It thus would be related to something more than episodes or actions, such as enduring states of persons (see Moser 2017, chap. 2). How are we to think of this moral experience with regard to its qualitative character?

Human moral conscience, being central to a morally good human life, would play a role, and the experience would include *being convicted* in moral conscience regarding selfishness on some occasion. On the positive side, the experience would include being convicted as being challenged, and thus being intruded upon, in conscience to cooperate with the source of the conviction, in loving others unselfishly, even one's enemies. It thus would be responsive to a challenge that includes uncoercive volitional pressure or nudging in intruding upon one, and it thereby would engage one's moral direction in life. It could do this by posing a sharp contrast in conscience with one's own moral shortcomings, leaving one with a decision to make: to cooperate or not to cooperate with the challenge. Being an intrusion upon one, the pressure would appear not to be of one's own making or doing. This kind of experience is widely neglected in contemporary philosophy of religion and theology, but it merits careful attention in a religious epistemology attentive to one's being led by God.

The self-presentation of God's moral character and will to someone could provide uncoercive nudging or challenging if it gives a sharp contrast with one's present character and will. It could occur in one's conscience when one experiences, or has one's attention attracted by, a sharp contrast between divine love toward oneself (as a kind of opponent or enemy of God) and one's lack of love for one's own enemies. If a person is cooperative and does not suppress the divine pressure, this self-manifestation would create a conflict of conscience and an existential dissonance for that person. It thus would call for a resolution, either in favor of enemy love (and God) or against it (and God). God would self-manifest the standard in a divine morally perfect personality or character to a human, and this indicative state for a person could ground an imperative for that person to be led by, or conformed to, God's moral character. So, a vital moral duty could arise from divine self-manifestation by which a person is cooperatively convicted.

Importantly, our moral experience is not empty or flat with regard to moral challenges in conscience. It is, instead, highly textured, with all of the ups and downs of an active conscience. Our world of moral experience did not have to be this way; it could have been very different. It could have been akin, for instance, to the morally uneventful world of goldfish or garden snakes. Perhaps the ongoing challenges in our moral experience indicate an intentional source of uncoercive challenge, beyond our human society, to our moral indifference and failure. At least this is a live option, and it deserves careful attention from responsible inquirers.

As direct evidence for *God's* reality and character, one's being convicted toward perfect goodness would not be a purely physical process, because it would be inherently purposive. The purposive or intentional component in being convicted by God could emerge saliently in experience, with human cooperation toward it, as the *goal-directedness* of one's being convicted emerges. If God seeks the perfecting of divine love in humans over time, and they cooperate with divine conviction toward that end, their experience will feature an *intentional increase* in loving others, in depth and in scope. This increase would rest on one's increasingly being convicted by God toward perfect moral goodness, including the love of one's enemies. Such an interpersonal process would be irreducibly purposive or intentional. In addition, by including love of my enemies, it would counter any suggestion that the process results just from my ordinary desires or imagination. It would, in fact, go against my natural desires. We thus might say that divine love is bigger than we are in a way that requires us to be led, via conviction, into this love by the morally perfect agent who has it perfectly.

The relevant type of "being convicted" is mentioned in John 16:8: "When [the Spirit of God] comes, he will convict the world concerning sin and righteousness and judgment" (RSV, using "convict" from the margin). It also emerges in

Revelation 3:19, portraying the Spirit of God as speaking: "As many as I love, I convict and instruct" (my translation). In addition, it is implicit in Psalm 139:1, in its talk of one's being "searched" and "known" by God. If there can be convicting a person as challenging that person *against* sin and evil, there also can be convicting a person as challenging, and thus intruding upon, that person *toward* righteousness, including righteous love. So, being convicted need not be simply a negative phenomenon; it can have a positive moral and interpersonal goal toward which one is challenged. John 16:8 suggests as much, although the point is widely neglected (cf. John 16:15). Being convicted toward loving others, in any case, need not be static over time but could deepen beyond self-interested goals over time. The deepening would include one's becoming *increasingly* loving toward others, even toward one's enemies. This is central to Paul's two short prayers noted above, and it agrees with the love commands issued by Jesus (Mark 12:30–31; cf. John 21:15–19).

The kind of "being convicted" under consideration differs from what some philosophers and theologians have called "conviction." We can gain some clarity by way of contrast. James McClendon and James Smith offer the following definition: "A 'conviction' ... is a persistent belief such that if X (a person or a community) has a conviction, it will not easily be relinquished and it cannot be relinquished without making X a significantly different person (or community) than before" (1975, p. 7). A "persistent belief" of that sort differs from being convicted in the manner indicated above, because such a belief need not include the passive experiential feature of an agent's *being* convicted. In particular, it need not include an intrusion from volitional pressure on an agent that appears not to be of the agent's own making or doing. A persistent belief could arise solely from one's active commitments without one's being *intruded upon* in the manner suggested. So, being convicted does not reduce to a persistent belief, even a persistent belief that would significantly change a believer upon its omission.

Willem Zuurdeeg has characterized conviction as follows: "We take the term 'conviction' to mean all persuasions concerning the meaning of life; concerning good and bad; concerning gods and devils; concerning representations of the ideal man, the ideal state, the ideal society, concerning the meaning of history, of nature, and of the All" (1958, p. 26). He identifies the following definition as "closest" to his usage: "a certainty of a thorough kind; a strong persuasion or belief; ... a state of being fully persuaded" (p. 25). If persuasions are just "strong beliefs," however, they will not capture the previous talk of being convicted, because they do not capture the component of an agent's being intruded upon in being convicted, beyond the agent's own making or doing. My strong persuasions can come from my own commitments without an apparent intrusion on me from beyond me and my making or doing. Being convicted has a feature of such intrusion that need not be present in persuasions as strong beliefs.

Zuurdeeg acknowledges the role of one's being "overcome" by a convictor in at least some convictions, and this moves in the right direction. As Chapter 1 noted, however, he misses the mark in characterizing a role for a convictor as follows: "People are convinced because a Good, a Cause, or a God has taken hold of them. They cannot help themselves; for they are drawn irresistibly" (p. 30). His previous definition of "conviction" does not require a convictor beyond the person with strong persuasions, but in adding an *irresistible* convictor the approach goes wrong. Being convicted by God, as Chapter 1 noted, would not require that God be irresistible, whereby people "cannot help themselves." A divine challenge or intrusion in conscience could allow for human rejection of it (if only by their turning away), thus preserving a role for genuine human agency in being convicted by God. The same point applies to the key idea of being led by (the Spirit of) God. Omission of a role for human agency will result in a coercive approach to the divine leading of humans; implausibly, it will omit the key role for human cooperation. Our understanding of conviction by God should preserve the role of human cooperation.

Edgar P. Dickie, as Chapter 1 indicated, has recommended a kind of conviction that omits a cooperative component. It arises from a coercive part of reality, and it does not depend on the will of a human. He illustrates: "We believe because we must, and we also believe that the coercion comes from God" (1954, p. 37). This is not the kind of conviction appropriate to a God of perfect love, who would aim to sustain the genuine agency of humans in relating to God. Without such agency, if we have a God, we would not have a God who supports interpersonal relations of love between God and human agents. Coercion of human wills regarding (reception of) God extinguishes an opportunity in this connection for a human to be a genuine responsible agent in a relation of love toward God.

Dickie offers the following position noted in Chapter 1: "[Divine] revelation produces conviction and the conviction so produced may be characterized by the sense that all is of God; that it is the divine truth itself which comes to the human heart to exercise a sway that cannot be challenged or gainsaid" (p. 19). This is misleading if God seeks interpersonal relationships with genuine responsible agents. The first problem arises from the suggested sense of the conviction that "all is of God." This is too abstract and sweepingly metaphysical as a characterization of a wide range of evident experiences of being convicted by God. A different sense of "being convicted" is more germane to God's moral character: the sense of being loved by a supreme being and nudged uncoercively by that being toward loving others. The latter sense helpfully removes the relevant experiences from the domain of abstract metaphysical reflection and locates them properly in actual moral experience, such as in uncoercive volitional pressure toward moral perfection.

In addition, it avoids any commitment to the dubious sense that "all is of God," on the assumption that some things evidently arise from God's enemies, and not from God (see Matt. 13:27–30).

The second problem with Dickie's position is its talk of truth in conviction that exercises "a sway that cannot be challenged or gainsaid." If, as Chapter 1 indicated, "to gainsay" means "to deny, oppose, or contradict," the conviction from a perfectly loving God who respects human agency in this area *could* be gainsaid by humans. Indeed, a lament from numerous Biblical writers is that God's effort to convict God's people is opposed or otherwise rejected by them. This lesson emerges from the prophets in ancient Israel, and it is true to familiar religious experience. Neither human experience nor its history gives us a good reason to deny that humans can oppose or otherwise reject a divine effort to convict them toward love for God and other humans.

The deepening or extending of being convicted to love others as God does would be crucial to the experience of being led by God in an *intentional*, goal-directed manner. The experience would not stop with a person's attitude or behavior toward one recipient of love, but it would extend over time to all available recipients. It would be an ongoing process moving *toward a goal*, thus making it intentional and not haphazard or otherwise nonpersonal. In being thus convicted, we would get evidence of an *intentional agent*, rather than a mere physical process, at work in guiding us toward loving others. This would take us beyond a story of mere efficient causation to a morally relevant experience of the purpose or intention of a loving agent in action.

The process of being convicted by God would be cooperative, in order to preserve responsible human agency in yielding to God. So, one would need to allow oneself to be convicted by God toward loving others, because the power in being convicted toward divine love would be uncoercive power. In that respect, it would be cooperative power and thus cooperative conviction. This would preserve the genuine interpersonality or interagency of the phenomenon of being convicted toward love. In this vein, Paul offers the following injunction: "Do not quench the Spirit" (1 Thess. 5:19; cf. Eph. 4:30, Isa. 63:10). We may paraphrase that injunction: Do not resist cooperative conviction from God. Humans thus can be challenged to cooperate in their being convicted toward divine love, and they can settle on a decision by way of response. So, this is no matter of coercive impulsion. Talk of "irresistible overwhelming" thus distorts what occurs in divine conviction in moral experience.

A person who perfectly exemplifies divine love for people will place no restriction on willing what is good all things considered for them, including forgiving them for any wrongdoing and accompanying guilt. Many humans, however, opt for restrictions in this area, owing to fear, insecurity, and selfishness. Conflict in human relationships then results. An intentional move beyond such restrictions can be a sign of the divine moral deepening of humans as co-workers with God in loving others. Without such deepening when an opportunity arises, divine love would not be guiding or leading human love. This deepening would be part of the perfecting of divine love in humans, as suggested by the writer of 1 John. Contrary processes would be at best counterfeits of the real article, that is, being led by God via conviction in moral experience.

Being led by God figures directly in divine lordship. If we are to know God *as God*, that is, as authoritative *Lord* over all of created reality, we would need to allow God to be known as Lord over us and our lives. So, we would need to allow God to *lead* us, and thus to convict us, in God's ways that bear on human life. Otherwise, God would not be *our* God in being *our* Lord, even if we acknowledge God's existence. Set on what is best for us, all things considered, God would lead us by convicting us uncoercively to exist and to behave in accordance with God's perfectly good character and will rather than our contrary will.

If we are not convicted in moral conscience by God, then God would not be Lord over us in any morally relevant way, and, in that regard, we would not be responsible children of God (as Rom. 8:14 implies). So, we could block our knowing God as Lord, if we wish, by not allowing ourselves to be convicted by God toward divine love for others. This lesson agrees with the aforementioned test for knowing God: "Whoever does not love does not know God, for God is love" (1 John 4:7–8). Such a test gains sharpness in conviction, by way of contrast with our ordinary tendencies, when it includes the New Testament command to love even one's enemies.

It would be misleading to try to reduce divine self-manifestation to (*de dicto*) propositional truths (that something is the case). That would omit the underlying nonpropositional reality of such truths: God's actual moral character of perfect goodness, including perfect love for all other agents. Wilhelm Herrmann has noted a danger here: "*Information concerning God*, although it may claim to be of divine revelation, can only bring that troubled piety that lives by no delivering act of God, but by men's own exertions" (1903 [1971], p. 58). We can identify the core of the relevant "delivering act of God" in human moral experience, in terms of cooperative human conviction by the self-manifesting God toward God's moral character.

The self-manifestation of divine love to a human person does not require the expression, divine or human, of a *de dicto* judgment that God loves a human person. Instead, it can be an expression of divine love in statement-free action of self-manifestation toward a human person. This seems to be part of an announcement attributed to God in Romans 10:20, citing Isaiah 65:1: "I have shown myself to those who did not ask for me." This kind of divine self-manifestation delivers moral power to human experience in a way absent from mere moral claims. Divine convicting of humans thus can include a self-manifestation on God's part without a verbal or propositional accompaniment.

God could offer a *de re* manifesting of divine love in order to create a sharp contrast with and a salient challenge to a selfish human state. Such a manifesting would include God's *de re* expression of the divine moral character in action toward an attentive person. A verbal or propositional interpretation from God may or may not join this expression. We are familiar with this distinction, in general, from cases where a human shows an act of striking kindness to an enemy without saying a word. A moral character presented in action can self-manifest moral goodness, and thereby the contours of a moral challenge and duty, for a person. So, not all significant content in being morally convicted is verbal or propositional. Qualitative experiential content lies at the base, and it can prompt verbal interpretation while not requiring it. This is not surprising if God is an intentional agent or spirit, and not just propositional information.

In being convicted by God, one would face the basis of an indicative and of an imperative in moral experience, that is, the basis of a gift and of a duty. The basis of an indicative or a gift would be the experienced presence of divine love for oneself (and others), and the basis of an imperative or a duty would be the experienced volitional pressure on one toward loving others, even enemies, as God does. This twofold basis could serve as one's experiential foundation for not only a theistic religion but also a theological ethics. I suspect that it is the most resilient and meaning-laden foundation available to humans, and that it could underwrite the epistemic status of some testimony from others about God's intervention in their moral experience.

The twofold basis could have an indispensable *practical* role in theistic religion and theological ethics for a person, that is, in living in accordance with one's religion and its ethics. It could bring religion and its ethics out of the domain of mere thought and talk into the domain of felt experience and moral struggle. A challenging historical model for the latter domain is Jesus in Gethsemane (see Mark 14:32–39; cf. Moser 2013, chaps. 1 and 3). Thought and talk may be cheap, but the reality of a challenging Gethsemane experience with God would be priceless for humans open to lived meaning or purpose in *agapē* (see Moser 2017, chaps. 4 and 5). We need to relate this conviction-oriented approach to spiritual discernment.

6 DISCERNING GOD

One's being cooperatively convicted in being led by God toward loving others would have evidential or epistemic significance regarding God's reality, at least directly for oneself. One thereby would allow what needs to be discerned (God's moral character and will of perfect love) to enter saliently, if elusively at times, into one's own domain of awareness and agency. In doing so, one would allow the showing or presenting of God's moral character and will directly to oneself, a character and will centered in righteous *agapē*. In resisting or ignoring cooperative conviction by God, one would disallow such entering of the experienced divine presence and thereby disadvantage the discerning of God's character and will from one's experiential perspective. One's volitional perspective then would be uncooperative or oppositional in ways that block vital available evidence regarding God's reality and will. Here we can acknowledge a relevant distinction between the evidence *available* to one and the evidence one actually *receives* regarding God's reality and moral character.

The writer of 1 John links one's cooperating with the perfecting of divine love with confidence toward God: "Love is perfected with us, in order that we may have confidence [before God]" (1 John 4:17, my translation). The confidence is based on the unique experiential evidence received directly from God in one's allowing oneself to be convicted and thereby led by God toward loving others.

We find a similar lesson about discerning God's reality and will in Paul's letter to the Romans: "I appeal to you therefore, brothers and sisters, by the mercies of God, to present your bodies as a living sacrifice, holy and acceptable to God, which is your spiritual worship. Do not be conformed to this world, but be transformed by the renewing of your minds, so that you may discern what is the will of God – what is good and acceptable and perfect" (Rom. 12:1–2). Discerning God's will thus calls for a transformation of one's mindset, or overall intellectual and motivational perspective on things. This transformation comes via cooperative participation in divine, self-sacrificial *agapē*: "Present your bodies as a living sacrifice, holy and acceptable to God." Here is where God's unique moral power would be experienced directly by humans. In allowing it to approach us directly in our being cooperatively convicted toward love, we would gain salient access to it, despite our selfish tendencies.

Paul, as indicated, endorses the epistemic significance of experienced *agapē* in connection with an offering or gift from God: "Hope [in God] does not disappoint us, because God's love (*agapē*) has been poured into our hearts through the Holy Spirit that has been given to us" (Rom. 5:5). Paul would say the same for faith in God: Its evidential anchor is in something to be received cooperatively from God, directly in experience, and that something is integral to God's moral character: perfect divine *agapē*.

The cooperative reception of faith in God is no mere armchair reflection. It is, instead, the thoroughgoing resolve, under cooperative conviction, to allow God to lead one to love others as God does. This includes a profound moral and spiritual transformation, a sea change, for ordinary humans, owing to the significant difference between perfect divine love and ordinary human ways. Even so, the transformation can proceed synchronically, with due attention to human obstacles and weaknesses. The goal of being perfected in divine love for humans does not come in an instant, if it comes at all.

The needed transformation for discerning God's reality and suffering can benefit from suffering, according to Paul (2 Cor. 4:6–8, 12:6–7; Rom. 8:17), by excluding boasting in oneself and by acknowledging *God's* unique power in *agapē*. Paul portrays God as hoping to nudge people toward *agapē* on a grand scale: "The creation was subjected to futility, not of its own will but by the will of the one who subjected it, in hope that the creation itself will be set free from its bondage to decay and will obtain the freedom of the glory of the children of God" (Rom. 8:20–21). As noted, the "children of God," according to Paul (Rom. 8:14), are people cooperatively led, and thus convicted, by the Spirit of God. In this perspective, ignoring or resisting the needed conviction will hinder the kind of transformation crucial to discerning God's will and perhaps even God's reality. In that case, important available evidence regarding God will be obscured or blocked by an uncooperative person. One then will obstruct and frustrate the "God who is at work in you, enabling you both to will and to work for his good pleasure" (Phil. 2:13).

Human discernment of God's reality and will, in one's cooperatively being convicted and led by God, does not entail anything near a full understanding of God's purposes, including divine purposes in allowing suffering and evil. No full theodicy is available to us now, despite the wide range of theodicies offered by philosophers and theologians. Even so, we need not concede skepticism about God's reality or will, because having salient evidence of God's reality and will does not require a full understanding of God's purposes in allowing suffering and evil. Having adequate evidence about God's reality, based in cooperative conviction toward *agapē*, does not require having full evidence about God and God's purposes. We can know in part without knowing in full. (Chapter 8 returns to this theme.)

Rufus Jones has pointed to an important kind of widely neglected evidence for God's reality:

I suspect with a good deal of reason that there is a divine push, a Godward striving, a divine *urge*, revealed in the central nucleus of my being.... I cannot explain the whole of myself without bringing in God.... And I do not look toward finding Him by going back in an infinite regress in time, but rather by going forward toward a Beyond within that forever draws me.... The monumental evidence of God is, I believe, the fact of spiritual personality through which divine traits of character are revealed (1931, pp. 215–17; cf. Moser 2010, chap. 4).

The divine "urge" mentioned by Jones fits with what I have called "being convicted and led" by God, as long as we do not regard the urge as coercing an agent's will. The relevant divine pressure on one's will could be rejected or ignored by one, if one so chooses.

An important role for inference to a best available explanation emerges in the claim that "I cannot explain the whole of myself without bringing in God." If the best available explanation of my being convicted toward *agapē* is that God seeks to lead me, and nothing in my experience defeats this explanation, we may endorse talk of suspecting "with a good deal of reason that there is a divine push." The foundational evidence will be in the (qualitative contents of the) convictional experience, but explanatory considerations can figure in an argument for a positive epistemic status. (Chapter 8 returns to this topic, with an example from moral conviction; see also Moser 2017, chap. 5.)

One can recommend a theistic interpretation of religious experience as being reasonable on an explanatory basis, so long as a person has the relevant experience. This consideration enables us to reject Arthur Campbell Garnett's talk in Chapter 6 of an interpretive "guess" here. An interpretive best available explanation for a person is no guess; it is an interpretation grounded in one's overall evidence. It is also common in the sciences, where the relevant evidence is socially readily shareable. We should not rule it out in principle in contexts of religious evidence.

7 CONVICTIONAL KNOWLEDGE

We now can introduce a notion of direct *convictional knowledge* of God: It is knowledge of God grounded directly in the convicting self-manifestation of the divine character of morally perfect love to a cooperative human. This kind of *de re* knowledge of God, involving a direct I–Thou acquaintance relation, differs significantly from theoretical knowledge that God exists, even though it can be the basis for knowledge (and well-grounded belief) that God exists.

A redemptive God would prefer direct convictional knowledge over theoretical knowledge for the following reason noted by David Forrest: "It is easy to disregard the divine when it is conceived as a theoretical truth, however conclusive the demonstration of it may seem to be, but not when it discloses itself as involved in what we *are*. It then becomes a 'presence not to be put by,' because the commonest incidents of every day contain intimations and reminders of it" (1906, p. 385). A perfectly loving God would not want to be easily disregarded by humans in need of God, and therefore would seek to give an experiential basis for convictional knowledge to receptive humans.

The rationale for God's preferring direct convictional knowledge among humans would be a divine aim for moral transformation and reconciliation from humans, based on divine leading toward God's character. As perfectly good, God would be resolute toward such transformation and reconciliation, and therefore would need to engage humans at a deep motivational level, with due respect for their cooperation as agents. Cooperative conviction would serve this divine purpose in a unique way, despite its widespread neglect in the literature of theology and the philosophy of religion. An excessive stress on the intellectual component of faith has led to the neglect of such conviction.

We now can see why morally transformative, convictional knowledge of God cannot be "impartial" in a way that omits human affections and volitional cooperation.

Robust moral transformation of a person involves not only one's thoughts but also one's affections and will. One must thereby be *sympathetic* in cooperation toward the moral goodness of God on offer. Here we find a contrast between theoretical scientific knowledge, as typically characterized, and morally transformative interpersonal knowledge. If convictional knowledge of God's reality and character is inherently morally transformative, it resists being included in theoretical scientific knowledge, owing to the role of one's affections and will in being cooperatively convicted toward God's moral character. Partiality toward the goodness on offer in being convicted by God would be no impediment to convictional knowledge of God and would be, in fact, a requirement. This follows from the role of sympathetic interpersonal cooperation in such knowledge. One's motivational base thus would be as important as one's informational base in convictional knowledge.

Convictional knowledge of God calls for a distinction between private and public evidence of God's reality and character. One can be cooperatively convicted by God without anyone else sharing in the evidence from one's experience of being thus convicted. So, convictional knowledge of God would not need to be socially shared or even readily shareable knowledge. Even so, it *could* be socially shared by people who cooperate with being convicted by God in the same manner. As a result, convictional knowledge could be edifying for a group of people and thereby contribute to a flourishing community. It can have a vital social role without being *inherently* social among humans.

In convictional knowledge of God, one knows *God* directly, and not just the effects of God. Such knowledge thus differs from the kind of knowledge typically proposed by natural theology, on the basis of arguments affirming a first cause of contingent events, design in nature, fine-tuning in nature, or consciousness in humans. The inherently personal moral character of God is missing from the proposed evidence underlying such arguments of natural theology.

This omission prevents the evidence from having the personal and moral robustness required of a God worthy of worship, and it leaves one at best with a lesser god.

A first cause, designer, or fine-tuner from natural theology gives no indication of having the kind of moral perfection required for worthiness of worship. Such an entity thus falls short of the morally perfect God acknowledged by the prominent versions of traditional monotheism. In addition, getting to a lesser god, *if* natural theology can, offers no well-grounded move toward a God worthy of worship; one still would need an account of that move. A perfectly good God, in any case, would have no need of the speculative and dubious arguments of natural theology (see Moser 2020 for further discussion).

If there is human knowledge of God available through the created world, it will include evidence of God's morally perfect character. Otherwise, the evidence would not be evidence of a God worthy of worship, that is, the God of traditional monotheism. So, the question is whether God could self-manifest the divine moral character through the created world. An affirmative answer would not yield natural theology of a traditional sort, because it would not assume that the created world *by itself* (i.e., as a strictly natural world) yields a good argument for God's reality. Instead, it assumes that *God* would self-manifest the divine moral character through some part of the created world. This fits with Paul's view in Romans 1:19 that *God* shows himself through the created world, without any assumption that the created world by itself does this or somehow yields a good argument for God's reality on the basis of strictly natural considerations.

A good place to look for evidence of God's reality in the created world is in the *personal agents* being cooperatively conformed to God's moral character. This fits with Paul's question to Christians at Corinth: "Do you not know that you are God's temple and that God's Spirit dwells in you?" (1 Cor. 3:16). It also agrees with his following remark to the

Corinthian Christians: "You yourselves are our letter, written on our hearts, to be known and read by all; and you show that you are a letter of Christ, prepared by us, written not with ink but with the Spirit of the living God, not on tablets of stone but on tablets of human hearts" (2 Cor. 3:2–3; cf. Matt. 5:16, John 13:35). These considerations point to inherently interpersonal evidence of God, beyond any nonpersonal effects of God. Elsewhere I have called this "personifying evidence of God's reality" as an alternative to natural theology (see Moser 2010; cf. Moser 2020). Convictional knowledge of God figures centrally in this alternative.

Given that convictional knowledge of God is inherently interpersonal, and not mechanical or coercive, human agents easily can miss out on it under certain circumstances. In particular, they can miss out on the relevant direct evidence of God's reality and moral character. Owing to the sharp contrast between God's moral character and typical human moral characters, we should expect some difficulty, struggle, and stress in the human appropriation of divine self-manifestation as evidence for God. We have no reason to suppose that the process would be easy or challenge-free. Its inherent challenge to us in our moral shortcomings can be difficult for us.

We would need to discern, attend to, and ultimately cooperate with the divine self-manifestation on offer. This demands that we look in the right place, where God's moral character would be self-revealed by God. We may not want to go there, however, preferring instead to avoid being convicted by God. So, with bluntness appropriate to some cases, John's Gospel remarks: "All who do evil hate the light and do not come to the light, so that their deeds may not be exposed [or convicted]" (John 3:20). We may think of this as a common human tendency toward conviction-avoidance and *agapē*-avoidance. This tendency, given the nature of convictional knowledge, can block a person from having direct evidence of God's reality and moral character.

We may prefer a mode of *self*-conviction or *self*-convincing to being convicted by God, owing to the moral and spiritual rigors of divine conviction. In that case, we may risk our own self-deceiving in omitting vital, existential truths about ourselves in relation to God. So, we sometimes may experience the hardness, even the severity, of learning to cooperate with God in being convicted toward a life of morally righteous *agapē*. (On divine severity, see Moser 2013.) We decide in favor of an alternative in some cases, and thereby avoid the kind of direct interpersonal experience of God found in cooperative conviction by God. We thus sidestep the important cognitive lesson of John 7:17 about Jesus and his Father: "Anyone who resolves to do the will of God will know whether the teaching is from God or whether I am speaking on my own."

Resolving to do the will of God can have not only moral value for humans but also cognitive value. It can be the cooperative doorway to receiving salient evidence of God's reality and moral character. Indeed, it may be the opening to God's providing a sui generis self-authentication and defense of divine reality and goodness. In this perspective, the ultimate "apologetics" or defense for theism comes in cooperative convictional knowledge, and not in anything speculative or abstract (see Moser 2017, chap. 5). It would come from the intervening God who self-manifests the perfect character of God, in *agapē* poured out in cooperative humans. This kind of cognitive process would be no mere academic matter. It would make a person morally new, after the moral character of God. An open but vital question is whether humans are willing to cooperate with the intervening divine self-manifestation.

Moral conviction of wrongdoing can make us feel small morally, and thus we tend to prefer to avoid it. Our moral pride often aims to cover our moral shortcomings, and, in doing so, it can obscure evidence of divine activity in our experience. Such pride can interfere with our candidly testing for God's reality and presence, with a kind of moral religious experiment. The moral experiment would be to examine whether one's moral experience does indeed indicate one's being led, via one's conscience, away from selfishness to righteous *agapē* in one's life with others, including one's enemies. This would require ongoing candor about one's moral standing toward others and one's moral experience. It thus would be easy to ignore or distort for the sake of moral comfort. Even so, there could be a vital role for such an experiment in religious life. (For relevant discussion, see Farrer 1966, chap. 6.)

8 GIFT FOR IMITATION

One might say that the divine self-presentation of *agapē* comes as an unconditional gift to a person, by divine grace rather than by human earning. The reality of the situation, however, would be more complicated. A perfectly caring God would not offer a gift in a way that the offer or the gift brings moral harm to potential recipients. An unconditional gift of God's caring presence could be abused by a person in a way that morally harms that person. For instance, one could use the gift for selfish purposes that morally corrupt oneself and bring harm to others. In such a case, human control over having a divine gift could oppose the purpose of the gift and empty it of redemptive value. As a result, a perfectly caring God could withdraw the gift from a person, in order not to bring moral harm to that person.

The divine gift in question would include *agapē* as a divine gift to humans, but ideally it would not be merely an event or episode of *agapē*. Instead, it ideally would include a divine offer of an *ongoing relationship* of *agapē* with humans for their moral benefit. A divine expectation, for the good of humans, would be human reciprocity in a relationship of *agapē* toward God (and other humans). So, the mutuality of *agapē* in an ongoing relationship would be God's goal in self-manifestation toward humans. Mere human knowledge that God exists would fall short of this goal. Such factual knowledge that God exists would serve only as a means to God's more demanding goal of an ongoing relationship of mutual *agapē* with humans. The latter goal would result from God's being perfectly good toward humans, and therefore seeking what is morally and spiritually best for them. (On this goal, see Moser 2017, chaps. 2 and 5.)

The ongoing relationship sought by God as Spirit would seek the reconciliation of humans to God, ideally without their depending on sight, touch, or any other sensory experience. This goal fits with God's not being a sensory object or depending on a sensory object for existence. It also fits with the theme from Paul that in relation to God "we walk by faith, not by sight" (2 Cor. 5:7). The result is the divine expectation for humans to work on a relationship without a sensory safety net. Even if sensory factors loom large when the relationship is young and immature, they are to drop off as maturity enters, for the sake of focus on God as Spirit (see Maltby 1921). The focus then becomes interpersonal and intervolitional, intentional will to intentional Will. God's morally perfect will then can relay power to a human will without interference or distraction from sensory factors. A real danger in relying on sensory factors as central to a relationship with God is idolatry: taking those factors to be as important as God. This calls for the ban on such idolatry in the first commandment of Exodus 20:4.

Working without a sensory safety net, in relation to God, does not reduce to working without an *evidential* net. God can supply evidence of divine reality and presence without relying on sensory evidence. God's self-presentation of the perfect divine will to a person, such as in moral conscience, does not depend on sensory evidence of God. So, fideism about divine evidence has no foothold here. Even so, the relevant evidence is anything but convenient and easy for typical humans. It calls for their extreme makeover, from a moral point of view.

It would be morally counterproductive for God to offer an ongoing relationship of *agapē* to humans if they would abuse it for their opposing selfish purposes. Such an offer also could strengthen, rather than weaken, human opposition to God, in cases where humans are set on their selfishness. So, God would wait for an opportune time to offer the relationship to humans, given a divine desire for human cooperation with it. This could include God's withdrawing an offer until humans are ready to cooperate with it. Such withdrawing, however, would not remove divine *agapē* toward humans. Instead, it would stem from divine *agapē* for them, including a sincere concern for what is morally best for them.

The divine offer of an ongoing relationship with humans, and the corresponding gift of grace in relationship, would be sensitive to human receptivity as cooperation. So, they would not qualify as ordinary, irrevocable "gifts." They would not be given by a perfectly good God without the prospect of withdrawal or retraction. Instead, they would be divine *entrustments* or entrusted gifts subject to God's withdrawal or retraction upon (impending) human abuse. So, it can be misleading to talk of divine grace in an offered relationship as a "gift" without qualification. In addition, such talk can have a negative effect on human attitudes toward God, leading people to take a divine gift of grace for granted, as if it did not come with divine expectations or conditions for its maintenance by them. The negative effect can lead to a neglect of the need for human perseverance in relation to God (on which, see Berkouwer 1958). As a result, human indifference toward divine grace can result, owing to neglect of its expected rigors. This lesson about grace in relationship has been largely neglected in theology and the philosophy of religion, to the detriment of our understanding the evidence for God's reality.

Divine self-manifestation as evidence for God's reality, in keeping with divine grace in relationship, would not be an unqualified gift. Instead, it would be an entrusted gift, or an entrustment, to humans. Owing to a divine redemptive purpose, such evidence would come and go in a manner sensitive to human receptivity as cooperation. As perfectly good, God would not be complicit in human abuse of this evidence. Otherwise, God's moral standing as worthy of worship, and thus perfectly caring for the good of humans, would be at risk. So, God would be discerning about the opportunities for divine self-manifestation to humans and would not be promiscuous in presenting such evidence of the divine reality and presence. Nothing good would be gained by evidential promiscuity in this area, and real harm could threaten if humans abuse, neglect, or trivialize the evidence they need for their flourishing. So, we cannot separate the subject of foundational evidence for God's reality from morally relevant considerations about its potential recipients, particularly their morally relevant attitudes toward it and its value.

Divine self-manifestation that yields static and irrevocable evidence for God's reality would not accommodate God's redemptive character or purposes toward humans. God thus would be selective at times in self-manifestation to humans for redemptive purposes. For instance, in cases where some people are not ready to handle divine self-manifestation in a cooperative manner, God would withhold self-manifestation for their benefit. This would be a kind of redemptive divine hiding, and it would falsify the view that occurrent evidence for God's reality is uniformly possessed by all people or always possessed by all people. Any theory of evidence that excludes such divine hiding would threaten God's morally perfect character and thus be inadequate to that extent. (Chapter 8 returns to this topic; see also Moser 2017, chap. 3.) Some proponents of traditional natural theology offer their arguments as if they can offer good evidence for all reflective people. This perspective does not fit well with the portrait of a redemptive God who hides at times for the good of some people. (For relevant misgivings toward that perspective, see Moser 2010, chap. 3; Moser 2020.)

A God worthy of worship, as suggested, would be a morally perfect agent with morally perfect goals. One of these intended goals would be to have the divine moral character cooperatively welcomed and reflected in human lives, for the moral good of humans. This would include an aim for *imitatio Dei*, the intentional imitation of God's moral character by humans, in attitude and in action. As responsible moral agents, humans would need to cooperate with God in the process of their moral maturation, but only on the basis of supporting evidence of God's trustworthiness. Otherwise, their needed moral development would rest on something no more stable than wishful thinking.

De re faith in God would include a favorable commitment with trust toward divine convicting and leading, such as in one's conscience. This would encompass a sympathetic commitment toward cooperating with the divine convicting and leading in one's moral experience. *De re* faith in God thus would be irreducible to factual knowledge that God exists, because its commitment with trust would exceed such knowledge. Its foundational (noninferential) evidential support would come from a self-manifestation of divine moral character in one's experience, and that manifestation would offer moral conviction and guidance to one, even when one has not categorized it as divine. Such faith, then, would have an evidential basis that is cognitively prior to faith itself. The evidential basis in question could have a causal influence on some human beliefs, but it would not be merely causal, given that it would, or at least could, confer epistemic status on a commitment. In addition, the relevant evidence need not be public, or socially shared, but could be private to a person. Similarly, it need not be reproducible by a human, given that, when veridical, its source would be God, and it would not be controllable by a human. God would be self-evidencing in presenting a living moral-character manifestation to humans, and this could serve as foundational evidence for them.

We now see the epistemic significance of one's conception of God, particularly of the moral features it ascribes to God. Those features figure centrally in the self-evidence that God would show to cooperative humans, and that evidence would be foundational (or noninferential) for belief that God exists and for belief in God. God's moral character thus would be epistemically relevant for such belief. The relevant conception of a morally perfect God would exceed a conception of God in mere theism or deism, and, in doing so, it would supply explanatory and evidential potential unknown to mere theism or deism.

Epistemic reasonableness, unlike truth, is person-variable, owing to variation in human experience that lies at the foundation of evidence. This consideration applies directly to the epistemic reasonableness of belief in God and belief that God exists. As a result, it is possible that belief in God is evidentially grounded for one person but not for another, given a difference in their overall experiences. This is no defect in belief in God; it is a consequence of the nature of evidence and epistemic reasonableness. This lesson does not challenge the integrity of evidentially grounded belief in God. Instead, it highlights that such belief owes its epistemic status to the actual evidence and grounding experience a person has. Actual experience thus matters, critically, in this domain, as in matters of evidence generally.

The epistemic reasonableness of a commitment, whether to God's existence or the existence of something else, depends on the absence of evidence that defeats or undermines the (evidence for) the commitment in question. It requires adequate support from the perspective of one's overall evidence rather than just part of one's evidence. In this respect, epistemic reasonableness is ultimately holistic relative to one's evidence. So, the epistemic reasonableness of theistic religious commitment depends on the bearing of defeaters on (evidence for) that commitment. We turn, then, to the topic of relevant defeaters of theistic religious commitment.

8

∾

Religious Experience Cognized

Defeaters

Chapter 7 explained how a theistic interpretation of religious experience could have an evidential basis in a person's moral experience. It identified divine self-manifestation in human experience as a potential source of foundational evidence that does not depend for its being evidence on an inference. It also acknowledged an intentional component in some experienced evidence that convicts a person toward God's moral character and thereby includes divine leading of a person in moral transformation. Such evidence is purposive in indicating a goal-directed move toward one's being perfected in divine love. Being thus purposive, the evidence indicates the activity of an intentional agent in the convicting and leading of a human person. Chapter 7 proposed that the evidence in question could figure in a best available explanation of one's religious experience in terms of a theistic interpretation.

A pressing question is whether the theistic evidence characterized in Chapter 7 faces defeaters that undermine it for all people who have it. Some skeptics about God's existence will offer an affirmative answer, and some theists will propose a negative answer. So, we need to look at some influential proposed defeaters regarding the evidence in question. This chapter will assess potential defeaters from three areas: evil in the world, divine hiddenness of a relevant kind, and religious diversity in beliefs found in religion. We shall see that the evidence in dispute is resilient against the proposed defeaters for some people in some contexts.

1 SKEPTICISM AND DEFEATERS

Any claim to epistemically justified belief in God will elicit challenges from skeptics of various persuasions. Skeptics can introduce a specific conception of epistemic justification that makes particular demands on such justification and thereby blocks justified belief in God. For instance, a conception of epistemic justification could require that all justified beliefs get their semantic meaning from sensory experience (as various proponents of Humean skepticism have suggested; on which, see Watkins 1984). In that case, justified belief in God will be ruled out, owing to supposed defects in the very idea of God. Typical notions of God, especially in traditional monotheism, are not defined by sensory experience. Similarly, if a conception of epistemic justification requires logical entailment for an evidential support relation, justified belief in God will be excluded. Such belief does not rest on such a demanding support relation, and that is not a defect in this case.

A serious problem arises for the skeptics in question. Nonskeptics are not required by reason or evidence to accept the stringent conceptions of epistemic justification offered by those skeptics. So far as reason and evidence go, they can proceed with alternative conceptions of epistemic justification, and some of those conceptions do not rule out justified belief in God.

Skeptics need not make their case on the basis of a disputed conception of epistemic justification. Instead, they can offer (potential) defeaters of justification for belief in God, while working within a widely accepted notion of epistemic justification. The typical defeaters on offer would undermine justification for one's belief in God when conjoined with one's supporting evidence. Defeaters can be direct, challenging the truth of a belief, or indirect, challenging the evidence for a belief. Defeaters, however, are not mere beliefs (contrary to Plantinga 2000, p. 485). If they were, one could create defeaters just by forming beliefs, but that would make defeat too easy in allowing for the defeat of any evidence one prefers to defeat. Evidence, of course, does not function in that easy way.

We can, and should, ask whether faith that God exists is correct in its interpretation of human experience bearing on God's existence. Correctness would entail fact-based truth and thus factuality, thereby going beyond justified belief about reality to an actual feature of reality. So, a correct interpretation must match the relevant facts. Departure from such a realist approach to truth is philosophically self-refuting (see Moser 1989, chap. 1; 1993, chap. 1), and nobody has explained how we can proceed coherently without such an approach. In particular, faith that God exists cannot be properly understood apart from the question of whether it is true or factual that God exists.

A compelling approach, from an epistemic point of view, to the question of whether faith that God exists is true fits with a broad approach to epistemic reasonableness, the kind of reasonableness suited to factual knowledge. As Chapter 7 suggested, this approach relies on *abduction*, an inference to a best available explanation of the relevant evidence for a person, as a central factor in epistemically reasonable belief (for details, see Moser 1989, 2008, 2017). A person need not always *draw* an inference to a best available explanation to have an epistemically reasonable belief. Instead, the epistemic reasonableness of a belief for a person can depend on there *being available* to that person an inference to a best available explanation from the person's evidence to the belief in question.

Foundational evidence for a person will consist of that person's base of experience. In addition, the nonfoundational evidence for a person will consist of that person's beliefs made epistemically reasonable (for that person) on the basis of the foundational evidence. An epistemic

connection between the two tiers can be an available inference to a best available explanation. One's *belief* that God
exists will be fully grounded when it is suitably based
on the relevant foundational evidence and on the epistemic
connection between that evidence and the belief. The *proposition* that God exists, however, could be epistemically
supported for a person on the basis of experience, even
though that person does not actually base a belief that
God exists on the supporting evidence or epistemic
connection.

An abductive approach to epistemic reasonableness relies
on explanation-seeking why-questions about foundational
evidence in a person's experience. A typical why-question
is: Why am I now having *this* experience, rather than no
experience at all or some other experience? This question
will prompt better or worse answers relative to a person's
overall experience and evidence. My current experience of
apparently being morally convicted, by an intentional
agent, in conscience of my selfishness invites the question
of why I am now having *this* experience rather than no
experience at all or some other experience. A bad answer,
from an abductive point of view, would be that I am now
eating raw onions. The latter answer would not suitably
explain why I am having the moral experience in question.
That answer's content does not suitably elucidate my
experience of being morally convicted in conscience of
my selfishness.

Some skeptics will suggest that my present experience of
being morally convicted in conscience by an intentional
agent could be just a dream or an illusion. On this basis,
they would recommend that I withhold judgment on the
matter. This recommendation, however, would be premature. If "could" indicates logical possibility, we have no
reason to deny the possibility, because neither epistemic
reasonableness nor knowledge rules out the logical possibility of being mistaken. Knowledge, given its truth
condition, rules out the *actuality* of being mistaken, but that

leaves intact the logical possibility of being mistaken. In contrast, epistemic reasonableness does not require truth, because there can be epistemically reasonable belief that is false. So, skeptics using a modal notion of a "possible mistake" would need to clarify the relevant domain of modality and then explain its actual bearing on my actual evidence of moral conviction.

My overall experiential evidence of being morally convicted in conscience does not give me any indication that I am now undergoing a dream or an illusion. I have had numerous dreams and illusory experiences, and, so far as my actual evidence goes, they always have been accompanied by indicators of being dreams or illusory experiences. So, I do not find myself wondering now, in genuine doubt, whether any of my actual experiences is, or has been, a dream or an illusion. I am able to tell, so far as my actual evidence goes, which experiences of mine were dreams or illusions, because my dreams and illusions, given my evidence, have had telltale indicators. Some of the familiar indicators are inconstancy, abruptness, indistinctness, and incongruity. I, among others, have been well aware of such indicators in connection with (what I know to be) dreams and illusions.

My overall present experience of being morally convicted in conscience of my selfishness does not include any of the telltale indicators of a dream or an illusion. So, my present experience does not include any evidence (or indicator) of its being a dream or an illusion. I logically *could* be undergoing a dream or an illusion, but that modal truth is not to the *epistemic* point now. It also logically could be the case that I am not now undergoing a dream or an illusion. Epistemic reasonableness for a person is determined by that person's *actual* truth indicators, and I do not have a truth indicator in my evidence of a dream or an illusion in the present case. The burden is on skeptics to identify an actual indicator of a dream or an illusion, and a mere modal claim will not discharge this burden. Without an actual truth indicator, skeptics will not be able to discharge the burden, and their skeptical challenge then will be neutralized.

We now can identify an important lesson about foundational evidence for faith that a worship-worthy God of perfect *agapē* exists. When I confront a certain kind of righteous *agapē* toward me that is challenging me in my experience, I should ask (at least from an epistemic point of view): Why am I having this *agapē* experience rather than no experience or a different experience? A responsible answer calls for close attention to my actual experience, and I may need to put myself in a suitable position to get such an answer. I may need, for instance, to curb any bias I have against the value of unselfish *agapē*, including such *agapē* directed toward me. I also may need to be willing to cooperate with such *agapē* in order to comply with what God intends it to accomplish.

A perfectly good God would intend divine *agapē* to launch or to sustain a relationship of fellowship or communion between God and a human that is in the best interest of that human. Indeed, God would seek to build a flourishing community or society of free people on the basis of interpersonal righteous *agapē*. If, however, a person is opposed or indifferent to divine *agapē*, God may hide from that person to avoid a kind of harmful rejection that hardens opposition or indifference to God. If God seeks human cooperation within divine *agapē*, God's self-manifestation of such *agapē* to a person would not aim for human responses that encourage fatal alienation or guilt relative to God. (On the relevant kind of communion, see Moser 2017, chap. 5.)

We should not assume that all humans would experience divine *agapē* in exactly the same way. Instead, we should allow for some variability, given distinctiveness in persons and their circumstances. Even so, an important issue will be whether one's experience of *agapē* includes an experience of personal traits suited to a God worthy of worship. Such traits would include the righteous love's being intentional, directed, and nudging without coercion toward a person's imitating and cooperating with it. A key issue will be whether a superhuman agent manifests such intentionality, directedness, and nudging in any human experience. This amounts to the question of whether the manifestation of righteous *agapē* in human experience is a personal disclosure that transcends a human source.

My experience of being presented with and guided toward divine *agapē* could be diachronic rather than just synchronic. In other words, it could take place over time, and not just at a moment. So, I could consider it over time regarding its source, without making a judgment about just a moment of experience. My experience over time could include my moral conscience being challenged, and perhaps even convicted, by the standard of experienced *agapē* over time, including my experienced failure to conform to that standard. In experiencing an attempt to lead me away from my selfishness, I could experience my falling short of the unselfish *agapē* directed toward me. This could create dissonance in my experience, including in my moral conscience. It also could challenge my moral self-understanding and thus create a moral crisis in my life. (For discussion of this kind of experience, see Farmer 1935, chaps. 1 and 11; Niebuhr 1941, chap. 9; and Garnett 1955, chaps. 5 and 6.)

My experience of righteous *agapē* could indicate my being intentionally challenged to replace my selfishness with unselfish love toward others, including my enemies. The apparently intentional challenge could oppose my own preferences and intentions, and it could come to me via my moral conscience without influence from another human. So, I could lack evidence that the *agapē* presented to me, including its apparently intentional challenge to me, comes from me or another human. In that situation, nothing in my experience would defeat my evidence that my experience of the challenge of *agapē* to me arises from a personal source independent of me and other humans. Given my

actual experience, I seem to be intentionally led, via conviction in conscience without coercion, toward unselfish love
for others and away from my selfishness. This happens to
be true of my own experience and conscience, and it indicates, if fallibly, the involvement of a personal agent other
than a human agent.

Given my overall evidence, I could reasonably decide
that an intervention from a perfectly good God figures in
a best available explanation (for me) of the challenging
and guiding *agapē* that troubles my conscience. I could
(and, I submit, do) lack the availability of a better or even
an equally good alternative explanation of this *agapē* presented to me. We have no good reason to deny this situation
of mine, so far as my actual evidence goes.

A skeptic could propose a purely natural explanation as a
defeater of my evidence for a theological explanation of my
moral experience. A skeptic might propose, for instance,
that I myself am creating my experience of the challenging
and guiding *agapē* in question. We can grant the logical
possibility of my creating this, even without our specifying
a mechanism, but actual evidence requires an actual
truth indicator, beyond mere possibility. So, a skeptic needs
somehow to base the critical proposal in my actual evidence. Otherwise, the proposal will not get epistemic support, at least for me, from the standpoint of my actual
evidence. Without a basis in my evidence, the skeptical
proposal of self-creation will not figure in a best available
explanation for me, relative to my evidence. It thus
will have an inadequate epistemic status for me, given my
evidence. The same holds for any other proposed merely
natural explanation. The alleged natural explainer will need
to figure in my evidence to gain epistemic standing, at least
for me. My own relevant experience, as it happens, does not
underwrite such an explainer.

Some skeptics will ask how the thesis of a morally perfect
God can be established from an "external" perspective that
is neutral relative to theistic positions. They will be

unmoved by an attempt from an internal perspective that favors a theistic position. An adequate response to such skeptics would begin with a clarification of what an "external" position includes. It also would distinguish between one's having adequate evidence for a position and one's establishing that position. In addition, we should distinguish between something's being external to beliefs of some sort and something's being external to evidence of some sort. The position on offer does not face a problem if we have in mind being external to theistic beliefs that entail God's existence. We have not built such beliefs into the relevant evidence from experience that supports belief in God. So, we have not imposed an "internal" perspective on this evidence as a starting point.

My experience of the challenging and guiding *agapē* presented to me could benefit, epistemically, from *evidentially grounded* reports from others. Such reports could come from well-grounded parts of a written religious tradition, such as well-grounded parts of the Bible, and from well-grounded testimony from my contemporaries. The explanatory coherence of such well-grounded reports, relative to my overall experience, can add to the positive epistemic status of the best available explanation for me. In contrast, *mere* reports or testimonies, like mere beliefs, would not add to positive epistemic status. They are epistemically arbitrary in a way that well-grounded reports are not. *Evidential* support is the key difference here, and such support can vary among people. Any testimonial report, however, would need ultimate support in foundational evidence.

Defeaters as underminers of epistemically reasonable belief for one can come from any relevant aspect or area of one's experience. Similarly, increased well-grounded explanatory coherence for a belief relative to any aspect or area of one's experience can increase the positive (defeasible) epistemic status of that belief for one. Epistemic abductivism is thus evidentially holistic for a person, with regard to positive evidence and defeaters. The ultimate epistemic status of (available) evidence for a person depends on all of that person's (available) evidence and potential defeaters. Epistemic reasonableness is relative to persons and their evidence in this way, and thus it differs from truth and factuality. It does not entail or otherwise guarantee truth, but it is the evidentially responsible, non-arbitrary way to aim at acquiring truth and avoiding error. In particular, it is responsible to one's overall indicators (or evidence) of what is true or factual, even if those indicators are fallible and defeasible.

Epistemic abductivism accommodates the truth that basic, foundational evidence in experience is not an argument or even a belief. The fact that the explanatory value of a belief relative to one's experience confers epistemic status on that belief allows that the basic evidence in experience is free of an argument or a belief. So, evidence from divine *agapē* in experience need not include an argument or a belief. It can anchor the epistemic reasonableness of a belief that serves in the best available explanation of that experiential evidence for a person. So, one's ultimate evidence for God's existence need not be an argument or a belief.

De dicto faith (that something is the case) can offer an interpretation of basic experiential evidence, for instance, by specifying what it is. In addition, that interpretation can figure crucially in a best available explanation of one's experience. When it does figure thus, in the absence of defeaters, such faith can be well grounded and hence epistemically reasonable for a person who has the relevant experience. Even when offering an interpretation and a best available explanation of experience, however, *de dicto* faith-in God will allow for incompleteness, perplexity, and mystery in explanation. Indeed, we should expect these phenomena when the object of faith is a God who cannot be fully comprehended by humans. After all, the God in question would transcend the created order and the understanding of reality its members enjoy.

Many agnostics and atheists would benefit from serious attention to the fact that some other people could (and arguably do) have significant evidence of God's existence, say, in their moral experience in the manner characterized by Chapter 7. This fact is compatible with the relevant agnostics and atheists lacking such evidence in their own experience. I have no reason to hold that these agnostics and atheists have salient evidence indicating that all theists lack the theistic evidence they acknowledge in their moral experience. At least, we would need to see that evidence if they have it. We know that evidence is often variable among people, and we seem not to have evidence to exclude its variability in the case of theistic belief. So, there is an epistemic gap in the agnostic or atheist story when it is generalized to all people. This gap recommends against a sweeping dismissal of religious commitment on evidential grounds.

2 EXPLAINING GOD AND EVIL

Many people blithely take the world's evil to be a defeater of theistic religious commitment, and they often show remarkable confidence in their doing so. On reflection, however, we humans should not expect to have now a theodicy that fully explains God's purposes in allowing evil. For us to have such a full theodicy, God would need to reveal divine purposes to us now in a way that bears on all cases of allowed evil. Our evidence, however, does not indicate such revealing to us, and we should not expect it to do so.

The absence of a full theodicy for us now does not entail a defeater of the kind of foundational theistic evidence offered in Chapter 7. Even so, the human limitations we face, including in the area of explaining evil, could serve a divine redemptive purpose. They could encourage a felt need for dependence on God (rather than just on a theory), thereby countering human pride and presumed self-sufficiency (on which, see Niebuhr 1949). Still, we shall explore how some explanation is available to us in this area, and what may account for our explanatory limitations.

Some theists find relief in saying that God *allows*, rather than causes, evil and its resulting suffering. This is cold comfort regarding God's moral character, however, because God would be morally responsible for what God allows as well as what God causes. That is, God would be responsible for allowing it rather than causing it, in cases where God is not the cause. So, God would need a higher moral end in allowing evil and its suffering for humans.

Can defenders of God's moral character be completely in the dark about the needed higher end? If they are, should they be agnostic about (part of) God's moral character? Even if they lack a full theodicy, they should have something illuminating to say about God's higher moral end, or at least about God's not revealing that end now to humans. If they have nothing to say, they will invite a recommendation of agnosticism about (an aspect of) God's moral character.

Many theists look for a higher moral end in God's seeking to build human moral character, that is, in "soul-making" for humans (see Hick 1977). We have, however, no settled account in this area. James S. Stewart explains:

We are still left with the question whether God could not have brought his sons and daughters to the same goal by some less tragic road. It is not the fact of suffering that baffles us, for we can see that we need it; it is the frightful excess of the thing which seems so cruel and senseless and superfluous. If God intends [human] sanctification [or purification], why could he not have thought out some kindlier way? (1940, p. 161)

Stewart raises a difficult question for any effort toward a full theodicy. In addition, much human suffering yields despair, including despair about God's reality or goodness, rather than an improved moral character. So, a rationally compelling theodicy would require more than an appeal to a divine purpose to build human moral character. The same holds for such divine purposes as challenging human sin, awakening human conscience, converting humans to God, and promoting human solidarity. The matter is complicated at best, and it resists any simple explanation.

After trying to identify God's purposes in allowing his suffering, Job confessed: "I have uttered what I did not understand, things too wonderful for me, which I did not know" (Job 42:3). The apostle Paul echoed the general attitude of Job toward God's apparently severe ways: "O the depth of the riches and wisdom and knowledge of God! How unsearchable are his judgments and how inscrutable his ways!" (Rom. 11:33).

The responses of Job and Paul suggest a question: Why do humans not (fully) understand why God, if real, allows all of the unjust suffering and evil in their lives, even if they understand the purposes behind *some* unjust suffering and evil? If God chooses not to reveal the divine purposes in allowing unjust suffering and evil in human lives, we humans will have real difficulty in identifying them. Without divine revelation to us, we seem not to have access to those purposes, nor, without divine revelation to us, should we expect to have such access.

Three options arise for the lack of human understanding of God's relevant purposes. First, the matter of God's allowing unjust suffering and evil is *constitutively complex* beyond our cognitive resources. Its elaborate nature, in virtue of its many parts and their interconnections, outstrips what we comprehend in the context of our cognitive limitations. Second, the matter is *morally profound* beyond our moral depth; it has a moral gravitas beyond our own. Job confesses lack of understanding on the ground that the relevant things are "too wonderful (or marvelous)" for him, and Paul remarks on the "depth" of the relevant wisdom and knowledge of God. They seem not to be commenting on mere constitutive complexity in creation.

Instead, they seem to have in mind something closer to moral profundity in God's purposes. Third, God hides from humans at least some divine purposes in allowing unjust suffering and evil, and this concealment blocks a full human understanding of the relevant divine purposes. It also should block a human expectation to have such a full understanding. This option can include the second option: God could hide a divine purpose because, upon being revealed to unprepared humans, its moral profundity would result in human distortion and resistance. This option also could acknowledge a partial role for constitutive complexity in the relevant lack of human understanding.

If we can explain why humans should not expect to understand the full purpose of God in allowing evil, we can remove the *intellectual* sting of their not fully understanding it. (The *psychological* sting, we shall see, is a separate matter.) Humans still would need the power to endure evil in their lives, but they would not need to suffer from a false expectation to understand now God's full purpose in allowing evil. Relief from that false expectation would disarm a common intellectual source of human resistance to God's moral character and even God's reality. In that regard, we may consider the effort at hand as *neutralizing* the problem of evil as an intellectual threat to human commitment to God.

We can look to some aspects of New Testament Christology to illuminate our not having a full theodicy, despite the widespread neglect of this important connection. Even if we cannot identify God's higher moral end in allowing all of the unjust suffering and evil in human lives, we can, given a certain Christological lesson, identify God's purpose in *not revealing* that end prior to its fulfillment in human experience. One part of that purpose, we shall see, would be to have humans acquire a felt, sympathetic understanding of the relevant divine end through their experience of its fulfillment. A felt, sympathetic understanding would differ from a merely verbal, conceptual, or intellectual understanding that fails to engage the affective or volitional center of a person.

A second part of the divine purpose in not revealing, we shall see, would be God's desire to save humans from a certain kind of counterproductive resistance to God and God's ends. The resistance, stemming from inadequate sympathetic understanding at least, would include a life-directing objection to God's ends in allowing unjust suffering and evil in human lives. We shall see that Jesus considered the resistance in question to be "adversarial" toward God in a manner to be identified.

A Christological Lesson

We sell New Testament Christology short when we limit its importance to atonement or redemption. It bears also on the intellectual problem of evil regarding God, particularly on the prospect for a full theodicy as an explanation of the full purpose in God's allowing unjust suffering and evil in human lives. Its bearing on a full theodicy, and thus on God's alleged culpability in allowing evil, merits our attention. We shall see that an important lesson from New Testament Christology illuminates the absence of a full theodicy owing to human limitations in properly understanding some divine purposes.

A pivotal exchange from Matthew's Gospel, closely following Mark's Gospel, involves Jesus and Peter:

Jesus began to show his disciples that he must go to Jerusalem and undergo great suffering at the hands of the elders and chief priests and scribes, and be killed, and on the third day be raised. And Peter took him aside and began to rebuke him, saying, "God forbid it, Lord! This must never happen to you." But he turned and said to Peter, "Get behind me, Satan! You are a stumbling block to me; for you are setting your mind not on divine things but on human things." (Matt. 16:21–23; cf. Mark 8:31–33)

Would God allow the unjust crucifixion of the innocent Jesus? Peter's explicit answer here: No. Jesus's implicit contrary answer: Yes.

We typical humans reflect Peter, in response to many cases of unjust suffering and evil. If Jesus is right, however, we often mind the wrong things (literally, "the things of humans") and thus are not in a position to understand properly "the things of God," particularly the divine purposes in allowing unjust suffering and evil. In case we miss the point, Mark's Gospel repeats that the disciples of Jesus did not "understand" Jesus's prediction of his death and resurrection (Mark 9:32; cf. Mark 10:33–38).

Luke's Gospel reiterates the teaching of Mark's Gospel that the disciples did not understand Jesus's prediction of his suffering. It adds: "Its meaning was concealed from them, so that they could not perceive it" (Luke 9:45). Using the divine passive voice, Luke suggests that *God* intentionally concealed the meaning from the disciples. In concealing this meaning, God concealed the full divine purpose in allowing the innocent Jesus to suffer. So, the disciples lacked a full theodicy for the unjust suffering of their Messiah. We can, and will, generalize on this case in connection with God's allowing unjust suffering and evil in human lives in general and our lacking a full theodicy.

Following Mark's Gospel, Luke's Gospel reaffirms that the disciples lacked understanding of Jesus's prediction that he would suffer at human hands: "They understood nothing about all these things; in fact, what he said was hidden from them, and they did not grasp what was said" (Luke 18:34; cf. Luke 24:25–26). Luke uses the divine passive to indicate that God hid the meaning of Jesus's prediction of suffering from the disciples. God did not hide from the disciples the *statement* that Jesus will suffer; Jesus made the statement directly to them. Instead, God concealed both (a) *the meaning* of the statement with regard to God's *full purpose* for allowing the Messiah's suffering and (b) *the statement of that meaning* and purpose. The divine hiding of

(a) and (b) leaves the disciples without a full theodicy for the death of their Messiah. They thus cannot explain why God did not choose a less destructive approach to the culmination of the earthly life of Jesus, nor can we, given the incompleteness of our relevant evidence.

Neither God nor Jesus offers anything near a full explanation of why Jesus would undergo, with God's allowance, unjust suffering and evil at human hands. Jesus does portray his own life and death as self-giving for others (Mark 10:45, 14:23–24; cf. Matt. 20:28, 26:27–28), but this broad portrayal falls short of a full explanation. The best account of this divine withholding of a full explanation is that the disciples were not *ready*, or *in a position*, to understand or otherwise handle it properly. Indeed, this is Jesus's suggestion in his aforementioned remark that the disciples mind, or value, human considerations in a manner at odds with properly minding, or valuing, the things of God (Mark 8:33, Matt. 16:23). Their inadequacy in minding the things of God colors their defective understanding of the relevant statements of Jesus in a way that leads to distortion and even counterproductive resistance.

One might suggest that Jesus himself lacked a full theodicy, in keeping with his cry of dereliction (Mark 15:34), but the matter is complicated. Jesus did not blame God for the evil in and among humans (see Matt. 13:24–30). If the historical Jesus did not have a full theodicy, we might ask: Why is this? Further questions arise. Would Jesus, as a human, have properly understood God's full purpose? If not, why not? Was this due to a lack of perfect divine love? Did Jesus have to learn such love, as a human work in progress, from the things he suffered? The author of the letter to the Hebrews claims that Jesus "learned obedience through what he suffered," and (thereby) was "made perfect" (Heb. 5:8–9). Perhaps the author has in mind a need to be made perfect in divine love (in keeping with a lesson of Chapter 7 above) and thereby in understanding. At any rate, it is doubtful that the historical Jesus had a full theodicy, and this would fit with his avowedly limited knowledge (see Mark 13:32).

A relevant lesson of divine concealment emerges from Jesus's use of parables, according to the Gospels of Mark and Matthew (Mark 4:11–13, Matt. 13:13–15; see Boucher 1977; Hultgren 2000; Snodgrass 2008). The idea, drawn from Isaiah 6:10, is that God blocks or limits understanding of the divine message for those who are not in a position to respond properly. In the case of the parables, the uncomprehending audience consists of "those outside" (Mark 4:11), whereas in the case of Jesus's prediction of suffering, the uncomprehending audience includes the disciples. Perhaps even the disciples can be "outside" the position needed for properly understanding the prediction of Jesus's suffering. If so, they can be recipients of divine concealment. At least Luke's Gospel indicates as much, taking its lead from Mark 9:31–32.

Peter may get some of the language right in his confession of who Jesus is (Mark 8:29–30, Matt. 16:15–17), but his understanding seems to be largely verbal or conceptual rather than profoundly sympathetic. He evidently does not understand the full meaning involved in God's allowing the Messiah to suffer and die. This shortcoming leads to his rebuking Jesus and, in turn, to Jesus calling him "satan" (or "adversary"). We must ask whether we typical humans would have a similar problem if God now stated a full theodicy for unjust suffering and evil in human lives. I suspect that we would, given our cognitive and moral shortcomings relative to God's perfect cognitive and moral character. Even so, we can appreciate, and perhaps even share, Peter's implicit protest that God should find a less destructive option for the culmination of the Messiah's earthly life. God *seems* to be allowing excessive suffering and destruction in this case, among many others. From a different perspective (perhaps God's), one might suggest that God's redemptive love for humans is costly beyond human understanding.

Perhaps, like Peter, we can gain *some* needed (incomplete) understanding *after* the fulfillment of God's enacted plan in human experience, but, in any case, it often comes late if at all. We find an example of this in John's Gospel: "The other disciple, who reached the tomb first, also went in, and he saw and believed; for as yet they [the disciples] did not understand the scripture, that he must rise from the dead" (John 20:9; cf. Luke 24:25–27). Their understanding was delayed, until the time of the experienced fulfillment of God's plan in their lives. God thus could withhold a full explanation of divine purposes before their fulfillment in human experience. We need to clarify why this is so.

Many people regard the crucifixion of Jesus as an unsurpassed injustice to an individual human, on the assumption that Jesus was innocent of wrongdoing. James Stewart remarks that the "cross [of Jesus] itself was the problem of evil at its worst, the most unpardonable, desperate deed that ever defaced the pages of history" (1996, p. 213). Jesus, however, does not give Peter an answer to the question of why he would undergo a crucifixion allowed by God, instead of a less vicious form of death. He reveals that he and his disciples will suffer, but not why he and they will suffer in the way indicated or why he and they will suffer as much as they will. Peter and the disciples receive no explanation of why the suffering allowed by God is morally fitting rather than excessive. We find a similar situation in the divine calling of Saul of Tarsus: "The Lord said to [Ananias], 'Go, for [Saul] is an instrument whom I have chosen to bring my name before Gentiles and kings and before the people of Israel; I myself will show him how much he must suffer for the sake of my name'" (Acts 9:15–16). Here, too, the apostle Paul does not receive an explanation of why his suffering allowed by God is fitting rather than excessive.

Paul was aware of the challenge to faith in God from unjust suffering and evil allowed by God (see 2 Cor. 1:8), but he neither proposes a full theodicy nor laments not having one. In addition, he shows no sign of expecting God to offer a full theodicy to humans now. Instead, he offers the following response:

Who will separate us from the love of Christ? Will hardship, or distress, or persecution, or famine, or nakedness, or peril, or sword? As it is written, "For your sake we are being killed all day long; we are accounted as sheep to be slaughtered." No, in all these things we are more than conquerors through him who loved us. (Rom. 8:35–37)

Paul highlights one's being able to endure, courtesy of God's power, the unjust suffering and evil in question, even in the absence of a full theodicy. He acknowledges that God "did not withhold his own Son, but gave him up for all of us," but he does not fault or doubt God's goodness for excessive tolerance in giving Jesus up to violent crucifixion by the Roman soldiers. Instead, he thinks of *some* cases of suffering as an opportunity to trust God: "We felt that we had received the sentence of death so that we would rely not on ourselves but on God who raises the dead" (2 Cor. 1:9).

Paul, as noted, finds a "depth" in God's redemptive plan that leaves God's full purpose "unsearchable" and "inscrutable" by humans now (Rom. 11:33). He does expect to have improved knowledge in the fullness of time (1 Cor. 13:12), but that does not yield anything near a full theodicy now. Even so, given his knowledge of God's moral character in Christ, Paul affirms: "We know that all things work together for good for those who love God, who are called according to his purpose" (Rom. 8:28). This affirmation, however, does not entail knowledge now of God's full purpose in allowing unjust suffering and evil in human lives. So, it does not yield or support a full theodicy now, nor does it figure in an objection to our not having a full theodicy now. Paul thus would disown full understanding now of God's costly redemptive love, including its presence in the cruel death of Jesus.

Paul's attitude toward a full theodicy fits with that of Jesus, who refrains from explaining God's full purpose in allowing unjust suffering and evil. Luke's Gospel illustrates:

There were some present who told [Jesus] about the Galileans whose blood Pilate had mingled with their sacrifices. He asked them, "Do you think that because these Galileans suffered in this way they were worse sinners than all other Galileans? No, I tell you; but unless you repent, you will all perish as they did. Or those eighteen who were killed when the tower of Siloam fell on them – do you think that they were worse offenders than all the others living in Jerusalem? No, I tell you; but unless you repent, you will all perish just as they did." (Luke 13:1–5)

In rejecting a bad theodicy, Jesus gives no hint of why God allowed the unjust suffering and evil in question. In addition, he does not suggest that God should reveal the relevant divine purpose now to humans. Instead, he redirects the topic to how humans as morally responsible persons now relate to God. He suggests that the inquirers about evil should focus now on turning toward responsible obedience to God. He thus responds as if God will not now give humans a full explanation of why God allows unjust suffering and evil in human lives.

John's Gospel offers a relevant comment, in connection with the raising of Lazarus by Jesus: "The sisters sent a message to Jesus, 'Lord, he whom you love is ill.' But when Jesus heard it, he said, 'This illness does not lead to death; rather it is for God's glory, so that the Son of God may be glorified through it'" (John 11:3–4). It may be tempting to generalize on this comment by Jesus, and thus to propose that all suffering and evil are "for God's glory." Such generalizing, however, would be a mistake.

Jesus is commenting on the particular case of Lazarus in relation to his own opportunity to raise Lazarus. He thus offers a purpose regarding himself: "so that the Son of God may be glorified through it." This case, then, is not reflective of suffering and evil in general. As a result, we do not find here any suggestion of a full theodicy. In the New Testament, Jesus consistently refrains from indicating a full theodicy for humans now. Instead, he suggests that typical humans are not in a position now to understand God's full purpose in allowing unjust suffering and evil. We turn to the importance of this lesson regarding two kinds of theodicy and neutralizing the intellectual problem of evil.

Two Kinds of Theodicy

Even in the absence of a full theodicy, we can neutralize the intellectual problem of evil. We can do so by removing false expectations for God's revealing, and for our having, a full explanation of why God allows unjust suffering and evil. According to the previous Christological lesson, God has a reason *not* to reveal to typical humans now the full divine purpose in allowing unjust suffering and evil in human lives. Part of the reason is that typical humans now would lack the understanding needed to handle (a statement of) the purpose aright. They would fail, as in the case of the apostle Peter, to understand properly, and therefore they would tend toward counterproductive resistance to God and God's purpose. Such resistance, broader in scope than the kind seen in Peter (and inviting the tag "satan" from Jesus), would be counterproductive by increasing harmful alienation of people from God. We have no good reason to hold that we would handle the relevant situation better than Peter did, even if we tend to think otherwise.

At the heart of our problem is a lack of felt, sympathetic understanding of the divine purpose, beyond any merely verbal or conceptual understanding. The problem thus exceeds a matter of our intellectual limitations, even if we have pertinent intellectual limitations. H. R. Mackintosh explains, in connection with the crucifixion of Jesus:

The great reason why we fail to understand Calvary is not merely that we are not profound enough, it is that we are not good enough. It is because we are such strangers to sacrifice that God's sacrifice leaves us bewildered. It is because we love so little that His love is mysterious. We have never forgiven anybody at such a cost as His. We have never taken the initiative in putting a quarrel right with His kind of unreserved willingness to suffer. It is our unlikeness to God that hangs as an obscuring screen impeding our view, and we see the Atonement [of Calvary] so often through the frosted glass of our own lovelessness. (1938, pp. 176–77; cf. Glover 1917, p. 182)

Our being strangers, in our own intentions and actions, to perfect self-sacrifice for others out of unselfish love, according to Mackintosh, results in our not properly, and sympathetically, understanding God's costly purpose in allowing the crucifixion of Jesus. We lack proper felt understanding of God's purpose of costly sacrificial love because we are deficient in having and practicing such love.

We do not face a problem simply of the constitutive complexity of God's purpose in allowing unjust suffering and evil. Given our own moral shortcomings regarding the kind of costly self-sacrificial love characteristic of God, we face a problem of our deficient moral profundity in relation to God's perfect moral character. Paul identifies a related problem in 1 Corinthians 2:14: "Those who are unspiritual do not receive the gifts of God's Spirit, for they are foolishness to them, and they are unable to understand them because they are spiritually discerned." The way to respond to our moral shortcomings, according to Paul, is not a self-help program toward goodness, but instead is a matter of receiving divine grace for proceeding without despair, typically in suffering.

Our neutralizing the problem of evil calls for our generalizing on the Christological lesson about our inadequate understanding of the crucifixion of Jesus. We have the same kind of deficiency in understanding God's purpose more generally, in its allowing many other cases of unjust suffering and evil. We would have, by way of response to God's purpose, a kind of resistance akin to Peter's regarding the predicted suffering of Jesus. Our response, however, would be broader in scope, and it would increase our harmful alienation from God.

The culprit is in what would be our improper understanding. It would yield a false expectation of what God should do, as opposed to what God has done, in allowing the world's suffering and evil or at least in failing to explain for us its full divine purpose. If we reasonably can set aside the misunderstanding and the resulting false expectation, we can neutralize the problem of evil by disabling its intellectual threat. We then may be in a position to grant God's goodness in allowing the unjust suffering and evil in human lives.

We have a Christological basis for neutralizing the problem of evil, a basis in what God did in Jesus. The life of Jesus, in a Christian perspective, identifies and manifests God's moral character as self-giving for the good of others, even for enemies of God. His life exemplifies God's giving humans what (or, better, *someone*) they need for correctly portraying and relating to God as worthy of worship and hence as morally perfect. On this basis, we can sympathize with Paul's illuminating question: "He who did not withhold his own Son, but gave him up for all of us, will he not with him also give us everything else?" (Rom. 8:32). The key point is that Christology properly understood manifests God's moral character as seeking to work things out for the good of all humans who are willing to receive what is good from God on divine moral terms (see Rom. 8:28). Such Christology thus offers a basis for avoiding agnosticism about God's moral character in the face of unjust human suffering and evil.

We should not expect now a full explanation of either why God allowed Jesus to suffer unjustly in Roman crucifixion or why God allows unjust suffering in general. Instead, the life and death of Jesus manifest God's character as bringing good out of allowed evil in ways that give lasting benefits to humans, *at God's appointed time*. These benefits would come, at God's preferred time, to all people who are willing to receive such benefits on God's moral terms. They exceed, in Paul's account, what are ordinarily called "reparations" and, as well, what are typical human expectations (see Rom. 8:18, 1 Cor. 2:9, drawing from Isa. 64:4).

The God of New Testament Christology can give lasting benefits via the resurrection of humans, after the model of the risen Jesus (Rom. 8:11). This would extend the available time for such benefits. So, there would be no limit to *earthly* human life for the divine provision of benefits in the wake of unjust suffering and evil. People who reject life with God, however, will thereby reject for themselves the resurrection and its benefits that depend on cooperative life with God. They thus will block God's effort to bring lasting good out of the unjust suffering and evil in their lives. As long as God honors their freedom to reject cooperative life with God, they can frustrate the divine effort to bring lasting good life to all people. When they do, they would interfere with God's intended costly redemption of humans.

According to the Gethsemane story in the Gospels, Jesus ultimately agreed to self-sacrifice for others on behalf of God, despite initial hesitation (Mark 14:36, Matt. 26:39). His disciples, according to Jesus and Paul, should follow suit in sacrificial suffering, despite any initial resistance they may have (Mark 10:39, 13:9–13, Phil. 1:29, Col. 1:24). This suffering does not await advance approval from the disciples, and the same would be true of the resurrection benefits. God would seek to bring people to reconciliation and cooperation with God *in* their suffering and in advance of the full resurrection benefits. This would be a moral prerogative of God so long as God offers the benefits of resurrection life for those who suffer. It thus would be presumptuous of humans, given their cognitive and moral limitations relative to God, to suppose that they should control either the precise timing of God's redemptive provisions or how costly those provisions should be to God.

The neutralizing on offer does not rest just on a promise of the benefits of resurrection life. Instead, it has an anchor in distinctive experiential evidence in the present, courtesy of religious experience in moral conviction. Paul thinks of the anchor as including experience of one's undergoing new creation by God now (2 Cor. 5:17–18), whereby one experiences God's life-giving moral character in the beginning of resurrection life now (Rom. 6:4, 11; cf. Rom. 5:3–5, Col. 3:1). (On the relevant kind of experience, see Forsyth 1909, pp. 195–208; Hubbard 2002; and Moser 2017, pp. 284–330; see also Chapter 7 above.)

One would need to be suitably cooperative toward God to receive the evidence in question properly, but this does not count against the reality of the evidence. Instead, it acknowledges that the evidence would not be forced upon those who refuse it. We should expect this of a God who seeks to retain the genuine agency of those who decide for or against God (cf. Rom. 10:21, 11:20). As a result, we should not expect to be able to control the relevant evidence in a way that convinces all people. So, our neutralizing effort toward the intellectual problem of evil does not pretend to silence all skeptics with overwhelming evidence of God's character or purpose. It properly leaves room for divine hiding for divine redemptive purposes. Some of those purposes, as we should expect, are beyond our full understanding, given our cognitive and moral limitations relative to God.

Our neutralizing the intellectual problem of evil does not offer, or intend to offer, a full theodicy of God's allowing unjust suffering and evil. That is, it does not offer or depend on what we may call a *full-explanation theodicy* regarding

God's full purpose in allowing unjust suffering and evil. Instead, the proposed neutralizing offers a different approach to theodicy: a *partial-justification theodicy* regarding God's hiding (without God's completely explaining) the full divine purpose in allowing suffering and evil. In keeping with the aforementioned lessons from Jesus and Paul, we now have at best the latter kind of theodicy, and not the former kind. The partial justification suggested does not support a claim to explain divine hiding in general or to refute all skeptics. Such a claim would be ungrounded and presumptuous. The partial justification, however, does remove some false expectations that figure in a common anti-theistic use of the intellectual problem of evil. It thereby neutralizes the intellectual problem in connection with that use, at least for those receptive to the available evidence.

If God intends to hide the full purpose in allowing suffering and evil, we might wonder why Jesus would have put Peter in a difficult position that prompted a rebuke for "satanic" resistance. If God's concealment of the full purpose aims to avoid such resistance, why would Jesus prompt it in the case of Peter? A plausible answer is that Peter is serving, by divine intent, as an instructive example for a larger audience. At least the authors of the Gospels of Mark and Matthew, arguably with the influence of Jesus, are using Peter as an example of how *not* to approach the matter of Messianic suffering. Peter was an important example in this regard, given the ongoing suffering and persecution of the earliest Christians, including the first recipients of Mark's Gospel facing persecution in Rome. So, this example has important practical value for its original audience, and perhaps for later similar audiences, too. It manifests typical human misunderstanding of how costly divine redemptive love is.

God would be able to hide the full purpose for allowing suffering and evil, and would need to do so despite the disciples' lack of understanding. The reason for the latter need is that revealing the full purpose would only exacerbate the disciples' difficulty, given their not being in a position to understand properly. Such revealing would add to the extent of inadequate understanding suffered by the disciples, without a corresponding redemptive gain. It thus would be a worse situation than their not being told now the full purpose in question. This lesson applies even to those who are not disciples, and thus the neutralizing can apply to people not acknowledging God's existence, despite their unawareness of the lesson.

In neutralizing the intellectual problem of evil, we do not remove all *psychological* problems regarding evil in relation to God. We are in no position to neutralize all such psychological problems, such as emotional problems, haunting people as a result of evil. Some people suffer emotional pain from evil, and our neutralizing the intellectual problem of evil leaves their emotional pain intact. They may want, and even expect, more comfort from God in their pain, and we are in no position to fault them, just as we may be in no position to comfort them in the way they need. So, a partial-justification theodicy regarding God's hiding is no panacea for the trials and tribulations of this world. It removes a nagging intellectual problem for many people, but it allows other problems to endure. Perhaps this is part of the mixed predicament of having a "treasure in earthen vessels," as Paul might suggest. In any case, it is doubtful that more divine *explaining* or *purpose-revealing* would supply the psychological comfort sought. Something of a different kind, such as divine comfort, seems needed, and any divine comfort would have to be at divine, rather than human, discretion.

Our neutralizing effort does not acquiesce to any evil in either accepting it or refusing to oppose it. Instead, it yields to human limitations in understanding God's full purpose in allowing evil. These two options differ, and we have no reason to suppose that yielding to human limitations in understanding entails the former acquiescence to evil. One may oppose evil, even as a moral duty, while

conceding an incomplete understanding of the full purpose in allowing it.

The neutralizing on offer can benefit from a perspective
akin to that suggested by James Stewart:

What is the Christian answer to the mystery of suffering?
Not an explanation but a reinforcing presence: Christ to stand
beside you, through the darkness, Christ's companionship to
make the dark experience sacramental – "Yea, though I walk
in death's dark vale, Yet will I fear none ill: For Thou art
with me." [Psalm 23] (1996, p. 124)

I mention a position "akin" to this perspective, because our
lacking a full explanation does not entail our lacking *all*
explanation. For instance, even in the absence of a full
theodicy, we could find some explanatory value in the
following remark by Helmut Thielicke: "The afflictions of
your life and mine are the hollow ground under our feet
which gives way because God wills to catch us" (1962,
p. 20). If God seeks to emerge as the ultimate rescuer of
humans from their afflictions, God could allow human
suffering to that end. The suggestion of Thielicke, in any
case, does not deny a threshold for the pain God would
allow in willing to catch people in their afflicted collapse.

Many anti-God arguments from evil stem from a dubious
assumption about the finality of suffering and evil. They
assume that the earthly suffering and evil allowed by God is
final in not being redeemable in the end. This assumption
begs a key question against proponents of theism. The
suffering and evil of this world would not be final for the
God of traditional monotheism, the God of Abraham,
Moses, Jesus, Paul, and Muhammad. This God could
redeem this world's suffering and evil after death in this
world. Resurrection of humans by God would allow for
this, as it would give God an opportunity to restore goodness in human lives after their suffering and death. We
humans lack the power for such restoration on our own,

but God's power would not be similarly limited. So, we should not assume that the finality of suffering and evil relative to our power transfers to God. This consideration can challenge an unduly negative assumption about the ultimate sting of suffering and evil, even if their ultimate redemption depends on human cooperation with God.

The previous approach to evil and God does not emerge just from intellectual reflection, however rigorous. Instead, it engages who (or what kind of person) one resolves to be *as a personal, moral agent before God*. So, what may have seemed to be mainly an intellectual puzzle, regarding evil and God, leads to existential questions about who one will resolve to be in relation to God. This should be no surprise if God cares about who one is as a responsible person, and not just as an explainer of intellectual difficulties.

Answers may not come easy in the area at hand, but having neutralized the intellectual problem of evil, we now can face the deeper questions with intellectual sincerity. We now have the intellectual space to allow the existential questions about our relating to God to emerge and to endure for our good. This is one vital benefit of neutralizing the intellectual problem of evil, courtesy of New Testament Christology. In this perspective, theodicy recapitulates Christology.

We now have the space to acknowledge that a person's experience of evil can be an opportunity for that person's becoming open to a religious experience of God. The experience of evil can prompt awareness of a person's seriously needing God, whether for redeeming the evil or for strengthening (or perhaps rescuing) the person faced with evil. Awareness of such a need can give one proper focus and seriousness in looking for relevant evidence of God's reality. It also can prompt due cognitive modesty in one's pursuit of such evidence. It might even encourage one to have a will open to cooperation with God's will. Such an attitude could aid one in apprehending evidence of God's will and thus God's reality.

This world's evil, as extensive as it is, does not remove or undermine all evidence from religious experience for God's reality. A person can have the kind of experiential evidence for God's existence characterized in Chapter 7 while the world has its extensive evil. We would find a defeater of the relevant experiential evidence (an indirect defeater) and of theistic belief (a direct defeater) if the world manifested *only* evil, with no goodness at all. The actual world, of course, is not like that; it manifests goodness as well as evil. So, we have no basis for a quick and easy dismissal of theistic religion on the basis of this world's evil.

3 DIVINE HIDDENNESS

We now face a potential defeater indicated by the familiar question of why God's reality is not more transparent to many humans. Why do some people seem to be without the needed experiential evidence of divine reality? One might propose that this problem of divine hiddenness is part of the general problem of evil for God's existence, on the ground that a truly good God would omit such hiddenness as being evil. Even so, many people report having an experience of God's absence in their lives or at least having no experience of God's presence in their lives. For many such people, I find no good reason to question their report.

Absence of evidence of divine reality for a person could come from two sources: a failure of God to supply the divine evidence to that person or a failure of that person to be in a position to receive the divine evidence on offer. I doubt that we have good reason to disregard either source in many cases. God could postpone giving evidence of divine reality to humans if they would only abuse it, to their own detriment. Still, that evidence could be *available* to them under certain circumstances, even if they do not actually have it. We should not suppose, however, that we are within reach of a full explanation of God's purposes in hiding from some humans at some times. Just as we do not have a full theodicy for God's allowing suffering and evil, we do not have a full theodicy for divine hiding from some people at times. The response of the book of Job (chaps. 38–42) still holds firm: We humans now have an explanation deficit in this area.

The convictional approach to foundational divine evidence in Chapter 7 enables us to illuminate human failure to be in a position to receive such evidence. It prompts two questions. Are we *willing* to be attentive to being convicted toward divine love and away from selfishness and other ways of being self-willed in opposition to God's will? Alternatively, do we *resist* being thus convicted by opting for diversions, including an unduly fast pace of life, beyond the speed of *agapē* toward God and others? If we do resist, we are being *agapē-resistant*, with the result that salient evidence for us of God's reality and challenge toward *agapē* will be highly elusive at best for us. So, we could suppress and obscure vital convictional evidence of God in conscience and thereby quench the evidential effort of God in our moral experience. In that case, God would seem to be hidden from us, even though *we* are the responsible cause of the hiddenness.

We should not assume the divine hiddenness would always be a matter of God's simply *appearing* to be hidden from some humans. A morally perfect God could actually hide from some humans for various perfectly good purposes. We should not presume to have a comprehensive list of those purposes, but we can imagine some of them. For instance, we can imagine that God uses divine hiding from some humans as a means to bring judgment (perhaps for the sake of correction) on those people for resolute wrongdoing. This would be a live option for God, but other options would be available to God, too. In some cases, God could hide just to give some people a sense of experiencing God's absence in contrast with experiencing God's presence. The main point, however, is that divine hiddenness for some people at some times does not undermine all

experiential evidence of God's reality. No easy generalization to a universal agnostic or atheist position is available
from divine hiddenness of the sort found in the
actual world.

How we value being morally convicted by God in *agapē*
may matter vitally. Indeed, this seems to be the "one thing"
prized by Jesus as needed by humans (Luke 10:41–42).
This focus of Jesus may matter crucially, because in New
Testament theology he is the one who not only sends God's
Spirit but also models the character of God's Spirit. He gives
human and moral shape to the Spirit of God, and thus saves
us from an anything-goes, morally amorphous mysticism.
At the same time, he is the one who ended his earthly life
with the desperate cry of affliction, "My God, my God, why
have you forsaken me?" (on which, see Rossé 1987). It thus
appears that some of his expectations for God in his own life
were frustrated, and he evidently experienced this frustration with considerable pain and suffering. Other humans
may have to follow suit in their experience, even after moral
conviction by God.

If God is hidden from some people at times, we should
expect a similar kind of hiddenness regarding the meaning
of life for some humans. God could hide that meaning from
people who are not ready to receive it and thus would
neglect it or use it destructively toward people. Making that
meaning obvious to all could trivialize it in a harmful way
for some people. This does not imply that one must earn or
merit access to the meaning of life. Instead, it implies that a
person may need to be prepared, at least in attitude, to
receive it as it is intended by God.

In a world governed by God, human attitudes toward
God and other people would matter. They would not be
disregarded for the sake of imparting mere information.
God would care about *how* people receive, in their deepest
attitudes, divine information and evidence on offer, from
the perspective of divine–human reconciliation. So, God
may wait for (some) people to feel the futility of life without

God in order to apprehend their need of God. This could be part of God's profound caring for people in need. Divine presence, then, is not God's only redemptive tool; divine absence can serve a redemptive purpose, too. So, we do not find a quick defeater of evidence for God's reality in divine elusiveness or hiddenness on various occasions.

4 RELIGIOUS DIVERSITY

Many people think of religious diversity, such as variation and conflict in religious beliefs and practices among humans, as supplying a defeater of religious commitment, including theistic commitment. This is puzzling, because human disagreement does not yield evidence by itself; instead, it yields beliefs of diverse and conflicting sorts. Mere beliefs need supporting evidence to gain a positive epistemic status, and defeaters likewise must have a positive epistemic status. Even so, a theistic religious perspective should offer some illumination of religious diversity.

A perfectly good God would aim to be Lord over human moral development without coercing humans. So, God would seek to lead or guide humans in their intentional imitation, *imitatio Dei*, toward the divine moral character with their cooperation. This would be central to being divine Lord in the moral domain, because a person's lord leads or guides that person. One could be led by God, via being morally convicted in conscience, while being an atheist or an agnostic regarding God's existence. Specifically, one's being led *de re* by God would not require one's accepting or even formulating correct *de dicto* content regarding God's reality.

One might use just minimal demonstratives regarding what morally convicts one in conscience, while lacking a notion of *God* as an intentional agent worthy of worship. This kind of case would not preclude one's being morally convicted and led by God *de re*, even though one's *understanding* of the influence on one's being led, and of its purpose, would be deficient. In any case, one's being thus led does not require one's adequately understanding the process of one's being led. Similarly, it does not require one's appreciating or recognizing one's evidence that the process is intentional in being indicative of an intentional agent, such as God, behind the convicting and leading.

The lesson here is important, because it would enable God to convict and lead people who come from a wide range of intellectual and religious perspectives, including atheists and agnostics. Such intellectually diverse people could have some experiences of God that are qualitatively the same, owing to a common influence from God's morally perfect character. They would explain those experiences differently, even though the experiences have an intrinsic quality in common. (Explaining experiences differently, however, does not entail doing so equally well.) Intellectual and religious diversity, then, would not preclude divine guidance for humans, and it thus would not undermine grounded theistic commitment of the kind presented in Chapter 7. An objection to theistic commitment from considerations of religious diversity can exaggerate the importance of (shared) *de dicto* belief regarding God. In contrast, God could work with *de re* belief (including trust) in God while allowing for extensive diversity in *de dicto* belief regarding God, including belief within nontheistic religions.

Evidence and knowledge can have *de dicto* and *de re* components, depending on what a person who has evidence and knowledge is related to (a judgment or something else). Bertrand Russell (1911) distinguished knowledge by description (being *de dicto*) and knowledge by acquaintance (being *de re*). In doing so, he identified a kind of knowledge that cannot be reduced to factual knowledge that something is the case. It is controversial among philosophers what the relevant *acquaintance* or *encounter* in knowledge by acquaintance encompasses, but it is at least *de re* in being causally related to an object different from a judgment or proposition.

In a theistic religious context, a prominent approach to *de re* knowledge emerges from Martin Buber's (1923) perspective (inspired by Kierkegaard's pseudonymous Climacus) on a direct "I–Thou" relation between a human and God. Since God is a personal "Thou" in this approach, the knowledge in question would be not just *de re* but also *de te*, in relation to a "You." The "object" of knowledge then would be not just an object, but also a *subject*, that is, a personal agent with self-consciousness and intentional self-determination. This would bear directly on the kind of evidence to be expected for human knowledge of God. Despite misgivings from some philosophers, we have no good reason to exclude evidence for a proposition from a nonconceptual and nonpropositional basis. Such a basis can exhibit properties in human experience that qualify as evidence for a person. (Chapter 7 offered an approach to divine evidence that illustrates this point.)

A personal encounter with God's self-manifestation would yield not objective or logical certainty but at most *interpersonal certitude*. Such certitude depends on one personal agent's relating to another personal agent with salient, or definite, interpersonal evidence (but not necessarily to all personal agents). Its salient evidence and assurance for one agent do not automatically generalize to such evidence and assurance for all relevant agents, even all agents who reflect carefully on the matter. As noted, God could hide, at least for a time, from some personal agents who are not prepared to receive God's self-manifestation in the way it is intended (by God). So, evidence and assurance from a personal encounter with God are not automatically generalizable to all relevant inquirers about God. Some inquirers can have evidence, assurance, and certitude regarding God that other inquirers lack, and this is no strike against God's goodness or reality.

Objective or logical certainty, such as that stemming from a mathematical proof, would require an evidential basis readily available to all capable inquirers. In contrast, God's self-manifestation, given its redemptive intent, would not be public or universal in that way. Instead, it would be selective in timing and scope for redemptive purposes, being sensitive to the receptivity of humans who would respond positively, negatively, or with indifference. If a person is opposed to any divine intervention or to divine existence itself, perhaps out of fear of losing "autonomy" of some kind (see Nagel 1997, p. 130), God could choose to refrain from self-manifesting to that person, at least until an opportune time.

The evidence from the self-manifestation of an elusive God, as suggested, would not reduce to the kinds of arguments found in traditional natural theology. Those arguments offer a kind of static evidence (however questionable) that does not intentionally bob and weave in the way a redemptive God would out of sensitivity to human receptivity. They thus illustrate a key difference between propositional evidence in arguments and interpersonal evidence from divine self-manifestation. A redemptive God would work with the latter evidence but have no requirement to use the former.

The divine redemption of humans would aim for something more profound and morally significant than intellectual acknowledgment of God's reality. It would aim for the *willing cooperation* of humans with God's perfect moral character and will, even if they lack intellectual acknowledgment of God's reality. A process of being cooperatively convicted and led by God, if only or primarily *de re*, would contribute to that aim. It also would allow for considerable diversity and even disagreement in human understanding or interpretation of the redemptive process. This is important, because social influences on humans will often result in such diversity and disagreement, even when humans have the best of intentions, including moral intentions. A perfectly good God would value good moral intentions over correct intellectual content regarding God. We should expect the evidence of God's reality to follow suit. It thus would give a key role to God's moral character and will, even when humans lack an adequate *de dicto* understanding or interpretation regarding God's purpose and intervention in human lives.

It is a live option, from the standpoint of the evidence of many people, that one God is at work in the presence of considerable intellectual and practical diversity among religions. Such a God could be after trust *de re* from humans, regardless of their intellectual commitments. In addition, the reality of such a God could figure centrally in a best available explanation of the moral experience of many people, who need not share religious beliefs. In that case, if they come to believe that God exists, this belief would not be a "guess," but would be an evidentially grounded commitment. The explanatory value attributed to (affirming) the reality of God would require that God have definite features that bear on human moral experience in a way that yields evidence of divine reality. The God in question, then, would not be an ineffable being of the sort proposed by some extreme versions of mysticism about religious experience. Even so, God could be incomprehensible in not being *fully* comprehensible by humans, say, with regard to full divine purposes toward humans. Such incomprehensibility does not entail divine ineffability as incompatibility with correct description.

5 GOD'S GAMBIT IN REDEMPTIVE DURESS

We can gain illumination by considering what would be central to God's overarching goal for humans in divine–human reconciliation. The goal would include some kind of divine communication with humans for the sake of their reconciliation to God. John Baillie has identified a likely difficulty for God regarding many people: "[A] great difficulty that confronts God in his desire to reveal himself to you and me, that thereby he may save us, is the difficulty of cutting through the dreadful tangle of dishonesty and lying and self-deception and pathetic make-believe with which we surround ourselves" (1941). This may seem to be a harsh assessment of humans, but we should be open nonetheless to a clash between the moral character of a perfect God and the moral character of typical humans. This clash could impede the human reception of divine revelation expressive of perfect goodness. As a result, God could adopt a strategy of some risk, a gambit, to counter this problem of human resistance.

According to my dictionary, a gambit is "a device, action, or opening remark, typically one entailing a degree of risk, that is calculated to gain an advantage; for instance, in chess: an opening in which a player makes a sacrifice, typically of a pawn, for the sake of some compensating advantage." Some near synonyms of "gambit" are: stratagem, scheme, tactic, maneuver. We should consider that God would enact a risky strategy of redemptive duress for God and humans, in order to establish and highlight the moral gravity of the divine redemptive effort. In this strategy, the risked duress would include the risked suffering of God and humans who face debilitating evil in the redemptive process aimed at divine–human reconciliation. A perfectly loving God would not forgo a redemptive effort to avoid a risk of costly suffering, including suffering as a result of evil.

The reality of divine suffering in redemptive duress would be understandable in a world like ours. Perfect *agapē* in a world of personal conflict would be "suffering love" in many situations, given one's frustrated goals for the good of other persons and the resulting grief for oneself. This would apply to God and to humans committed to a life of perfect *agapē* in interpersonal relationships. If God is inherently loving toward morally imperfect humans, suffering as grief or frustration would be part of God's own psychological and moral character. Such costly suffering would underlie a divine offer of forgiveness to humans doing wrong, and related suffering would underlie the human reception of forgiveness as a means to reconciliation with God.

Even if God is not causally responsible for all suffering and evil, God as Lord intentionally would *allow* the suffering and the evil that occur. In addition, it would be puzzling if human suffering and evil had no purpose while God could stop it. God could allow suffering and evil in order to participate in it somehow (without causing it) and thereby to redeem it by bringing good out of it. God's own costly suffering would be a self-chosen limitation, and not a case of a greater power imposing suffering on God against what God allows. So, divine suffering would not threaten God's lordship. Instead, God's lordship would supply a rationale for divine and human suffering, even if humans, given their cognitive limitations, do not fully understand it.

The suffering of Jesus and the evil inflicted on him by humans can illustrate how God would use costly redemptive duress in connection with suffering and evil. H. Wheeler Robinson explains: "The evil [of the Cross of Jesus] was permitted to triumph over the good that the evil might show its own nature and its utter futility when matched with the good. The Cross was a focal point of victory wrought by the goodness of Jesus against the evil of the world, though at a spiritual cost which we cannot measure" (1939, p. 169). Given this kind of redemptive transformation, according to Robinson, "the Cross of Christ shows us that the order of [God's] spiritual world reverses that of the physical. It moves not from life to death, but from death to life" (p. 174). Divine redemption thus would undermine selfish human power to make room for life-giving divine power, even in the midst of suffering, evil, and death.

In a Christian religious perspective, the divine pattern of redemption moving from death to life finds its high point in the death and resurrection of Jesus, but this is not its only manifestation. It would recur wherever divine redemption is at work. Michael Ramsey thus proposes: "The Christlikeness of God means that [Christ's] passion and resurrection are the key to the very meaning of God's own deity.... The [events of] self-giving [in] the suffering love were not ... mere incidents in the divine history" (1969, pp. 99–100). Why, however, is *this* the pattern for divine redemptive self-manifestation, when something less severe seems preferable to us?

The answer, if incomplete now, is in the ultimate motive and goal of divine redemption: *self-sacrificial agapē* among persons in relating to God and others, as something needed for meeting and living with God. John's Gospel represents Jesus as saying: "God so loved the world that he *gave* his only Son, so that everyone who believes in him may not perish but may have eternal life" (John 3:16). Similarly, Paul remarks that God "did not withhold his own Son, but gave him up for all of us" (Rom. 8:32), and that "God proves his love for us in that while we still were sinners Christ died for us" (Rom. 5:8). The writer of 1 John concurs: "God's love was revealed among us in this way: God sent his only Son into the world so that we might live through him. In this is love, not that we loved God but that he loved us and sent his Son to be the atoning sacrifice for our sins" (1 John 4:9–10). We thus should consider the sacrificial suffering of Jesus as reflecting the sacrificial suffering of *God* in sending Jesus to die for us. To say that God is love, then, is to say that God is costly self-sacrifice for the good of others. This fact would underwrite redemptive duress on God's part.

God's giving his unique Son for the sake of our having life with God would be inherently self-sacrificial love for us. Christ's self-giving death and resurrection offer a distinctive model for the unique divine love at work for humans. Such love calls for the end, the death, of all competing human power, for the sake of lasting human life in *God's* power. Paul identifies the divine aim in limiting human power in ways that involve redemptive suffering in human life: "We have this treasure in clay jars, so that it may be made clear that this extraordinary power belongs to God and does not come from us" (2 Cor. 4:7). This fact would underwrite redemptive duress in the lives of God's people.

Regarding one case of redemptive suffering, Paul puts the divine aim thus: "We felt that we had received the sentence of death so that we would rely not on ourselves but on God who raises the dead" (2 Cor. 1:9). This divine aim concerns what we ultimately *trust*: either God or ourselves. Human power that opposes or otherwise competes with divine power faces God's self-sacrificial love that calls for a reordering of typical human priorities, including what and how we trust and love. This requires death to old ways for the sake of new, divinely empowered ways. In that case, our ultimate self-trust would give way to ultimate trust in God, and our self-inadequacy or collapse in suffering could encourage us to welcome this shift toward God.

God's gambit of redemptive duress is illustrated in the allegorical parable of the wicked tenants attributed to Jesus in the synoptic gospels (Mark 12:1–12, Matt. 21:33–46, and Luke 20:9–19). Matthew's Gospel offers the parable as a model of how "the kingdom of God" approaches and challenges people who tend to resist God's plan for reconciliation, including God's aim for human cooperation in obedience. The divine kingdom is on loan to people, but it comes with God's expectations for their conforming to it rather than abusing it. The parable illustrates God's taking a calculated risk of abusive and murderous freedom among humans, including toward God's representatives in desired reconciliation.

God risks abusive human freedom by allowing distance between God and humans. In this portrait, God "went away" from the relevant humans (see Mark 12:1, Matt. 21:33) but still expected responsible behavior from them. God's gambit is in taking the risk of human abuse for the sake of showing God's faithfully redemptive character and action under duress. The costly redemptive death of Jesus is, according to the main New Testament message (and the parable of the wicked tenants), central to this gambit.

God's gambit presented in the New Testament opposes any easy story of a "quick-fix-it" God, who would not leave the time or opportunity for redemptive duress. Instead, it offers a God who risks and even patiently oversees human opposition, failure, and collapse for the sake of human redemption as reconciliation to God. Paul puts the gambit as follows: "The creation was subjected to futility, not of its own will but by the will of the one who subjected it, in hope that the creation itself will be set free from its bondage to decay and will obtain the freedom of the glory of the children of God" (Rom. 8:20–21). Paul thus suggests that God, without causing evil, subjects various human efforts and plans to futility or frustration, in order to draw people to appropriate the freedom in becoming children of God. In their failure and the resulting suffering, according to this view, people can find in God a better alternative for their well-being.

Helmut Thielicke has offered comments that elucidate the divine gambit:

In setting over against himself a being to whom he gave freedom and power, [God] risked the possibilities that the [human] child would become a competitor, that the child would become a megalomaniacal rival of the Creator.... This venture of God in which he bound himself to man – and exposed himself to the possibility of being reviled, despised, denied, and ignored by man – this venture was the first flash of his love. God ventured, as it were, his own self. He declared himself ready to suffer the pain the father endured when he let the prodigal son go into the far country, when he allowed deep wounds to be inflicted upon his heart, and still would not give up his child of sorrows. This line reaches its end in Jesus Christ. There God exposed himself to his rebellious children, put himself at their mercy, and let his most beloved die by their hand but for them. (1961, pp. 60–61).

These remarks cohere with Thielicke's aforementioned suggestion that "the afflictions of your life and mine are the
hollow ground under our feet which gives way because
God wills to catch us" (1962, p. 20).

God, we might say, would want reconciliation and
fellowship with humans "through thick and thin." So, there
must be both thick and thin if God is to test for the effect-
iveness of the divine redemptive gambit. In that case,
people would face a test of what (by way of response) *they
will do*, in relation to God, with the duress and the evil they
face, however extensive and tragic. Our learning love and
trust that endure toward God under redemptive duress
would call for tragic suffering on our part.

A likely question is whether the redemptive effort is
worthwhile in the end. Would it have been better not to
have lived at all? As Job responds in initial protest: "Why
was I not buried like a stillborn child, like an infant that
never sees the light? There the wicked cease from troubling,
and there the weary are at rest" (Job 3:16–17). Somehow
Job's protest gives way to his about-face response to God:
"I have uttered what I did not understand, things too wonderful for me, which I did not know. I had heard of you by
the hearing of the ear, but now my eye sees you; therefore,
I despise myself, and repent in dust and ashe" (Job 42:3–6).
Evidently, a transformative religious experience intervened.

The difficulty of redemptive duress offends many people
and calls for some comment. Thielicke has offered some
helpful remarks:

Here lies the solution of the problem of why God apparently
makes it so hard for us, of why he does not shout down
from heaven: "I am the chief of the cosmic general staff;
don't get excited when a tactical situation in your life is
incomprehensible!" If that were so, the kingdom of God would
be like the apparatus of a welfare state. Everything
would click, everything would be taken care of; but then we
would not need to bother about the *thing* [or the *One*] that took

care of us, because it would only be an anonymous apparatus and an apparatus has no heart. Instead of a loving heart, there would be nothing but a filing cabinet. (1961, pp. 54–55)

The relevant difference here is between a quick-fix-it God and a God who patiently seeks reconciliation and fellowship with people in righteous *agapē*. The latter God would oversee, guide, and participate in costly redemptive duress for the good of all concerned, even in cases of human despair and collapse. The redemption would come ultimately from divine restorative power, even in the absence of human success and progress. The supporting evidence for a human response of trust would come in the context of one's cooperatively knowing the God in question, even if one could not confirm the details of God's redemptive plan for the future.

God would seek a reconciled relationship with humans but not constant experience of God by them. Religious experience can become an idol in relation to God, because God would not be a religious experience and would be distorted and neglected in some religious experiences. As the history of religion shows, religious experiences range from the bizarre to the boring, and they include many counterfeits. God would seek loyal and obedient human commitment to God's morally perfect character and will for the sake of human benefit and meaning. God would seek and value such commitment even while one is not having a religious experience of God. Perhaps this lesson figures, at least for Jesus, in Jesus's cry of dereliction from the cross, but we are not in a position to settle this.

6 NORMATIVE MEANING IN RELIGIOUS EXPERIENCE

What remains now of overarching meaning in religion, of the kind outlined in Chapter 1? We end up with two pressing questions. Why, all things considered, should the overarching meaning for life offered by a religious perspective be normative for *my* life? In addition, why, all things considered, should the overarching meaning for life offered by a religious perspective be normative for *all* human lives, universally? In short, why should I and others conform to the meaning proposed by a religious position? Inquirers will face such questions sooner or later, and they do well to face them directly with candor. Such questions can invite *relativism* about religious meaning, the view that such meaning bears on people not universally but at most locally, relative to their varying religious commitments. Many proponents of religion, however, do not settle for that kind of relativism. They think of "the meaning of human life" as bearing on all people, regardless of variation in religious beliefs. Is that position sustainable?

A theistic religion could supply a distinctive kind of overarching meaning for human life. It could do so via *God's* overarching intention for divine–human (including human–human) reconciliation in human lives universally. Such an intention would lead to morally relevant religious experiences for humans, at least for those humans open to, or cooperative with, the reconciliation on offer. God would rely on such experiences to advance the overarching project of reconciliation (and resulting *koinōnia*, or fellowship) between God and humans and, on that basis, among humans.

The divine purpose of reconciliation would bear on my life, for instance, because I am a member of the group for which God would seek divine–human reconciliation. In addition, it would bear on human lives universally, because a perfectly loving God would seek to include all humans in the grand reconciliation. If one's evidence provides access to God's priorities for humans, one could rely on those priorities for responsible decisions, all things considered, bearing on life's meaning. So, a theistic religion could avoid some clear threats of relativism about the normativity of meaning in religious experience. Many inquirers will consider this a benefit of a theistic religion.

Chapter 7 characterized the kind of moral experience that would include divine intervention aimed at moral conviction and leading toward God's moral character. The process would be inherently intentional owing to God's redemptive purpose. Even so, humans could resist the divine effort and thereby obscure the relevant evidence of God's redemptive effort in their experience. Humans who choose not to resist, in contrast, could enter a meaningful relationship with God (and others) that brings lasting purpose or meaning to human life. The purpose would be to sustain, deepen, and expand divine–human reconciliation (and, as a result, human–human reconciliation) in human lives. Some advocates of theistic religion, including Paul and Tolstoy, have testified to the reality and moral power of such a relationship. Similarly, the theistic religions of Moses, Muhammad, and Krishna can acknowledge the divine redemptive effort in human moral experience. One God can work in diverse contexts of theological interpretation. So, the kind of redemptive evidence of God characterized in this chapter and Chapter 7 should not be restricted to just one context of religious interpretation.

We should not settle for the following pragmatic argument for a theistic religion: Humans need an alternative to relativism about religious meaning; theism (alone) provides that alternative; therefore, we should endorse a theistic religion. Many inquirers rightly will be unmoved by such an argument, because they demand evidence for the *reality* of the God in question, the God whose singularity of overarching purpose can undermine relativism. It is not adequate for evidentially grounded belief that God exists to identify a human *need* that God (alone) would satisfy. The relevant need may end up unsatisfied, even if an existing God *would* satisfy it.

We should ask whether a theistic religion would be more effective than a nontheistic religion in countering relativism about the religious meaning of life. Nontheistic religions, we have seen, propose overarching meaning for human life in virtue of being religions, but they do not acknowledge God's reality, at least with regard to life's meaning. So, they do not acknowledge a God whose overarching redemptive purpose for humans gives value and meaning to human life in general.

Clearly, a purpose embraced by an individual human does not automatically have normative value for humans in general. My aim to buy an inexpensive ghost town in North Dakota, for instance, does not automatically bear on the meaning of your life. You may have nothing to do with my adventurous aim, and you may even consider it to be bizarre. God's purposes, however, would differ from my purposes in their normative status, because God would be involved at least as Creator in the lives of all people. God's purposes thus would have a moral relevance for all people in a way that my purposes do not.

Nontheistic religions that reject relativism need to explain what gives general normative significance to their acknowledged sources of meaning for life. One might appeal to humanly shared values as a basis for general meaning, but one will need to explain why *these* values rather than others yield life's meaning for all involved. Many inquirers plausibly will demand a convincing explanation in this area, if only to avoid an arbitrary position on the meaning of life. The absence for many people of such an explanation contributes to widespread religious disagreement and diversity, and we have no quick or easy way to bring about agreement in this area. Our various religious communities illustrate this fact, enduringly. Some people will embrace relativism about the religious meaning of life and let matters stand there. Others will seek a deeper unity for such meaning, as an alternative to relativism.

We have linked religion to a proposal about "the meaning of life" for humans on the basis of religious experience. The definite article "the" is crucial here. A religion does not propose simply *a* meaning for human life or just *my* (or just *your*) meaning for human life. Otherwise, it would amount to the kind of meaning found in nonreligious proposals for meaning *in* human life, rather than *the meaning of* human life. The key issue, then, is: What exactly gives singularity to the meaning of life, and why? For any proposal, why is *that*, rather than something else, the proposed base for meaning? In other words, why is that the (alleged) singular value for the meaning of human life? These are urgent questions for any religion, because it is inherent to a religion to offer overarching meaning for human life. As a result, a religion should offer a firm base in something valuable for its singular proposal for the meaning of life.

We have suggested that a theistic religion can ground its proposal for the meaning of life in the singular character and purpose of God. A nontheistic religion will not invoke that ground, but it will need to find a different ground to avoid relativism. In offering a different ground, such as some relevant value or other, a nontheistic religion will need to account for the special relevance of the value proposed. As suggested, many people will wonder why that proposed value, rather than some other, has the singular role of grounding the meaning of human life. The answer will need to have some perceived relevance for inquirers, and not be just a dogma or a doctrine. It will have to be the kind of consideration that makes sense to inquirers, even if they have their doubts about its truth. Here we have a big remaining task for nontheistic religions. Given space limitations, we must leave it as unfinished business for such religions.

Chapter 3 asked whether traditional monotheism is too demanding of humans in connection with the love-commands and required absolute submission to God. The concern is that ordinary humans lack the power to meet the demands in question. A response should distinguish human power that depends on God's power and human power that does not. Even if the latter kind of power will fail, it is not clear that the former kind of power will always fail. In any case, a perfectly good God would encourage

humans to rely on divine power for their moral improvement. In addition, such a God would offer forgiveness in
cases of human failure. So, monotheism need not be harmful or unjust in this area.

Regarding a human need for power, Chapter 4 noted
the following confession of Confucius: "That I have not
cultivated virtue, that I have learned but not explained, that
I have heard what is right but failed to align with it,
that what is not good in me I have been unable to change –
these are my worries" (*Analects* 7.3). The worry relevant
now is that "what is not good in me I have been unable to
change." This is a worry about the power needed to change
what is not good in oneself. Confucius apparently lacks
confidence that he has the needed power. His candor
should prompt our consideration of whether divine power
is needed where human power is dubious. The same consideration should bear on Gautama's recommended exclusive path for *self*-purification toward self-Awakening.
A nontheistic interpretation of religion must face the worry
of Confucius with candor, whatever the outcome. In any
case, my own experience supports that worry as fitting
and appropriate for typical humans, in their volitional and
moral weakness.

Some people disavow their having any religious experience, theistic or nontheistic. We have no firm ground to
reject their disavowal, at least in many cases. As a result,
some people will persist in being nonreligious, at least by
their own acknowledgment. This consideration is no threat
to a durable religious perspective. We have no good reason
to suppose that everyone does or should have a religious
experience. In the case of theistic religion, as noted, divine
hiding is pertinent. God could have good reasons not to
intrude at present in the awareness of some people, such
as people resistant to God's presence in their experience.
So, God could postpone a religious experience for such
people. They still could have moral experiences, even

relative to moral laws, but those experiences need not include the sensed presence of God. So, the reality of some people without religious experience is compatible with a theistic religion well-grounded for other people.

Diversity of religious evidence and experience is a fact of life among humans. We have no good reason to deny it or to disparage it. Acknowledgment of such diversity invites an important lesson: We can reject relativism about religious *truth* while acknowledging variability in what is *reasonable* relative to religious evidence and experience among humans. Truth and reasonableness do not always walk together, inside or outside religion. Reasonableness in religion for a person is ultimately a function of that person's (available) religious evidence and thus of that person's religious experience, or the lack thereof.

Since religious evidence and experience can vary among humans, what is reasonable from a religious point of view can likewise vary among humans. So, a claim to a single religious position required of all reasonable people entails a tall order. Such a claim must find a common basis of religious evidence and experience for all people, and that is no small task. Indeed, it seems to be a task in conflict with our empirical evidence about actual humans and their religious evidence and experience. At least, I find no firm ground to reject the evident variation in religious evidence and experience. Any competition about the reasonableness of religious perspectives, I recommend, should be tempered by the evident variation in religious evidence and experience among actual humans.

We have seen that religion seeks overarching meaning for life on the basis of religious experience. Such meaning, when grounded in suitable value, is significant for humans in various ways, including for the integration of purposes in human lives. Inquirers are therefore well advised to be vigilant about the availability and the reality of religious experiences in their lives. They thus could find a deep, value-based reason for living their lives, beyond just persisting in a fragmented life. In that case, religious experience would yield new, meaningful life for their good. We will do well, then, to be attentive to the potential value of religious experience for our lives, even if this demands considerable effort on our part. The value may justify the effort for us and for others, as well. If it does, religious experience will merit our ongoing attention, perhaps even in our practical lives.

References

Abe, Masao. 1993. "Buddhism." In *Our Religions*, edited by Arvind Sharma, pp. 69–137. New York: HarperCollins.

Armstrong, Karen. 2001. *Buddha*. New York: Viking Penguin.

2009. *The Case for God*. New York: Knopf.

Arnold, Matthew. 1883. *Literature and Dogma*. London: Smith, Elder. Online at: https://en.wikisource.org/wiki/Index:Literature_and_Dogma.

Aubrey, Edwin. 1933. "The Authority of Religious Experience Re-examined." *Journal of Religion* 13, 433–49.

Baillie, John. 1929. *The Interpretation of Religion*. Edinburgh: T&T Clark.

1939. *Our Knowledge of God*. London: Oxford University Press.

1941. Sermon cited in Torrance 1961.

Barth, Karl. 1925 [1962]. "The Principles of Dogmatics According to Wilhelm Herrmann." In Barth, *Theology and Church*, trans. Louise Pettibone Smith, pp. 238–71. London: SCM Press.

Berkouwer, G. C. 1958. *Faith and Perseverance*, trans. R. D. Knudsen. Grand Rapids, MI: Eerdmans.

Bhagavad-Gita, trans. Edwin Arnold. New York: Truslove, Hanson, & Comba, 1900. Online at: www.gutenberg.org/files/2388/2388-h/2388-h.htm.

Bhagavad-Gita (contemporary translation). Online at: www.holy-bha gavad-gita.org/.

Boucher, Madeleine. 1977. *The Mysterious Parable*. Washington, DC: Catholic Biblical Association.

Brown, William Adams. 1930. *Pathways to Certainty*. New York: Charles Scribner's Sons.

Brunner, Emil. 1962. *The Christian Doctrine of the Church, Faith, and the Consummation: Dogmatics*, vol. 3, trans. David Cairns. London: Lutterworth Press.

Buber, Martin. 1923. *I and Thou*, trans. R. G. Smith. New York: Charles Scribner's Sons, 1958.

Bultmann, Rudolf. 1951. *Theology of the New Testament*, vol. 1, trans. Kendrick Grobel. New York: Charles Scribner's Sons.

Confucius. *Analects*. Online at: www.indiana.edu/~p374/Analects_of_Confucius_(Eno-2015).pdf.

Conze, Edward, ed. 1959. *Buddhist Scriptures*. London: Penguin Books.

Dawkins, Richard. 1996. *River out of Eden*. New York: Basic Books.
2006. *The God Delusion*. New York: Houghton Mifflin.

De Burgh, W. G. 1939. *Knowledge of the Individual*. London: Oxford University Press.

Dennett, Daniel. 2006. *Breaking the Spell: Religion as a Natural Phenomenon*. New York: Viking Penguin.

Dhammacakkappavattana Sutta 56. Online at: www.dhammatalks.org/suttas/SN/SN56_11.html.

Dhammapada 12. Online at: www.dhammatalks.org/suttas/KN/Dhp/Ch12.html.

Dickie, Edgar P. 1954. *God Is Light: Studies in Revelation and Personal Conviction*. New York: Charles Scribner's Sons.

Dunn, James D. G. 1998. "Discernment of Spirits – A Neglected Gift." In Dunn, *The Christ and the Spirit*, vol. 2, pp. 311–28. Grand Rapids, MI: Eerdmans.

Dvedhāvitakka Sutta, Majjhima Nikāya 19. Online at: www.dhammatalks.org/suttas/MN/MN19.html.

Eichrodt, Walther. 1967. *Theology of the Old Testament*, vol. 2, trans. J. A. Baker. Philadelphia: Westminster Press.

Eliade, Mircea. 1959. *The Sacred and the Profane*, trans. W. R. Trask. New York: Houghton Mifflin.

Farmer, H. H. 1929. *Experience of God*. New York: Doubleday.
1935. *The World and God*. London: Nisbet.
1942. *The Servant of the Word*. New York: Charles Scribner's Sons.

Farrer, Austin. 1966. *A Science of God?* London: SPCK.

Fitzmyer, Joseph. 1993. *Romans*. New York: Doubleday.

Fodor, Jerry. 1998. *In Critical Condition*. Cambridge, MA: MIT Press.

Forrest, David W. 1906. *The Authority of Christ*. Edinburgh: T&T Clark.

Forsyth, P. T. 1909. *The Person and Place of Jesus Christ*. London: Independent Press.
1912. *The Principle of Authority*. London: Hodder and Stoughton.

Freud, Sigmund. 1913. *Totem and Taboo*. New York: Norton, 1990.
1927 [1961]. *The Future of an Illusion*, trans. James Strachey. New York: Norton.
1930 [1961]. *Civilization and Its Discontents*, trans. James Strachey. New York: Norton.
1933. "A Philosophy of Life." In Freud, *New Introductory Lectures on Psychoanalysis*. New York: Carlton House.
1939 [1967]. *Moses and Monotheism*, trans. Katherine Jones. New York: Random House.

Gale, Richard. 1991. *On the Nature and Existence of God*. Cambridge: Cambridge University Press.

Garnett, Arthur Campbell. 1945. *God in Us*. Chicago: Willett, Clark.
1952. *The Moral Nature of Man*. New York: Ronald Press.
1955. *Religion and the Moral Life*. New York: Ronald Press.

Glover, T. R. 1917. *The Jesus of History*. London: Association Press.

Gould, Stephen Jay. 1992. "Impeaching a Self-Appointed Judge." *Scientific American* 267, pp. 118–21. Online at: www.stephenjay gould.org/reviews/gould_darwin-on-trial.html.
1999. *Rocks of Ages: Science and Religion in the Fullness of Life*. New York: Ballantine.

Hardy, Alister. 1979. *The Spiritual Nature of Man: Study of Contemporary Religious Experience*. Oxford: Oxford University Press.

Herrmann, Wilhelm. 1903 [1971]. *The Communion of the Christian with God*, trans. J. Sandys Stanyon and R. W. Stewart; ed. Robert T. Voelkel. Philadelphia: Fortress Press.

Heschel, Abraham Joshua. 1996. "A Preface to an Understanding of Revelation." In Heschel, *Moral Grandeur and Spiritual Audacity*, edited by Susannah Heschel, pp. 185–90. New York: Farrar, Straus and Giroux.

Hick, John. 1977. *Evil and the God of Love*, 2nd ed. New York: Macmillan.

Hood, Ralph W., Peter C. Hill, and Bernard Spilka. 2009. *The Psychology of Religion*, 4th ed. New York: Guilford Press.

Hubbard, Moyer. 2002. *New Creation in Paul's Letters and Thought*. Cambridge: Cambridge University Press.

Hultgren, Arland J. 2000. *The Parables of Jesus*. Grand Rapids, MI: Eerdmans.

James, William. 1890. *Principles of Psychology*. New York: Henry Holt.
1902. *Varieties of Religious Experience*. New York: Modern Library.
1909. *A Pluralistic Universe*. London: Longmans.

Jataka. Online at: www.sacred-texts.com/bud/j1/index.htm.

Jones, Rufus. 1931. *Pathways to the Reality of God*. New York: Macmillan.

The Junzi Practices Ritual. Online at: www.indiana.edu/~p374/Ana lects_of_Confucius_(Eno-2015).pdf.

Kant, Immanuel. 1783 [1978]. *Lectures on Philosophical Theology*, trans. A. W. Wood and G. M. Clark. Ithaca, NY: Cornell University Press.

Käsemann, Ernst. 1980. *Commentary on Romans*, trans. G. W. Bromiley. Grand Rapids, MI: Eerdmans.

Kierkegaard, Søren. 1846. *Concluding Unscientific Postscript to Philosophical Fragments*, trans. H. V. Hong and E. H. Hong. Princeton, NJ: Princeton University Press, 1992.

Kyburg, Henry. 1970. *Probability and Inductive Logic*. New York: Macmillan.

Lash, Nicholas. 1990. *Easter in Ordinary*. Notre Dame, IN: University of Notre Dame Press.

Lehmann, Paul. 1963. *Ethics in a Christian Context*. New York: Harper and Row.

Leslie, John. 1979. *Value and Existence*. Oxford: Blackwell.

Levenson, Jon D. 2016. *The Love of God*. Princeton, NJ: Princeton University Press.

Mackintosh, H. R. 1921. *The Divine Initiative*. London: SCM.

　　1929. *The Christian Apprehension of God*. London: SCM.

　　1938. "An Indisputable Argument." In Mackintosh, *Sermons*, pp. 171–79. Edinburgh: T&T Clark.

Mahā Assapura Sutta 39. Online at: www.dhammatalks.org/suttas/MN/MN39.html.

Majjhima Nikaya 36. Online at: www.dhammatalks.org/suttas/MN/MN36.html.

Majjhima Nikaya 100. Online at: www.metta.lk/tipitaka/2Sutta-Pitaka/2Majjhima-Nikaya/Majjhima2/100-sangarava-e1.html.

Maltby, William Russell. 1921. *The Meaning of the Resurrection*. London: Epworth Press.

Marshall, I. Howard. 2008. *Aspects of the Atonement*. Milton Keynes: Paternoster.

Martin, Ralph P. 1981. *Reconciliation: A Study of Paul's Theology*. Atlanta, GA: John Knox Press.

Matthews, W. R. 1936. "Who Is God?" *The Modern Churchman* 26, 176–82.

McClendon, James Wm., Jr., and James M. Smith. 1975. *Understanding Religious Convictions*. Notre Dame, IN: University of Notre Dame Press.

Meadors, Edward. 2006. *Idolatry and the Hardening of the Heart*. Edinburgh: T&T Clark.

Moser, Paul K. 1989. *Knowledge and Evidence*. Cambridge: Cambridge University Press.

　　1993. *Philosophy after Objectivity*. New York: Oxford University Press.

　　2008. *The Elusive God*. Cambridge: Cambridge University Press.

　　2010. *The Evidence for God*. Cambridge: Cambridge University Press.

　　2013. *The Severity of God*. Cambridge: Cambridge University Press.

　　2017. *The God Relationship*. Cambridge: Cambridge University Press.

　　2020. "Natural Theology: A Deflationary Approach." In *Natural Theology: Five Views*, edited by James K. Dew and R. P. Campbell. Grand Rapids, MI: Baker Academic. Forthcoming.

Moser, Paul K., and J. D. Trout, eds. 1995. *Contemporary Materialism*. London: Routledge.

Moule, C. F. D. 2011. "The Energy of God." In Moule, *Christ Alive and at Large*, edited by Robert Morgan, pp. 93–110. London: Canterbury Press.

Murphy, Jeffrie, and Jean Hampton. 1988. *Forgiveness and Mercy*. Cambridge: Cambridge University Press.

Nagel, Thomas. 1997. *The Last Word*. New York: Oxford University Press.

Neusner, Jacob. 1993. "Judaism." In *Our Religions*, edited by Arvind Sharma, pp. 291–355. New York: HarperCollins.

Niebuhr, Reinhold. 1940. "Why the Christian Church Is not Pacifist." In *The Essential Reinhold Niebuhr*, edited by Robert McAfee Brown, pp. 102–19. New Haven, CT: Yale University Press, 1986.

1941. *The Nature and Destiny of Man*, vol. 1. New York: Charles Scribner's Sons.

1949. *Faith and History*. New York: Charles Scribner's Sons.

1966. "Faith as the Sense of Meaning in Human Existence." In *Niebuhr, Faith and Politics*, edited by R. H. Stone, pp. 3–13. New York: George Braziller, 1968.

Otto, Rudolf. 1923. *The Idea of the Holy*, trans. J. W. Harvey. London: Oxford University Press.

Pascal, Blaise. 1658 [1966]. *Pensées*, trans. A. J. Krailsheimer. London: Penguin Books.

Plantinga, Alvin. 2000. *Warranted Christian Belief*. New York: Oxford University Press.

Plato. 1997. *Phaedo*, trans. G. M. A. Grube. In *Plato: Complete Works*, edited by J. M. Cooper, pp. 49–100. Indianapolis, IN: Hackett.

Quine, W. V. O. 1990. *Pursuit of Truth*. Cambridge, MA: Harvard University Press.

Qur'an, trans. Talal Itani. Online at: www.clearquran.com/.

Railton, Peter. 1986. "Moral Realism." *Philosophical Review* 95, 163–207.

Ramsey, Michael. 1969. *God, Christ, and the World*. London: SCM Press.

Rescher, Nicholas. 2010. *Axiogenesis*. Lanham, MD: Lexington Books.

Robinson, H. Wheeler. 1939. *Suffering: Human and Divine*. London: Macmillan.

Robinson, N. H. G. 1956. *Christ and Conscience*. London: Nisbet.

Rossé, Gérard. 1987. *The Cry of Jesus on the Cross*, trans. S. W. Arndt. New York: Paulist Press.

Russell, Bertrand. 1903. "A Free Man's Worship." In Russell, *Mysticism and Logic*, pp. 44–54. New York: Doubleday, 1957.

1911. "Knowledge by Acquaintance and Knowledge by Description." *Proceedings of the Aristotelian Society* 11, 108–28.

Samyutta Nikaya 12. Online at: www.dhammatalks.org/suttas/SN/SN12_65.html.

Snodgrass, Klyne. 2008. *Stories with Intent*. Grand Rapids, MI: Eerdmans.

Stewart, James S. 1940. *The Strong Name*. Edinburgh: T&T Clark.

1996. *Walking with God*, edited by Gordon Grant. Edinburgh: Saint Andrew Press.

Taylor, Vincent. 1946. *Forgiveness and Reconciliation*, 2nd ed. London: Macmillan.

Thielicke, Helmut. 1961. *How the World Began*, trans. J. W. Doberstein. Philadelphia: Muhlenberg.

1962. *Out of the Depths*, trans. G. W. Bromiley. Grand Rapids, MI: Eerdmans.

1982. *The Evangelical Faith, vol. 3: Theology of the Spirit*, trans. G. W. Bromiley. Grand Rapids, MI: Eerdmans.

Tolstoy, Lev (Leo). 1882 [1921]. *My Confession*, trans. Aylmer Maude. London: Oxford University Press.

1882 [1983]. *My Confession*, trans. David Patterson. New York: Norton.

Torrance, T. F. 1961. "A Living Sacrifice: In Memoriam, John Baillie." *Religion in Life* 30, 329–33.

Watkins, John. 1984. *Science and Scepticism*. Princeton, NJ: Princeton University Press.

Wei-ming, Tu. 1993. "Confucianism." In *Our Religions*, edited by Arvind Sharma, pp. 139–227. New York: HarperCollins.

Zuurdeeg, Willem F. 1958. *An Analytical Philosophy of Religion*. Nashville, TN: Abingdon Press.

Index

Aaron, 77
abandoned by God, 250
Abba, 89, 172
abduction, 24, 286
Abe, Masao, 103
Abiathar, 131
Abraham, 75, 80, 86, 90, 118, 126,
    168, 174, 252, 311
adoption, 89, 172
adoration, 74, 113, 115
affections, 272
afflictions, 311, 326
agapē, 88, 124, 220, 235, 248–50, 254,
    258, 268–71, 275–78, 288–92,
    314–15, 321, 323, 327
agapē experience, 288
agency, 40–41, 128, 161, 164–65, 230,
    245, 253, 256, 258, 262, 264, 268,
    308
agnostics, 243–44, 250, 293, 317
aliens, 119, 130, 132
Allah, 90
altar, 78
altruistic love, 235
ambassadors, 124
amorphous mysticism, 315
Analects, 62–63
angels, 92, 94, 127
anthropology of morals, 212
anti-God arguments, 311
anti-religious diagnosis, 202, 209
anti-religious sentiment, 196

apologetics, 276
apologists, 250
apostle, 83
appearance–reality distinction, 49
Aristotle, 13, 36
Arjuna, 68–70, 164, 203
Armstrong, Karen, 53, 103
Arnold, Matthew, 210
assurance, 89, 156, 187, 225, 250,
    318
atheists, 243–44, 250, 293, 317
atonement, 77–80, 82, 84–86, 89, 96,
    116–18, 120, 123, 167, 203, 219,
    297, 305
attention-attraction, 7, 47, 76
autonomy, 167, 319
Awakening, 53–58, 60–61, 98, 105–8,
    154–55, 157–59, 199, 218, 332

Baillie, John, 221, 225–31, 320
baptism, 122
Barth, Karl, 37–39
becoming, 58, 199
behavior, 104
being commanded, 92, 125, 174, 176,
    206, 220
being convicted, 9, 260–61, 263
being mistaken, 286
being morally convicted, 267,
    286–87, 315–16
belief in God, 102, 127, 175, 197, 243,
    282, 284, 291

benevolence, 65–66, 109–10, 160–61,
    198, 223
best available explanation, 25, 31,
    233, 271, 283, 285–86, 290–92,
    320
Bhagavad-Gita, 68
biology, 139, 142
bliss, 71, 113, 202
Brahma, 72
Brunner, Emil, 39
Buber, Martin, 241, 318
Buddhism, 14, 24, 52, 67, 103. *See also*
    Gautama

call, 203
Calvary, 248, 250, 305
Canaan, 75–76, 204
celibacy, 115, 165
certainty, 94, 151, 163, 190, 262, 318
certitude, 318
cessation, 54, 56, 105
change, 56
chemistry, 139, 142, 148
children, 89, 112, 132, 168, 172–73,
    185, 255–56, 266, 270, 325
Christ, 39, 83–85, 87, 89, 97, 121–22,
    124, 133, 170–71, 205, 220, 251,
    253, 257, 275, 302, 311, 322–23,
    325
Christian theism, 8, 239
Christianity, 8, 16, 24, 52
Christlikeness of God, 322
Christological lesson, 296, 304, 306
Christology, 296–97, 306, 312
Civilization and Its Discontents, 187,
    191
civitas Dei, 226
clairvoyance, 144
Climacus, 318
clinging, 55
clock winder, 214
coercion, 89, 244, 256, 263
cognitive modesty, 143, 146, 178,
    312
cognitively responsible, 181, 243
color concepts, 23

communication, 23, 91, 112, 172, 178,
    320
community, 90, 112, 247, 261, 273,
    288
companionship, 226
concept, 21, 50
    descriptive, 24
    explanatory, 23
conceptions of God, 98
conceptual diversity, 22
conflict of conscience, 259
Confucian self, 109
Confucianism, 14, 24, 62, 67
Confucius, 27, 62–67, 70, 74–76,
    80, 96, 98, 104, 109–12, 121,
    159–64, 183, 200, 202, 218, 222,
    239, 332, 336–37. *See also*
    Analects
conscience, 41, 89, 119, 191, 205, 207,
    227, 231, 234–37, 259, 262, 277,
    281, 286–87, 289–90, 295, 314,
    316
    critical, 234
    traditional, 234
consciousness, 54–56, 74, 115,
    164–65, 199, 273, 318
Constant-Adoration Theism, 68, 74,
    89, 97, 164
contemplative, 107
converts, 255
conviction, 8–9, 11, 13, 40, 186, 191,
    224, 261–62
conviction-avoidance, 275
convictional evidence, 314
convictional knowledge, 272–73,
    275–76
    social role, 273
cooperation, 82, 273
cooperative conviction, 265, 268–70,
    276, 319
cooperative maturation, 258
cooperative power, 265
core religious experience, 7, 42, 52,
    100
Corinth, 122–23, 274
Corinthian church, 122

cosmic physicalism, 143
court of law, 161
covenant, 77, 80, 82, 116, 120, 123, 167–68, 220
creation, 93, 171, 270, 290, 295, 308, 325
creator, 92, 193
cross of Christ, 88, 322
crucifixion, 84, 87, 298, 301–2, 305–7
cry of dereliction, 250, 299, 327
curse, 79

Damascus, 83–84, 88, 220
dao, 62, 65, 218
Daoism, 14
Dawkins, Richard, 140, 150–53, 177–78, 184, 208, 216, 246
Day of Atonement, 78
de dicto faith, 292, 317
de dicto features, 46
de re faith, 281
de re features, 46, 48, 267, 318
de te features, 318
death, 54, 122, 248
decision, 11
    all things considered, 35, 99
    epistemically responsible, 35, 99, 135
defeaters, 282–84, 291–92, 316
    direct, 284
    indirect, 284
deficient moral profundity, 305
deism, 214, 242, 282
delusions, 183, 189–90, 208
Democritus, 177
demons, 144
Dennett, Daniel, 142–44, 153, 177–78
design in nature, 273
designer, 250, 274
despair, 54–55, 58, 141, 294, 305, 327
Deuteronomy, 118–19, 130
devotion, 69, 74, 113, 235
diachronic, 258, 289
Dickie, Edgar P., 40, 263–64
disbelievers, 126

discernment, 55, 71, 155, 175, 250, 268, 270
dissonance, 289
divided self, 16
divine agency, 165
divine approval, 85–87, 96
divine command, 94
divine concealment, 300
divine elusiveness, 99, 217, 316
divine grace, 86, 121, 277, 279, 305
divine hate, 132
divine hiding, 280, 298, 308–9, 314, 332
divine holiness, 78
divine intervention, 76, 142, 220, 237, 290, 319, 329
divine law, 95
divine love, 132–33, 205, 248, 250, 252–53, 255, 257–60, 264–69, 283, 299, 314, 323
divine power, 71, 75, 202, 214–15, 248, 252–53, 322, 324, 327, 332
divine presence, 76, 114, 119, 165, 268
divine purposes, 214, 270, 293, 295, 297–98, 301, 320
divine revelation, 91, 149, 196, 266, 295, 321
divine self-authentication, 251–52
divine self-manifestation, 72, 202–3, 206, 230, 246, 259, 266, 275–76, 280, 283, 319
divine severity, 276
divine superintendence, 216–17
divine testing, 247
dogmatism, 25, 32, 39, 163, 170
dream, 286–87
dues, 96
Dunn, James D. G., 255
duty, 10, 114, 227, 235, 259, 267, 310
dying, 18, 29, 59, 84, 87, 122, 133

earning, 80, 85–87, 95, 121, 125, 277
effluents, 58

ego, 191–92
egocentric perspective, 44
Egypt, 75–76, 119, 167, 203
Egyptians, 76–77
Eichrodt, Walther, 119
eightfold path, 56, 106, 158
Eliade, Mircea, 26, 28
eliminativism, 44, 144
empirical test, 215
empiricism, 144, 146–47, 177
encounter, 317–18
ends in themselves, 129
enemies, 132–33, 135, 249, 259–61,
    264, 266–67, 277, 289, 306
enemy-love, 132, 260
  Jesus, 132
  Jewish Bible, 132
  Paul, 133
  Qur'an, 133
Enlightenment, 27, 53. See also
    Awakening
entrusted gifts, 279
epistemic abductivism, 291
epistemic assessment, 243
epistemic gap, 293
epistemic reasonableness, 282,
    285–86, 292
eschatological, 82, 88, 198
Eucharist, 122
evidence, 35, 98, 287
  available, 99, 313
  foundational, 271, 282, 285
  having, 240
  person-relativity, 246
  presenting, 240
  private, 273
  public, 178, 273
  readily available, 35
  reproducible, 281
  socially readily shareable, 201
  standard for, 245
  subjective, 178
  truth-indicator, 287
  undefeated, 240
evidential arbitrariness, 135
evidential promiscuity, 280
evidential support relation, 284

evil, 4, 7, 15, 27–28, 36, 68, 99, 107,
    132–33, 136, 140, 154, 192, 225,
    227, 248, 261, 270, 275, 283, 293,
    295–303, 305–13, 321–22, 325,
    335; see also psychological
    problem of evil
  experience of, 312
  problem of, 296, 304, 306, 309–10,
    312
existential dissonance, 259
exodus, 77, 84, 219
experience, 48
  apparent, 50
  of evil, 312
experimentation, 146
explanation, 25, 177
explanatory value, 211, 292,
    311, 320
external world, 43

fabrications, 57
facts, 44
faith, 86–87, 94, 121
  in God, 269, 281
fallibilism, 145, 147, 163
fallibility, 44
false gods, 254
Farmer, H. H., 6, 289
fate, 189
father figure, 189, 193–94, 201–2,
    205, 207
fear, 37, 39, 68, 76, 89, 95, 118, 121,
    126, 172, 182, 189–90, 203, 222,
    232, 258, 265, 311, 319
fellowship, 88, 205, 212, 220, 230,
    288, 326–28
fideism, 33, 152, 163, 170, 217, 240,
    278
fine-tuner, 250, 274
fine-tuning in nature, 273
first cause, 250, 273
Fitzmyer, Joseph, 255
Fodor, Jerry, 140
forgiveness, 79, 117, 134, 205, 230,
    305, 321, 332
Forrest, David, 251, 272
fossil record, 215

foundational evidence, 285, 288, 291
Freud, Sigmund, 149, 180–86,
        188–209, 225, 232
fulfillment, 83
futility of life, 315
future, 82
Future of an Illusion, The, 181, 187–88

Gabriel, 92
Gale, Richard, 245–46
Galileans, 50, 303
gambit, 321, 324–25
Garnett, Arthur Campbell, 230–37,
        271, 289
Gautama, 27, 52–62, 64–67, 70,
        74–76, 80, 96, 98, 104–5, 107–8,
        112, 121, 154–59, 183, 199–200,
        202, 218, 222, 239, 332
Genesis, 169, 171
genetic diagnosis, 201
Gentiles, 83, 86, 132, 301
Gethsemane, 248, 268, 307
ghosts, 144
given, the, 46
glory, 70, 81, 171–72
goal-directed, 102
God, 45, 66, 69, 75, 115
    arguments for, 244, 250, 274, 292
    being known, 249
    candidates, 245
    causal power, 142
    conceptions of, 98
    creator, 330
    enemy-love, 133
    evidence, 89, 178, 274
    factual knowledge, 278
    faith in, 121, 123, 127
    false, 28
    hiding, 94, 98, 153, 280, 288, 296,
        298, 313, 318
    immanence, 244
    is love, 254
    knowledge of, 74
    led by, 89, 172, 205–6, 244, 255–57,
        259, 262, 264–65, 268, 270, 316,
        319
    monarch, 222
    moral character, 134
    moral prerogative, 308
    personal agent, 205
    power, 41
    promiscuous, 280
    public evidence, 153
    responsible, 294
    self-authenticating, 252
    self-evidencing, 252, 281
    self-manifesting, 70, 89, 104, 153, 229
    sensory evidence, 278
    sensory safety-net, 278
    suffering, 323
    superintendent, 217
    testing, 247
    title, 22, 242, 249
God's absence, 313–14
God's gambit, 320, 324–25
Godward striving, 271
Golden Rule, 110
Good News, 253
goodness, 110, 313
gospel, 122, 170, 253
Gould, Stephen Jay, 210–17
grace, 85, 87, 125, 170
    gift, 279
guesses, 163, 234, 320
guilt offering, 117

Hajj, 126
happiness, 20, 115, 165, 190–91, 197,
        222–24, 229
Hardy, Alister, 45
heart, 40, 58, 62, 65, 70, 72–73, 80,
        91–92, 94, 113, 115, 118–19, 121,
        129–31, 160, 167–68, 218, 224,
        226–27, 237, 247, 263, 325, 327
Heaven, 62
Hebrew Bible, 75, 84–85
Herodians, 131
Herrmann, Wilhelm, 266
Heschel, Abraham, 78
heterogenous personality, 16
higher Will, 232
Hinduism, 24, 68
historical explanation, 148
Holocaust, 248

holy life, 57–58, 60–61, 70, 113–14, 127, 154, 158
holy nation, 77
holy water, 102
holy will, 222
Homo interrogatus, 42–43
Homo religiosus, 18
Homo sapiens, 215
Homo teleologicus, 18
hope, 6, 20, 42, 83, 88, 141, 270, 325
Horeb, 81
human agency, 41
human freedom, 80, 230, 233, 324
human maturation, 258
human priorities, 324

I, 44
idolatry, 278
illusions, 48, 182–85, 194–95, 286
imitatio Dei, 281, 316
imitation, 124
impartial concern, 235
imperturbability, 58, 156–57, 159
improper understanding, 306
impurity, 60–61, 154
incomprehensible, 223, 320, 326
India, 53, 68
ineffability, 320
infantile helplessness, 189–90
infantile need, 194
infantile wish, 200
Infinite Will, 226
inner person, 171
inspiration, 141, 148–49, 177, 195, 235
instinctual renunciation, 192–93
instrumental value, 129
intellectual problem of evil, 310
intention, 11
intentional action, 101–2
intentional agent(s), 128, 154, 173, 181, 241
intentional habits, 112
intentional state, 101
internalizing, 80
interpersonal evidence, 246, 275, 318–19
interpersonal inquiry, 241
interpersonal meeting, 89

interpersonal virtue, 109, 111–12, 162
interpretation, 43, 46–47
intrinsic value, 114, 129
introspection, 184, 186
introversion, 236
intuition, 149, 184, 186, 195
inwardness, 115, 118, 126
Isaac, 75, 80, 118, 174
ISIS, 27–28, 30, 34–35, 50, 136, 225
Islam, 24, 90, 92, 94, 126–27, 206
Israel, 40, 75–78, 86, 118, 129–30, 132, 167–68, 205, 219, 264, 301
Israelites, 76–77, 204
I–Thou relation, 241, 272, 318

Jacob, 75, 80, 118, 174
James, William, 16, 20, 26, 43
Jerusalem, 84, 297, 303
Jesus, 83–85, 90, 122–24, 130–34, 150, 170–71, 174, 205, 220, 237, 248, 250, 257, 261, 268, 276, 297–307, 309, 311, 315, 322, 324–25, 327
  life of, 299, 306
jhāna, 156
Job, 18, 248, 295, 314, 326
Job's protest, 326
John's Gospel, 275, 301, 303, 323
Jones, Rufus, 270–71
Judaism, 24, 52, 75, 78, 82–83
junzi, 65, 109

Kant, Immanuel, 221–23, 225, 227–31, 237
Kierkegaard, Søren, 241, 318
kindness, 267
kingdom of God, 172, 324, 326
knowledge, 148–49, 195–96, 240, 249
  by acquaintance, 317
  by description, 317
koinōnia, 88
Krishna, 67–74, 89, 97–98, 104, 112–15, 164–66, 183, 202, 204, 219, 329

Last Day, 127, 175
Last Supper, 84
law of God, 94
Law-Based Theism, 89

law-governed, 14, 82, 144
laws of science, 141–43
legalism, 80
li, 66, 109, 160
life's meaning, 1, 12, 18, 36, 97, 121, 128. *See also* meaning of life; overarching meaning
life-directed, 12
liturgy, 63
loneliness, 225
Lord, 242, 266
Lord's Supper, 122–24
love, 118–20, 170, 251
  enemies, 132
love-commands, 129–32, 135, 331
lovelessness, 305
loyal reciprocity, 65, 109, 111–12, 161, 163, 200–1, 218
loyalty, 64, 167–68, 201
Luke's Gospel, 298, 300, 303
Luther, Martin, 20

Mackintosh, H. R., 39, 305
map of meaning, 120
Mark's Gospel, 297–98, 309
materialism, 139
Matthew's Gospel, 122, 297, 324
Matthews, W. R., 250
maze of options, 2
McClendon, James, 261
meaning; *see also* meaning of life
  ascribed, 50
  discovered, 50
  fragmentary, 82
  God, 5
  incomplete, 82
  life-diminishing, 30
  life-enhancing, 30
  religious, 24
  transformative, 29
meaning in life, 1
meaning of life, 1, 3, 12, 213, 330; *see also* life's meaning; overarching meaning
  control, 19
  gift-like, 19
Mecca, 126
meditation, 105, 114–15

mercy, 128, 232, 325
merely sensed value, 10
merit, 81, 86, 95
Messiah, 83–84, 89, 124, 133, 170, 205, 298, 300
Messianic suffering, 309
methodological monism, 149
methodological naturalism, 145, 159, 163, 169, 176, 178
methodology, 24, 146
middle way, 105–6
mind, 51, 58, 72, 107, 114, 119, 130, 155–56, 165, 171–72, 184, 195, 237, 297, 299
mind–body dualism, 172
mindfulness, 56, 106, 155–56, 158
miracle, 177, 213
monotheism, 60, 68, 90, 194–95, 243, 274, 284, 311, 331
moral challenge, 253, 267
moral conscience, 251, 259, 266, 278, 289
moral conviction, 186, 201, 207, 271, 276, 281, 287, 308, 315, 329
moral decency, 50
moral depth, 295
moral effort, 227
moral experience, 200–1, 229–30, 232–33, 236–37, 239, 249, 251, 258, 260, 263, 265–67, 277, 281, 283, 286, 290, 293, 314, 320, 329
moral experiment, 277
moral facts, 15
moral goodness, 27–28, 36–37, 42, 235, 238, 260, 267, 273
moral improvement, 15–16, 59
moral indifference, 243
moral perfection, 242–43, 249, 253–54, 258, 263, 274
moral power, 235, 252, 266, 269, 329
moral pride, 276
moral realism, 228
moral rebel, 231
moral relativism, 15
moral self-understanding, 289
moral strength, 124, 128
moral transformation, 272–73, 283
moral weakness, 128, 332

morally perfect character, 128, 171,
    222, 224, 230, 248–49, 253, 274,
    280, 317, 327
morally perfect will, 205, 252, 278
Mosaic Law, 78–80, 82–83, 85, 87–88,
    90, 95, 116–20, 124, 129, 132,
    167–68, 170, 203, 205, 220
Moses, 67, 75–77, 79–81, 89–90,
    96–98, 104, 116, 118, 121,
    167–70, 173–74, 183, 191, 203–4,
    219, 311, 329
Moses and Monotheism, 191
motivational base, 273
motivational power, 244
Muhammad, 67, 90–98, 105, 125–27,
    173–75, 183, 206–7, 220, 311, 329
Muslim, 90
mystical vision, 251

natural theology, 89, 165, 244, 250,
    273–74, 280, 319
naturalism, 137, 139, 142–43, 145–49,
    154, 157–58, 162–63, 165–66,
    169–70, 172–73, 175, 177,
    179–80, 228
    extreme, 148
    methodological, 145
    ontological, 143
naturalized epistemology, 144
nature, 145, 147, 150, 169
need for protection, 182, 197
Neoplatonism, 14
Neusner, Jacob, 120
new creation, 83
Niebuhr, Reinhold, 16, 289, 294
Nirvana, 27, 53
Noah, 91
NOMA. See non-overlapping
    magisteria
non-naturalism, 145
non-overlapping magisteria
    (NOMA), 211, 213–15, 217
nonpropositional reality, 266
nonreductive physicalism, 144
nontheistic religion, 329, 331
norm-fitting, 104, 108

obedience, 86–87, 96, 116, 121–22
oceanic feeling, 187–89
ontological naturalism, 143, 157, 166,
    169
ontology, 47, 145, 158
Otto, Rudolf, 26, 28
overall meaning, 3
overall value, 4
overarching meaning, 1, 4–5, 7–8, 10,
    13, 18–20, 30, 56, 75, 88, 91, 115,
    125, 200, 327, 329, 331, 333. See
    also life's meaning; meaning of
    life

pacifism, 16
Pāli Canon, 53
parable of the wicked tenants,
    324–25
parables, 300
Pascal, Blaise, 101
passion, 17, 101
Passover, 84
past lives, 156–58
Paul, 20, 36, 67, 83–86, 88–89, 96–98,
    105, 121–24, 128, 133–34, 170–72,
    183, 205–6, 220, 253, 255–57, 261,
    265, 269–70, 274, 278, 295, 301–3,
    305–11, 323, 325, 329
penance, 70
perfecting, 252–53, 258, 260, 265, 268
perfection, 73, 82, 132
persecution, 127, 302, 309
personal God, 236
personal identity, 16
personal responsibility, 79
personifying evidence, 275
persons, 44, 128, 154
    value of, 130
person-variability, 19
Peter, 297, 300–1, 304, 306, 309
Pharaoh, 76, 167
Pharisee, 83, 131, 205–6
phenomenology, 253
physical bodies, 171–72, 176
physicalism, 138–39, 143–45, 157,
    163, 166, 169, 171, 175

physics, 20, 23, 139, 141–42, 148
piety, 266
Pilate, 303
pilgrimage, 126
Plato, 5, 13, 18, 25, 36, 171
Platonic Form, 145
polytheism, 59–60, 90
polytheists, 243
possible mistake, 287
postulate, 204
power, 41, 45, 71, 74, 76, 87–88, 90,
    161, 219, 234, 251, 253, 302
practical reason, 224, 229
practice, 100
prayer, 45, 63, 70, 125–26, 175, 257
pride, 236
priests, 78, 84, 131, 297
primitive man, 193
probabilities, 151–52, 216
proclamation, 122, 124
projection, 225
prophet, 75, 81, 90–91, 93, 176
propositional evidence, 319
Proverbs, 133
Psalm 23, 61, 311
psychiatric delusions, 183, 194
psychoanalytic explanation, 188,
    201, 209
psychological insulation, 58, 62,
    113
psychological problem of evil, 20, 29,
    32, 38–40, 53–54, 58, 62, 80, 101,
    109, 113, 119, 126, 138, 144, 154,
    158, 180–82, 188, 191, 193,
    197–98, 209, 220, 241, 296, 310,
    321
psychology, 25, 39, 148, 179–81, 188,
    193, 208, 212, 241
  of religion, 212
purity, 60–61, 69, 126, 154, 156

qualitative awareness, 8, 199, 202
qualitative content, 47–48
quasi-personal purposes, 15
quick-fix-it god, 327
Quine, W. V. O., 144–47

Ramsey, Michael, 322
rationality, 224
reasonableness, 49
reciprocity, 64, 109, 111, 163, 218,
    277
reconciliation, 77, 79, 82, 84, 88–89,
    116–17, 119–20, 122–24, 133,
    167, 169–70, 173, 198, 203, 205,
    219, 230, 243–46, 252, 254, 272,
    278, 307, 315, 320–21, 324,
    326–28
redeemer, 174
redemption, 85, 87, 122, 167, 171,
    174–75, 205, 243, 297, 307, 312,
    319, 322, 325, 327
redemptive duress, 321–23, 325–27
redemptive effort, 77, 116, 321, 326,
    329
redemptive evidence, 329
redemptive love, 300, 303, 309
redemptive opportunity, 248
redemptive program, 124
redemptive testing, 246
reduction, 144, 209, 217, 221
reflective guidance, 103
reincarnation, 157
relativism, 22, 28, 112, 328–31, 333
religion, 25, 37, 212
  common core, 26
  concepts, 21
  ethical theory, 26, 37, 210, 219,
    221, 224, 236
  evil, 27
  holy, 26
  institutional, 19, 42
  moral values, 225
  moralized, 209
  morally good, 27, 34
  natural phenomenon, 142
  naturalized, 136
  nontheistic, 331
  philosophy, 26
  reason for, 33
  reformers, 42
  sacred, 26
  and science, 143

religion (cont.)
  social, 42
  sound object, 28
  taxonomy, 25, 30
  unsound object, 28
  worship, 27
religious action, 102
religious commitment, 12, 27, 30–31,
    38–39, 41, 103, 170, 179–81, 183,
    185, 187–88, 190, 193–95,
    198–99, 202–3, 206, 208, 218,
    231, 236, 238–39, 245, 282, 293,
    316
  direct, 31
  indirect, 31
religious customs, 102
religious diversity, 283, 316–17
religious epistemology, 253, 259
religious evidence, 178, 186–87, 196,
    201, 207, 271, 333
religious experience, 41, 46, 48, 52,
    75, 83, 91, 97, 173–74, 179, 221,
    332
  cognized, 240
  core, 7
  and evidence, 151
  as ground, 45
  naturalism, 137
  nonveridical, 10
  object, 28
  private, 44
  and probability, 151
  theistic interpretation, 271
  transformative, 29
  two extremes, 37
  unveridical, 48
  veridical, 10, 48
religious interpretation, 46, 96
  nontheistic, 52, 60, 67, 105
  theistic, 52, 67, 70, 97, 105
religious needs, 189
religious personality, 235
religious practice, 100, 122, 133, 135
  normative assessment, 136
  primacy, 103
ren, 65–66, 109–10, 160, 218

responsible action, 162
restraint, 108
resurrection, 84, 87, 90, 150, 172, 298,
    307, 322–23
revelation, 92, 169, 176, 244
righteousness, 85–86, 88, 122–23,
    127, 175, 225, 260
ritual, 109, 112, 124
Robinson, H. Wheeler, 89, 322
Rome, 309
Russell, Bertrand, 140–41, 317

sabbath, 131
sacred, 27, 193
sacrifice, 70, 114, 116, 127, 269, 305
sanctification, 294
Satan, 297
Saul of Tarsus, 83, 301
Schleiermacher, Friedrich, 37
science game, 144
science textbooks, 139, 164, 212
sciences, 43, 139, 142, 157, 166–67,
    173, 179, 186, 207, 213, 271
  laws of, 143
scientia, 148
scientific cosmology, 146
scientific evidence, 139, 141, 143,
    152–53, 159, 164, 177, 186–87,
    200–1, 203–4, 207–8, 216–17,
    246
scientific explanation, 148, 212
scientific fact, 150, 216
scientific knowledge, 273
scientific methods, 146, 150
scientific objects, 246
scientific vision, 140
self/selves, 44, 108, 154, 157
  token, 157
  type, 157
self-clinging, 61
self-commitment, 31
self-concentration, 60, 109, 155
self-control, 65
self-cultivation, 66, 109
self-determination, 66, 76, 82, 98
self-engaging, 12

self-evidencing law, 228
self-examination, 162
self-giving love, 88
self-help program, 76, 305
selfhood, 61
self-insulation, 155–56, 158
self-manifesting, 70, 89, 104, 153, 229
self-protecting love, 134
self-purification, 59–60, 332
self-sacrifice, 305, 307, 323
self-sufficiency, 80, 294
selfish tendencies, 250, 269
selfishness, 111, 259, 265, 277, 279, 286, 289, 314
semantic meaning, 284
sensemaker, 4
sensemaking, 3, 5, 8, 17, 24, 29, 31, 49–51
sensuality, 55, 58, 105, 156, 236
Shema, 85
signs, 93
sin, 74, 88, 116–17, 122, 261
sin offering, 78, 117
singularity, 118
skepticism, 49, 97, 270, 284
skeptics, 283–84, 286–87, 290, 308–9
slavery, 77
Smith, James, 261
social influences, 319
socially readily shareable, 152, 186, 201, 204, 215–16, 246, 271
socially shared, 19
society, 192, 227, 247, 260, 262, 288
Socrates, 25, 36
Son of God, 84, 303–4
Son of Man, 131
soul-making, 294
sovereign will, 119, 128
sowing to the Spirit, 256
space-time, 138–39
Spirit of God, 89, 172, 255, 260, 270, 315
spiritual being, 176
spiritual blindness, 254
spiritual body, 172
spiritual personality, 271

Stephanas, 122
Stewart, James S., 294, 301, 311
strangers, 119, 130, 132, 134, 305
stress, 58, 106
struggle, 8, 175, 233, 268, 275
submission, 90, 95–96, 125, 128
suffering, 18, 24, 53–55, 57–58, 60, 62, 88, 99, 108, 155, 158–59, 190, 199, 248, 270, 294–98, 300–3, 305–9, 311, 314–15, 321–23, 325–26
suicide, 8
super-ego, 191–92
superintendence of nature, 215
supernatural, 25, 31, 142, 145, 169, 177
supervenience, 138, 144
symmetry of tolerance, 213
sympathetic understanding, 296–97, 304
synagogue, 131
synchronic, 289

telepathy, 144
temple, 141, 274
testimony, 25, 182, 267, 291
Thales, 177
thanksgiving, 117
theism, 8, 52, 62
theistic evidence, 238, 246, 283, 293
theists, 14, 89, 151, 239, 242, 244–45, 250, 283, 293–94
theodicy, 257, 270, 293–94, 296–304, 308, 310–12, 314
  full-explanation, 308
  partial-justification, 309
Thielicke, Helmut, 256, 311, 325–26
things, 6, 144
threefold practical method, 57, 158
Tian, 62–64
token-identity, 157
Tolstoy, Leo, 8–10, 12–17, 19, 35, 40, 42, 45, 48, 51–52, 59, 183, 329
Torah, 78
Totem and Taboo, 180
transformation, 269–70

trespasses, 88, 124, 253
trials, 77, 256, 310
trust, 82, 85, 302, 320, 327
truth, 21, 44, 51, 99, 285
truth condition, 286
truth indicator, 241, 287, 290

Unconditional, 229
undefeated evidence, 240
understanding, 43
unity of religions, 97
universal love, 134–35
universal system of ends, 222

value commitments, 209
value of life, 3
value-based reason, 334
value-meaning, 210–11
value realism, 5
Vedas, 70, 114
vengeance, 133
violence, 16
virtue, 27, 64, 68
virtuous relationships, 109–10
visions, 151
volitional pressure, 259, 261, 263, 267
volitional receptivity, 89

wages, 95
"walk by the Spirit," 256
Way of life, 62, 64
way of practice, 57
Webb, Beatrice, 45
Wei-ming, Tu, 109, 112
wish fulfillment, 183, 195, 197–99,
    201–5, 207
witches, 144
witness, 89, 172
Word of God, 38–39
works, 85, 121
world religions, 14–15, 51–52, 67,
    100
worldview, 18
worship, 22, 27, 30, 45, 69,
    73–74, 76, 78, 85, 89, 94, 113–15,
    129, 164–65, 202, 206, 219,
    221, 242–44, 247, 249, 252–53,
    258, 269, 274, 280, 288, 306,
    316
wrath, 133

yogi, 72, 114, 165
Yom Kippur, 78

Zuurdeeg, Willem, 40, 262